Asthma
SOURCEBOOK

Fourth Edition

Health Reference Series

Fourth Edition

Asthma
SOURCEBOOK

Basic Consumer Health Information about Allergic, Exercise-Induced, Occupational, and Other Types of Asthma, Including Facts about Causes, Risk Factors, Symptoms, and Diagnostic Tests and Featuring Details about Treating Asthma with Medication and Other Therapies, Minimizing Indoor and Outdoor Asthma Triggers, Recognizing and Handling Asthma Attacks, Monitoring Symptoms and Developing an Action Plan, and Dealing with Co-Existing Conditions

Along with a Detailed Look at Childhood Asthma Concerns and Asthma in Pregnant Women, Minority Populations, and Clinical Trials, a Glossary of Related Terms, and a List of Resources for Additional Help and Information

OMNIGRAPHICS

615 Griswold, Ste. 901 Detroit, MI 48226

Bibliographic Note
Because this page cannot legibly accommodate all the copyright notices, the Bibliographic
Note portion of the Preface constitutes an extension of the copyright notice.

* * *

Omnigraphics, Inc.
Editorial Services provided by Omnigraphics, Inc.,
a division of Relevant Information, Inc.

Keith Jones, *Managing Editor*

* * *

Library of Congress Cataloging-in-Publication Data

Names: Omnigraphics, Inc.

Title: Asthma sourcebook : basic consumer health information about allergic,
exercise-induced, occupational, and other types of asthma, including facts about
causes, risk factors, symptoms, and diagnostic tests and featuring details about
treating asthma with medication and other therapies ....

Description: Fourth edition. | Detroit, MI : Omnigraphics, Inc., [2016] | Series:
Health reference series | Includes bibliographical references and index.

Identifiers: LCCN 2015049034 (print) | LCCN 2015050101 (ebook) | ISBN
9780780814806 (hardcover : alk. paper) | ISBN 9780780814790 (ebook)

Subjects: LCSH: Asthma--Popular works.

Classification: LCC RC591 .A84 2016 (print) | LCC RC591 (ebook) | DDC
616.2/38--dc23

LC record available at http://lccn.loc.gov/2015049034

Table of Contents

Part II: Recognizing and Diagnosing Asthma

Part III: Medications and Asthma Management

Part VI: Asthma in Other Special Populations

Part VII: Additional Help and Information

Preface

About This Book

Asthma is a chronic disorder characterized by inflammation of the air passages, resulting in the temporary narrowing of the passageways that transport air to the lungs. Although asthma can be managed with proper prevention and treatment, poorly controlled asthma can lead to reduced productivity, missed days at work or school, and acute medical emergencies, or even death.

The number of people with asthma in the United States is large and growing. According to the American Academy of Allergy Asthma and Immunology, approximately 23 million Americans, including almost 6 million children—an average of one out of every ten school-aged children—have asthma.

Despite asthma's prevalence, many Americans are unaware of the basic facts about the disorder and the progress being made in preventing and controlling it. New forms of treatment are being developed that make asthma easier to control, and with increased understanding of the causes and triggers of the disease, it is easier to prevent a flare-up.

Asthma Sourcebook, Fourth Edition provides basic consumer information about the different types of asthma and how they are diagnosed and treated. It includes information about the most common asthma triggers and suggests strategies for minimizing or avoiding them. It provides tips for managing asthma at school and in daily life and discusses common asthma concerns among pregnant women, older adults, and other minority populations. The book concludes with a glossary of related terms and a list of resources for further help and information.

How to Use This Book

This book is divided into parts and chapters. Parts focus on broad areas of interest. Chapters are devoted to single topics within a part.

Part I: Asthma Basics explains how the lungs work and describes what happens when asthma occurs. It discusses what is known about the causes of asthma and describes the most common asthma triggers. Finally, it provides statistics on the prevalence of asthma in the United States.

Part II: Recognizing and Diagnosing Asthma describes what asthma attacks are and explains what to do when one occurs. It provides details about the different types of asthma and describes the tests and procedures most often used to diagnose the disorder.

Part III: Medications and Asthma Management discusses the different types of medications used to treat asthma. It explains the adverse effects related to the use of asthma medications and describes how the different medication delivery mechanisms should be used and maintained. Alternative and complementary asthma therapies and the latest developments in asthma treatment are also discussed.

Part IV: Living with Asthma provides tips on overcoming the challenges that are part of living with asthma. It describes asthma triggers and explains how to minimize or avoid them. It discusses the conditions that most commonly co-occur with asthma and offers suggestions for keeping asthma under control through lifestyle modification. Finally, it outlines strategies for safely traveling with asthma.

Part V: Pediatric Asthma deals with common concerns about asthma in children. It explains how asthma is diagnosed in babies and young children and discusses the safety and effectiveness of the different treatments for children. It provides tips for handling asthma flare-ups in children and discusses how to deal with asthma at school and when children are participating in sports and other physical activity.

Part VI: Asthma in Other Special Populations discusses the particular challenges of managing asthma in pregnant women. It describes the differing incidence rates of asthma among minority populations and discusses the disorder's disproportionate effect on low-income populations.

Part VII: Additional Help and Information includes a glossary of terms related to asthma and a directory of resources for further help and support.

Bibliographic Note

This volume contains documents and excerpts from publications issued by the following U.S. government agencies: Agency for Healthcare Research and Quality (AHRQ); Agency for Toxic Substances and Disease Registry (ATSDR); Centers for Disease Control and Prevention (CDC); Federal Bureau of Prisons (BOP); National Cancer Institute (NCI); National Center for Advancing Translational Sciences (NCATS); National Center for Complementary and Integrative Health (NCCIH); National Heart, Lung, and Blood Institute (NHLBI); National Institute of Allergy and Infectious Diseases (NIAID); National Institute of Arthritis and Musculoskeletal and Skin Diseases (NIAMS); National Institute of Biomedical Imaging and Bioengineering (NIBIB); National Institute of Environmental Health Sciences (NIEHS); National Institutes of Health (NIH); Occupational Safety and Health Administration (OSHA); Office of Disease Prevention and Health Promotion (ODPHP); Office of Minority Health (OMH); U.S. Environmental Protection Agency (EPA); U.S. Department of Health and Human Services (HHS); U.S. Food and Drug Administration (FDA); and WhiteHouse.gov.

It may also contain original material produced by Omnigraphics, Inc. and reviewed by medical consultants.

About the Health Reference Series

The *Health Reference Series* is designed to provide basic medical information for patients, families, caregivers, and the general public. Each volume takes a particular topic and provides comprehensive coverage. This is especially important for people who may be dealing with a newly diagnosed disease or a chronic disorder in themselves or in a family member. People looking for preventive guidance, information about disease warning signs, medical statistics, and risk factors for health problems will also find answers to their questions in the *Health Reference Series*. The *Series*, however, is not intended to serve as a tool for diagnosing illness, in prescribing treatments, or as a substitute for the physician/patient relationship. All people concerned about medical symptoms or the possibility of disease are encouraged to seek professional care from an appropriate health care provider.

A Note about Spelling and Style

Health Reference Series editors use *Stedman's Medical Dictionary* as an authority for questions related to the spelling of medical terms and the *Chicago Manual of Style* for questions related to grammatical structures, punctuation, and other editorial concerns. Consistent adherence is not always possible, however, because the individual volumes within the *Series* include many documents from a wide variety of different producers, and the editor's primary goal is to present material from each source as accurately as is possible. This sometimes means that information in different chapters or sections may follow other guidelines and alternate spelling authorities.

Medical Review

Omnigraphics contracts with a team of qualified, senior medical professionals who serve as medical consultants for the *Health Reference Series*. As necessary, medical consultants review reprinted and originally written material for currency and accuracy. Citations including the phrase,
"Reviewed (month, year)" indicate material reviewed by this team. Medical consultation services are provided to the *Health Reference Series* editors by:

Dr. Senthil Selvan, MBBS, DCH, MD
Dr. K. Sivanandham, MBBS, DCH, MS (Research), PhD

Our Advisory Board

We would like to thank the following board members for providing initial guidance to the development of this series:

- Dr. Lynda Baker, Associate Professor of Library and Information Science, Wayne State University, Detroit, MI

- Nancy Bulgarelli, William Beaumont Hospital Library, Royal Oak, MI

- Karen Imarisio, Bloomfield Township Public Library, Bloomfield Township, MI

- Karen Morgan, Mardigian Library, University of Michigan-Dearborn, Dearborn, MI

- Rosemary Orlando, St. Clair Shores Public Library, St. Clair Shores, MI

Health Reference Series *Update Policy*

The inaugural book in the *Health Reference Series* was the first edition of *Cancer Sourcebook* published in 1989. Since then, the *Series* has been enthusiastically received by librarians and in the medical community. In order to maintain the standard of providing high-quality health information for the layperson the editorial staff at Omnigraphics felt it was necessary to implement a policy of updating volumes when warranted.

Medical researchers have been making tremendous strides, and it is the purpose of the *Health Reference Series* to stay current with the most recent advances. Each decision to update a volume is made on an individual basis. Some of the considerations include how much new information is available and the feedback we receive from people who use the books. If there is a topic you would like to see added to the update list, or an area of medical concern you feel has not been adequately addressed, please write to:

Managing Editor
Health Reference Series
Omnigraphics, Inc.
615 Griswold, Ste. 901
Detroit, MI 48226

Part One

Asthma Basics

Chapter 1

What Is Asthma?

Chapter Contents

Section 1.1

Asthma: An Overview

Text in this section is excerpted from "What Is Asthma?" National
Heart, Lung, and Blood Institute (NHLBI), August 4, 2014.

Asthma is a chronic (long-term) lung disease that inflames and
narrows the airways. Asthma causes recurring periods of wheezing
(a whistling sound when you breathe), chest tightness, shortness of
breath, and coughing. The coughing often occurs at night or early in
the morning.

Asthma affects people of all ages, but it most often starts during
childhood. In the United States, more than 25 million people are known
to have asthma. About 7 million of these people are children.

Overview

To understand asthma, it helps to know how the airways work. The
airways are tubes that carry air into and out of your lungs. People who
have asthma have inflamed airways. The inflammation makes the
airways swollen and very sensitive. The airways tend to react strongly
to certain inhaled substances. When the airways react, the muscles
around them tighten. This narrows the airways, causing less air to flow
into the lungs. The swelling also can worsen, making the airways even
narrower. Cells in the airways might make more mucus than usual.
Mucus is a sticky, thick liquid that can further narrow the airways.

This chain reaction can result in asthma symptoms. Symptoms can
happen each time the airways are inflamed.

Sometimes asthma symptoms are mild and go away on their own
or after minimal treatment with asthma medicine. Other times,
symptoms continue to get worse. When symptoms get more intense
and or more symptoms occur, you're having an asthma attack.
Asthma attacks also are called flareups or exacerbations. Treating
symptoms when you first notice them is important. This will help
prevent the symptoms from worsening and causing a severe asthma
attack. Severe asthma attacks may require emergency care, and they
can be fatal.

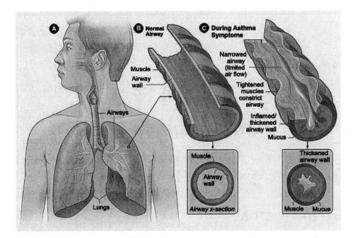

Figure 1.1. *Inset image A shows the location of the lungs and airways in the body. Inset image B shows a cross-section of a normal airway. Inset image C shows a cross-section of an airway during asthma symptoms.*

Outlook

Asthma has no cure. Even when you feel fine, you still have the disease and it can flare up at any time. However, with recent days' knowledge and treatments, most people who have asthma are able to manage the disease. They have few, if any, symptoms. They can live normal, active lives and sleep through the night without interruption from asthma. If you have asthma, you can take an active role in managing the disease. For successful, thorough, and ongoing treatment, build strong partnerships with your doctor and other health care providers.

Section 1.2

How the Lungs Work

Text in this section is excerpted from "What Happens
When You Breathe?" National Heart, Lung, and Blood
Institute (NHLBI), July 17, 2012.

What Are the Lungs?

Your lungs are organs in your chest that allow your body to take
in oxygen from the air. They also help remove carbon dioxide (a waste
gas that can be toxic) from your body.

The lungs' intake of oxygen and removal of carbon dioxide is called
gas exchange. Gas exchange is part of breathing. Breathing is a vital
function of life; it helps your body to work properly.

Other organs and tissues also help make breathing possible.

The Respiratory System

The respiratory system is made up of organs and tissues that help
you breathe. The main parts of this system are the airways, the lungs
and linked blood vessels, and the muscles that enable breathing.

Airways

The airways are pipes that carry oxygen-rich air to your lungs.
They also carry carbon dioxide, a waste gas, out of your lungs. The
airways include your:

- Nose and linked air passages (called nasal cavities)

- Mouth

- Larynx, or voice box

- Trachea, or windpipe

- Tubes called bronchial tubes or bronchi, and their branches

Air first enters your body through your nose or mouth, which wets
and warms the air. (Cold, dry air can irritate your lungs.) The air then

travels through your voice box and down your windpipe. The windpipe splits into two bronchial tubes that enter your lungs.

A thin flap of tissue called the epiglottis covers your windpipe when you swallow. This prevents food and drink from entering the air passages that lead to your lungs.

Except for the mouth and some parts of the nose, all of the airways have special hairs called cilia that are coated with sticky mucus. The cilia trap germs and other foreign particles that enter your airways when you breathe in air.

These fine hairs then sweep the particles up to the nose or mouth. From there, they're swallowed, coughed, or sneezed out of the body. Nose hairs and mouth saliva also trap particles and germs.

Lungs and Blood Vessels

Your lungs and linked blood vessels deliver oxygen to your body and remove carbon dioxide from your body. Your lungs lie on either side of your breastbone and fill the inside of your chest cavity. Your left lung is slightly smaller than your right lung to allow room for your heart.

Within the lungs, your bronchi branch into thousands of smaller, thinner tubes called bronchioles. These tubes end in bunches of tiny round air sacs called alveoli.

Each of these air sacs is covered in a mesh of tiny blood vessels called capillaries. The capillaries connect to a network of arteries and veins that move blood through your body.

The pulmonary artery and its branches deliver blood rich in carbon dioxide (and lacking in oxygen) to the capillaries that surround the air sacs. Inside the air sacs, carbon dioxide moves from the blood into the air. At the same time, oxygen moves from the air into the blood in the capillaries.

The oxygen-rich blood then travels to the heart through the pulmonary vein and its branches. The heart pumps the oxygen-rich blood out to the body.

The lungs are divided into five main sections called lobes. Some people need to have a diseased lung lobe removed. However, they can still breathe well using the rest of their lung lobes.

Muscles Used for Breathing

Muscles near the lungs help expand and contract (tighten) the lungs to allow breathing.

These muscles include the:

- Diaphragm
- Intercostal muscles
- Abdominal muscles
- Muscles in the neck and collarbone area

The diaphragm is a dome-shaped muscle located below your lungs. It separates the chest cavity from the abdominal cavity. The diaphragm is the main muscle used for breathing.

The intercostal muscles are located between your ribs. They also play a major role in helping you breathe.

Beneath your diaphragm are abdominal muscles. They help you breathe out when you're breathing fast (for example, during physical activity).

Muscles in your neck and collarbone area help you breathe in when other muscles involved in breathing don't work well, or when lung disease impairs your breathing.

What Happens When You Breathe?

Breathing In (Inhalation)

When you breathe in, or inhale, your diaphragm contracts (tightens) and moves downward. This increases the space in your chest cavity, into which your lungs expand. The intercostal muscles between your ribs also help enlarge the chest cavity. They contract to pull your rib cage both upward and outward when you inhale. As your lungs expand, air is sucked in through your nose or mouth. The air travels down your windpipe and into your lungs. After passing through your bronchial tubes, the air finally reaches and enters the alveoli (air sacs). Through the very thin walls of the alveoli, oxygen from the air passes to the surrounding capillaries (blood vessels). A red blood cell protein called hemoglobin helps move oxygen from the air sacs to the blood.

At the same time, carbon dioxide moves from the capillaries into the air sacs. The gas has traveled in the bloodstream from the right side of the heart through the pulmonary artery.

Oxygen-rich blood from the lungs is carried through a network of capillaries to the pulmonary vein. This vein delivers the oxygen-rich blood to the left side of the heart. The left side of the heart pumps the blood to the rest of the body. There, the oxygen in the blood moves from blood vessels into surrounding tissues.

Breathing Out (Exhalation)

When you breathe out, or exhale, your diaphragm relaxes and moves upward into the chest cavity. The intercostal muscles between the ribs also relax to reduce the space in the chest cavity.

As the space in the chest cavity gets smaller, air rich in carbon dioxide is forced out of your lungs and windpipe, and then out of your nose or mouth.

Breathing out requires no effort from your body unless you have a lung disease or are doing physical activity. When you're physically active, your abdominal muscles contract and push your diaphragm against your lungs even more than usual. This rapidly pushes air out of your lungs.

What Controls Your Breathing?

A respiratory control center at the base of your brain controls your breathing. This center sends ongoing signals down your spine and to the muscles involved in breathing.

These signals ensure your breathing muscles contract (tighten) and relax regularly. This allows your breathing to happen automatically, without you being aware of it.

To a limited degree, you can change your breathing rate, such as by breathing faster or holding your breath. Your emotions also can change your breathing. For example, being scared or angry can affect your breathing pattern.

Your breathing will change depending on how active you are and the condition of the air around you. For example, you need to breathe more often when you do physical activity. In contrast, your body needs to restrict how much air you breathe if the air contains irritants or toxins.

To adjust your breathing to changing needs, your body has many sensors in your brain, blood vessels, muscles, and lungs.

Sensors in the brain and in two major blood vessels (the carotid artery and the aorta) detect carbon dioxide or oxygen levels in your blood and change your breathing rate as needed.

Sensors in the airways detect lung irritants. The sensors can trigger sneezing or coughing. In people who have asthma, the sensors may cause the muscles around the airways in the lungs to contract. This makes the airways smaller.

Sensors in the alveoli (air sacs) can detect fluid buildup in the lung tissues. These sensors are thought to trigger rapid, shallow breathing.

Sensors in your joints and muscles detect movement of your arms or legs. These sensors may play a role in increasing your breathing rate when you're physically active.

Lung Diseases and Conditions

Breathing is a complex process. If injury, disease, or other factors affect any part of the process, you may have trouble breathing.

For example, the fine hairs (cilia) that line your upper airways may not trap all of the germs you breathe in. These germs can cause an infection in your bronchial tubes (bronchitis) or deep in your lungs (pneumonia). These infections cause a buildup of mucus or fluid that narrows the airways and limits airflow in and out of your lungs.

If you have asthma, breathing in certain substances that you're sensitive to can trigger your airways to narrow. This makes it hard for air to flow in and out of your lungs.

Over a long period, breathing in cigarette smoke or air pollutants can damage the airways and air sacs. This can lead to a disease called COPD (chronic obstructive pulmonary disease). COPD prevents proper airflow in and out of your lungs and can hinder gas exchange in the air sacs.

An important step to breathing is the movement of your diaphragm and other muscles in your chest, neck, and abdomen. This movement lets you inhale and exhale. Nerves that run from your brain to these muscles control their movement. Damage to these nerves in your upper spinal cord can cause breathing to stop, unless a machine is used to help you breathe. (This machine is called a ventilator or a respirator.)

A steady flow of blood in the small blood vessels that surround your air sacs is vital for gas exchange. Long periods of inactivity or surgery can cause a blood clot called a pulmonary embolism (PE) to block a lung artery. A PE can reduce or block the flow of blood in the small blood vessels and hinder gas exchange.

Section 1.3

Social Impact of Asthma

This section includes excerpts from "Asthma's Impact on the Nation," Centers for Disease Control and Prevention (CDC), May 9, 2012; text from "Data, Statistics, and Surveillance," Centers for Disease Control and Prevention (CDC), April 23, 2015; text from "Most Recent Asthma Data," Centers for Disease Control and Prevention (CDC), April 23, 2015; text from "FastStats," Centers for Disease Control and Prevention (CDC), January 20, 2015; and text from "2013 National Health Interview Survey (NHIS) Data," Centers for Disease Control and Prevention (CDC), February 13, 2015.

Is asthma really a problem?

Yes. Asthma is a serious health and economic concern in the United States. It's expensive.

- Asthma costs the United States $56 billion each year.
- The average yearly cost of care for a child with asthma was $1,039 in 2009.

It's common.

In 2010:

- 18.7 million adults had asthma. That's equal to 1 in 12 adults.
- 7 million children had asthma. That's equal to 1 in 11 children.

It's deadly.

- About 9 people die from asthma each day.
- In 2009, 3,388 people died from asthma.

What makes a person more likely to have asthma?

Gender:

Women are more likely to have asthma than men.
In children, boys are more likely to have asthma than girls.

Age:

Adults ages 18 to 24 are more likely to have asthma than older adults.

Race and ethnicity:

Multi-race and black adults are more likely to have asthma than white adults.

Black children are 2 times more likely to have asthma than white children.

Education level:

Adults who didn't finish high school are more likely to have asthma than adults who graduated high school or college.

Income level:

Adults with an annual household income of $75,000 or less are more likely to have asthma than adults with higher incomes.

Behavioral risk factors:

Smokers are more likely to have asthma than non-smokers.
Obese adults are most likely to have asthma.

How does asthma disrupt daily life?

Asthma keeps people out of work and school:

- Nearly 1 in 2 children miss at least 1 day of school each year because of their asthma.
- Nearly 1 in 3 adults miss at least 1 day of work each year because of their asthma.

Asthma interferes with daily activities:

- Nearly 3 in 5 people with asthma limit their usual activities because of their asthma.

Asthma Surveillance Data

Asthma surveillance data includes collection of asthma data at both the national and the state level. National data is available on asthma prevalence, activity limitation, days of work or school lost, rescue and control medication use, asthma self-management education, physician visits, emergency department visits, hospitalizations due to asthma, and deaths due to asthma from National Center for Health Statistics (NCHS) surveys and the Vital Statistics System. Asthma surveillance data at the state level include adult and child asthma prevalence from the Behavioral Risk Factor Surveillance System (BRFSS) and in-depth state and local asthma data through implementation of the BRFSS Asthma Call-back Survey (ACBS).

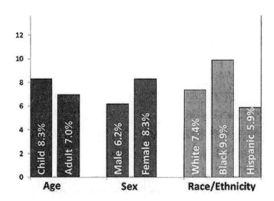

Figure 1.2. *Current Asthma Prevalence Percents by Age, Sex, and Race/ Ethnicity*

Recent Asthma Data

The following tables feature the latest national and state statistics on the burden of asthma among children and adults. The data are from national and state surveillance systems administered by the Centers for Disease Control and Prevention (CDC). Links to sources are provided with each table to assist with finding additional information on the data and relevant tables and reports.

Table 1.1. National Current Asthma* Prevalence (2013)

Characteristic**	Number with Current Asthma (in thousands)	Percent with Current Asthma
Total	22648	7.3%
Child (Age <18)	6109	8.3%
Adult (Age 18+)	16540	7.0%
Age Group		
0–4 years	826	4.2%

Table 1.1. Continued

Characteristic**	Number with Current Asthma (in thousands)	Percent with Current Asthma
5–14 years	4080	9.9%
15–19 years	1761	8.6%
20–24 years	1585	7.2%
25–34 years	2764	6.6%
35–64 years	8914	7.3%
65+ years	2719	6.3%
Child Age Group		
0–4 years	826	4.2%
5–11 years	2833	9.8%
12–17 years	2449	9.9%
Young Teens (12–14 years)	1247	10.0%
Teenagers (15–17 years)	1203	9.8%
Adolescents (11–21 years)	4024	8.9%
Young Adults (22–39 years)	5141	6.9%
Sex		
Males	9430	6.2%
Boys (Age <18)	3489	9.3%
Men (Age 18+)	5940	5.2%
Females	13218	8.3%
Girls (Age <18)	2619	7.3%
Women (Age 18+)	10599	8.6%
Race/Ethnicity		
White NH	14383	7.4%
Child (Age <18)	2920	7.5%
Adult (Age >18)	11463	7.3%
Black NH	3712	9.9%
Child (Age <18)	1344	13.4%
Adult (Age >18)	2368	8.6%
Other NH	1397	5.8%
Child (Age <18)	538	7.9%
Adult (Age >18)	859	4.9%
Hispanic	3157	5.9%

Table 1.1. Continued

Characteristic**	Number with Current Asthma (in thousands)	Percent with Current Asthma
Child (Age <18)	1307	7.4%
Adult (Age >18)	1850	5.2%
Puerto Rican†	686	14.6%
Child (Age <18)	275	20.7%
Adult (Age >18)	411	12.2%
Mexican/Mexican American†	1612	4.7%
Child (Age <18)	690	5.6%
Adult (Age >18)	922	4.1%
Federal Poverty Threshold		
Below 100% of poverty level	5321	10.9%
100% to less than 250% of poverty level	6260	7.0%
250% to less than 450% of poverty level	5208	6.2%
450% of poverty level or higher	5859	6.6%

Note: *NH = Non-Hispanic*

Includes persons who answered "yes" to the questions: "Have you EVER been told by a doctor or other health professional that you had asthma?" and "Do you still have asthma?"

**Numbers within selected characteristics may not sum to total due to rounding

†As a subset of Hispanic

Source: 2013 National Health Interview Survey (NHIS)

(Note: Child Age Group data analyzed separately)

Table 1.2. National Prevalence of Asthma Attacks (2013)

Characteristic	Number of persons with current asthma* who reported having one or more asthma attacks (in thousands)	Percent of persons with current asthma* who reported having one or more asthma attacks
Total	**11294**	**49.9%**
Child (Age <18)	3524	57.9%
Adult (Age 18+)	7770	47.0%

Includes persons who answered "yes" to the questions: "Have you EVER been told by a doctor or other health professional that you had asthma?" and "Do you still have asthma?"

Source: 2013 National Health Interview Survey (NHIS)

Asthma Statistics

Data are for the United States.

Morbidity: Adults

- Number of adults who currently have asthma: 18.7 million

Table 1.3. Current Asthma Population Estimates–in thousands by Age, United States: National Health Interview Survey, 2013

Characteristic†	Adults Age 18+	Age (years)			
		20–24	25–34	35–64	65+
Male	5940	619	1080	3058	895
Female	10599	966	1684	5856	1823
White Non-Hispanic:	11463	919	1822	6449	1995
Male	4069	324	673	2303	639
Female	7394	595	1150	4146	1356
Black Non-Hispanic:	2368	297	364	1217	359
Other Non-Hispanic:	881	151*	109	391	126
Female	1487	145	255	825	233
Other Non-Hispanic:	859	120*	140	415	145
Male	307	74*	62*	136	33*
Female	553	46*	78	279	112
Hispanic:	1950	249	437	833	220
Male	684	69*	236	227	98
Female	1166	180	201	605	122
Puerto Rican:a	411	22*	108*	187	72
Male	183	**	101*	60*	**
Female	228	**	**	126	56
Mexican/Mexican-American:a	922	141	186	430	86

Table 1.3. Continued

Characteristic†	Age (years)				
	Adults Age 18+	20–24	25–34	35–64	65+
Male	320	45*	84*	100*	47*
Female	602	96*	101	330	40*
Region:					
Northeast	3436	238*	473	1995	640
Midwest	3909	440	780	1998	539
South	5301	431	844	2829	992
West	3893	476	667	2092	548
Ratio of Family Income to Poverty Threshold:b					
0–0.99	3377	440	526	1735	419
1.00–2.49	4390	452	723	2043	1014
2.50–4.49	3926	435	683	1986	773
4.50 and above	4847	258*	833	3150	513

Source: National Health Interview Survey, National Center for Health Statistics, CDC
All relative standard errors are <30% unless otherwise indicated.
* Relative standard error of the estimate is 30%-50%; the estimate is unreliable.
** Relative standard error of the estimate exceeds 50%.
† Numbers within selected characteristics may not sum to total due to rounding.
a As a subset of Hispanic.
b Missing responses imputed.

- Percent of adults who currently have asthma: 8.0%

Table 1.4. Current Asthma Prevalence Percents by Age, United States: National Health Interview Survey, 2013

Characteristic	Age (years)				
	Adults Age 18+	20-24	25-34	35-64	65+
Male	5.2	5.8	5.3	5.2	4.7
Female	8.6	8.6	8.0	9.4	7.6

Table 1.4. Continued

Characteristic	Adults Age 18+	Age (years)			
		20-24	25-34	35-64	65+
White Non-Hispanic:	7.3	7.4	7.6	7.9	5.8
Male	5.4	5.2	5.6	5.8	4.2
Female	9.2	9.5	9.5	10.1	7.2
Black Non-Hispanic:	8.6	9.4	7.1	8.5	9.8
Male	7.2	10.8	4.7	6.1	8.7
Female	9.9	8.2	9.1	10.6	10.6
Other Non-Hispanic:	4.9	7.1*	3.7	4.6	6.5
Male	3.8	8.0*	3.7*	3.2	3.4*
Female	6.0	5.9*	3.6	5.9	8.9
Hispanic:	5.2	5.4	5.1	4.8	6.7
Male	6.8	3.1*	5.3	2.6	6.9
Female	6.5	7.6	4.9	6.9	6.6
Puerto Rican:a	12.2	5.4*	15.0*	11.6	14.1
Male	10.9	**	25.4*	7.9*	**
Female	13.5	8.3*	**	14.9	22.7
Mexican/Mexican-American:	4.1	4.6	3.3	4.0	5.2
Male	2.9	3.0*	2.9*	1.8*	6.7*
Female	5.5	6.1*	3.7	6.3	4.1*
Region:					
Northeast	8.3	6.8*	7.3	9.1	7.8
Midwest	7.3	8.7	7.9	7.5	5.5
South	6.1	5.2	5.5	6.3	6.1
West	7.2	9.2	6.7	7.5	6.1
Ratio of Family Income toPoverty Threshold:b					
0–0.99	10.5	8.0	8.1	12.8	9.9
1.00–2.49	6.7	6.0	6.1	7.1	6.9
2.50–4.49	6.0	7.8	5.5	5.9	6.3
4.50 and above	6.6	7.6	7.7	6.8	4.3

Source: National Health Interview Survey, National Center for Health Statistics, CDC All relative standard errors are <30% unless otherwise indicated.

* Relative standard error of the estimate is 30%-50%; the estimate is unreliable.
** Relative standard error of the estimate exceeds 50%.
A As a subset of Hispanic.
b Missing responses imputed.

Morbidity: Children

- Number of children who currently have asthma: 6.8 million
- Percent of children who currently have asthma: 9.3%

Physician office visits

- Number of visits to physician offices with asthma as primary diagnosis: 14.2 million

Emergency department visits

- Number of visits to emergency departments with asthma as primary diagnosis: 1.8 million

Hospital inpatient care

- Number of discharges with asthma as first-listed diagnosis: 439,000
- Average length of stay: 3.6 days

Mortality

- Number of deaths: 3,630
- Deaths per 100,000 population: 1.1

Section 1.4

How Asthma Works: A Physiological View

Text in this section is excerpted from "What Happens
When You Breathe?" National Heart, Lung, and Blood
Institute (NHLBI), March 2013.

Asthma symptoms result from ongoing inflammation (swelling) that
makes your airways super sensitive and more narrow than normal.
Although inflammation is a helpful defense mechanism for our bodies,
it can be harmful if it occurs at the wrong time or stays around after
it's no longer needed. That is what happens when you have asthma.

The airways in your lungs are more sensitive to things that they see
as foreign and threatening—such as tobacco smoke, dust, chemicals,
colds or flu, and pollen—also called asthma "triggers." Your immune
system overreacts to these things by releasing different kinds of cells
and chemicals that cause the following changes in the airways:

The inner linings of the airways become more inflamed (swollen),
leaving even less room in the airways for the air to move through.

The muscles surrounding the airways get bigger and tighten.
This squeezes the airways and makes them smaller. (This is called
bronchospasm.)

Glands in the airways produce lots of thick mucus, which further
blocks the airways.

These changes can make it harder for you to breathe. They also can
make you cough, wheeze, and feel short of breath.

If the inflammation associated with asthma is not treated, each time
your airways are exposed to your asthma triggers, the inflammation
increases, and you are likely to have symptoms that may get worse.

The normal airway is open, so the air you breathe moves in and out
of your lungs freely. When you are exposed to your asthma triggers,
the sides of your airways become more inflamed or swollen, and the
muscles around the airways tighten, leaving less room for the air to
move in and out.

Your asthma can be controlled: Discuss your asthma with your
doctor. Together, you can create a treatment plan that will help you:

- **Reduce impairment**—so you can keep asthma symptoms away, keep up with your usual daily activities, and sleep through the night.

- **Reduce risk**—so you can prevent asthma attacks, stay out of the emergency room or hospital, and have fewer side effects from your medicines.

Managing your asthma effectively means working closely with your doctor, taking your medicines as prescribed, avoiding your asthma triggers, and watching for any changes in your asthma. These steps will help you to reduce impairment and risk so you can gain—and keep—control of your asthma. You should expect nothing less.

Chapter 2

Asthma Causes and Risk Factors

Chapter Contents

Section 2.1

What Do We Know about the Causes of Asthma?

This section includes excerpts from "Explore Asthma," National
Heart, Lung, and Blood Institute (NHLBI), August 4, 2014; text from
"So You Have Asthma," National Heart, Lung, and Blood Institute
(NHLBI), March 2013; text from "Childhood Obesity Causes and
Consequences," Centers for Disease Control and Prevention (CDC),
April 27, 2012; and text from "AsthmaStats," Centers for Disease
Control and Prevention (CDC), August 14, 2013.

What Causes Asthma?

The exact cause of asthma isn't known. Researchers think some
genetic and environmental factors interact to cause asthma, most often
early in life. These factors include:

- An inherited tendency to develop allergies, called atopy

- Parents who have asthma

- Certain respiratory infections during childhood

- Contact with some airborne allergens or exposure to some viral
  infections in infancy or in early childhood when the immune system is developing

If asthma or atopy runs in your family, exposure to irritants (for
example, tobacco smoke) may make your airways more reactive to
substances in the air.

Some factors may be more likely to cause asthma in some people
than in others. Researchers continue to explore what causes asthma.

Your Asthma Triggers and How to Avoid Them

Avoiding the things that bring on your asthma symptoms—your
asthma triggers—is another important action to control your asthma.
Avoiding your asthma triggers can help reduce the inflammation in
your lungs, your symptoms, and even your need for medicine.

Some of the most common things that bring on asthma symptoms are airborne allergens and irritants, viral infections, and exercise.

Airborne allergens are substances that you breathe in and that can cause you to have an allergic reaction. That is, in some people, the immune system sees them as "foreign" or "threatening" and reacts in an overly strong way to protect the body against them.

Some of the most common allergens that affect people who have asthma are:

- Cockroach droppings
- Dust mites—tiny bugs (too small to see) that thrive in dust, mattresses, upholstered furniture, carpets, and stuffed animals
- Warm-blooded animals, including pets such as cats and dogs—which have allergens in their dander (flakes of skin), urine, feces, and saliva
- Pollen from trees, grass, and weeds
- Molds, both indoor and outdoor

Irritants are things in the environment that may irritate your lungs. Some of the most common irritants are:

- Tobacco smoke
- Air pollution, including ozone
- Formaldehyde and other chemicals (called volatile organic compounds) from newly installed linoleum flooring, synthetic carpeting, particleboard, wall coverings, furniture, and recent painting
- Gas stoves and other appliances not vented to the outdoors
- Fumes from buses, wood-burning appliances, or fireplaces
- Strong odors or sprays, such as perfume, talcum powder, hairspray, and paints.
- Changes in weather and exposure to cold air.

Other things that bring on asthma symptoms in some people include:

- Exercise and other physical activity
- Viral respiratory infections, including colds, respiratory syncytial virus (RSV), and the flu

- Medicines such as aspirin or other nonsteroidal anti-inflammatory drugs (NSAIDS) like ibuprofen, and betablockers that are used in high blood pressure and glaucoma medicines

- Bacterial respiratory infections, including Mycoplasma and Chlamydia

- Sulfites used as preservatives in food (dried fruit, instant potatoes, or shrimp) or drinks (wine or beer)

- This is not a complete list of all the things that can bring on your asthma symptoms. It is important to learn what causes problems for you

Ask your doctor to help you find out what else makes your asthma worse. Then decide with your doctor what steps you will take.

Who Is at Risk for Asthma?

Asthma affects people of all ages, but it most often starts during childhood. In the United States, more than 22 million people are known to have asthma. Nearly 6 million of these people are children.

Young children who often wheeze and have respiratory infections—as well as certain other risk factors—are at highest risk of developing asthma that continues beyond 6 years of age. The other risk factors include having allergies, eczema (an allergic skin condition), or parents who have asthma.

Among children, more boys have asthma than girls. But among adults, more women have the disease than men. It's not clear whether or how sex and sex hormones play a role in causing asthma.

Most, but not all, people who have asthma have allergies.

Some people develop asthma because of contact with certain chemical irritants or industrial dusts in the workplace. This type of asthma is called occupational asthma.

Why You?

Probably the most important factor in the development of asthma is atopy. This is the inherited tendency to be allergic. If other people in your family have allergies, you may have inherited a tendency to be allergic, and your chances of developing asthma are greater than average.

Researchers also are beginning to see that exposure to certain irritants when you are very young plays a role in the development of asthma. For example, if you have a family history of asthma or allergies and your mother was exposed to certain irritants, such as tobacco smoke, when she was pregnant with you, you may be more likely to develop asthma.

Exposure to certain indoor allergens in early childhood may also play an important role in the development of asthma. In many places, exposure to dust mites appears to have this effect. Other indoor allergens that may play an important role in the development of asthma include cat and dog dander (flakes of skin or dried saliva), cockroach droppings, and mold.

Certain viral respiratory infections in early life also appear to play a part in the development of asthma and of ongoing wheezing.

Exposure to irritants, certain chemicals, or substances in your workplace may increase your chances of developing occupational asthma.

Changes in the way we live and work in the United States nowadays may also increase our contact with these allergens and irritants. We now spend far more time indoors than we used to, and we've reduced ventilation in our homes and workplaces to conserve energy. This may trap allergens and irritants inside.

On the other side of the coin, medical research has shown that children who are exposed to certain types of infections and environments during the first year or two of life may be less likely to develop asthma. Such exposures may be protective factors against asthma. For example, some children who grow up on or near farms have been shown to be less likely to develop asthma and allergies. Asthma and allergies also appear to be less common among children who have two or more older siblings or who attend daycare during their first 6 months.

This discovery has led to the theory that our western lifestyle—with its emphasis on hygiene, sanitation, and indoor living and working— has resulted in changes in our living conditions and an overall decline in infections in early childhood. Many young children no longer experience the same types of environmental exposures and infections that children did in years past. This affects the way their immune systems develop during very early childhood and may increase their chances of developing atopy and asthma. This is especially true of people who have close family members with one or both of these conditions.

This theory is called the hygiene hypothesis. It may help explain why asthma has been increasing in recent years.

The "Hygiene Hypothesis"

One theory researchers have for what causes asthma is the "hygiene hypothesis." They believe that our Western lifestyle—with its emphasis on hygiene and sanitation—has resulted in changes in our living conditions and an overall decline in infections in early childhood.

Many young children no longer have the same types of environmental exposures and infections as children did in the past. This affects the way that young children's immune systems develop during very early childhood, and it may increase their risk for atopy and asthma. This is especially true for children who have close family members with one or both of these conditions.

Obesity Causes and Consequences

Obesity is a complex health issue. It occurs when a person is well above the normal or healthy weight for his or her age and height. The main causes of excess weight in youth are similar to those in adults, including individual causes such as behavior and genetics. Behaviors can include dietary patterns, physical activity, inactivity, medication use, and other exposures. Additional contributing factors in our society include the food and physical activity environment, education and skills, and food marketing and promotion.

Behavior

Healthy behaviors include a healthy diet pattern and regular physical activity. Energy balance of the number of calories consumed from foods and beverages with the number of calories the body uses for activity plays a role in preventing excess weight gain.

Community Environment

- Advertising of less healthy foods.
- Variation in licensure regulations among child care centers.
- No safe and appealing place, in many communities, to play or be active.
- Limited access to healthy affordable foods.
- Greater availability of high-energy-dense foods and sugar sweetened beverages.
- Increasing portion sizes.
- Lack of breastfeeding support.

Obesity is a risk factor for the development of asthma

Obesity is associated significantly with the development of asthma, worsening asthma symptoms, and poor asthma control. This leads to increase medication use and hospitalizations. In 2010, the obesity rate among adults with current asthma (38.8%) was significantly higher than the rate among adults without current asthma (26.8%).

Obesity rates differ from state to state. The rate among adults with current asthma was significantly higher than the rate among adults without current asthma in almost all states (except AL, AR, DE, KS, MN, ND, NE, and NY), Puerto Rico, and the two territories. The highest obesity rates are clustered in the Midwest and South.

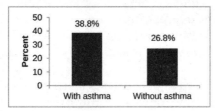

Figure 2.1. Percentage of adults who are obese with and without asthma.

Section 2.2

Genetics of Asthma

Text in this section is excerpted from "Asthma and Its Environmental Triggers," National Institute of Environmental Health Sciences (NIEHS), February 2012; and text from "Depression During Pregnancy Linked to Child's Asthma Risk," U.S. Department of Health and Human Services (HHS), March 9, 2015.

Does Asthma Run in Families?

Asthma does run in families, which suggests that genetics play an important role in the development of the disease. If one or both parents have asthma, the child is much more likely to develop the condition—this is known as genetic susceptibility. An NIEHS study of 615 Mexico City families showed that variations in two genes, ORMDL3 and GSDML, were associated with an increased risk of childhood asthma. These results confirm a similar study conducted among European populations.

Mother's Depression a Risk Factor in Childhood Asthma

A child may face an increased risk of asthma if the child's mother experienced depression during her pregnancy or she took an older antidepressant to treat her condition, new research suggests.

However, more than 80 percent of the women in the study who were prescribed antidepressants were given one of a newer class of drugs known as selective serotonin reuptake inhibitors (SSRIs). And those medications were not linked to any increased risk for asthma in the child.

How maternal depression affects asthma risk in the offspring is unknown, but the mechanism could involve hormone changes or changes in lifestyles. The most significant finding in the study is that the [overall] antidepressant use during pregnancy did not increase the risk of asthma in general.

But it was a different story when the researchers looked only at older antidepressants, known as tricyclic antidepressants. They were linked to the same level of increased risk for asthma as depression during pregnancy, the researchers said. In the study, roughly 8 percent of the women took the older medications.

Some examples of these older antidepressants include Norpramin (desipramine), Tofranil (imipramine), and Pamelor (nortriptyline).

Depression affects between 7 percent and 13 percent of pregnant women, according to background information in the study, and antidepressant use during pregnancy has risen in recent years.

SSRIs are the most commonly prescribed medications for depression. Some examples of SSRIs include Zoloft (sertraline), Prozac (fluoxetine) and Celexa (citalopram).

On an analysis of the medical records of more than 733,000 Danish children born between 1996 and 2007, more than 21,000 of the children's mothers either had a diagnosis of depression or received a prescription for antidepressants while they were pregnant.

Children born to mothers who had depression were 25 percent more likely to develop childhood asthma, the findings revealed.

Among the nearly 9,000 children whose mothers were prescribed antidepressants during pregnancy, the children of those women who received older antidepressants had a 26 percent increased risk of asthma.

The study did not prove that older antidepressants caused the asthma risk, just that there was an association between the two. The researchers pointed out that tricyclic antidepressants are typically prescribed for more severe depression, which has been linked to asthma in past research.

And the study also only found an association between depression and asthma risk, not a cause-and-effect link.

Tricyclic antidepressants have different pharmacokinetic properties than SSRIs, but the association may be confounded by the underlying severity of depression.

In other words, it might be that the reason for the increased asthma risk is that mothers who are prescribed tricyclic antidepressants already have more severe depression and that it is the depression—not the drugs—that contributes to asthma risk.

It's not clear, however, how a mother's depression might contribute to a child's asthma risk. The link might be explained partly by biology, with something happening during pregnancy, by involving environmental or genetic factors, or all three.

The researchers also found that depression in fathers slightly increased children's risk of asthma, which suggested that some kind of environmental or genetic factors might be involved.

The study findings should not change any woman's decision to treat depression during pregnancy, however.

This study asks some interesting questions that deserve further study, but there is no evidence here that antidepressants cause asthma. Women should have their depression treated so they can function better for themselves, their families and their newborns.

Section 2.3

Respiratory Syncytial Virus Can Increase Risk of Asthma

Text in this section is excerpted from "Asthma: The Hygiene
Hypothesis," U.S. Food and Drug Administration (FDA),
January 26, 2015.

What does RSV have to do with the hygiene hypothesis?

Respiratory syncytial virus (RSV) is often the first viral pathogen
encountered by infants.

RSV pneumonia puts infants at higher risk for developing childhood
asthma. (Although children may outgrow this type of asthma, it can
account for clinic visits and missed school days.)

RSV carries a molecule on its surface called the F protein, which
flips the same immune system "switch" (TLR4) as do bacterial
endotoxins.

It may seem obvious that, since both the RSV F protein and lipo-
polysaccharides (LPS) signal through the same TLR4 "switch," they
both would educate the infant's immune system in the same beneficial
way. But that may not be the case.

The large population of bacteria that normally lives inside humans
educates the growing immune system to respond using the TLR4
switch. When this education is lacking or weak, the response to RSV
by some critical cells in the immune system's defense against infections—called "T-cells"—might inadvertently trigger asthma instead
of protecting the infant and clearing the infection.

In order to determine RSV's role in triggering asthma, our laboratory studied how RSV blocks T-cell proliferation.

Studying the effect of RSV on T-cells in the laboratory, however,
has been very difficult. That's because when RSV is put into the same
culture as T-cells, it blocks them from multiplying as they would naturally do when they are stimulated. To get past this problem, most

researchers kill RSV with ultraviolet light before adding the virus to T-cell cultures.

The first major discovery was that RSV causes the release from certain immune system cells of signaling molecules called Type I and Type III interferons that can suppress T-cell proliferation.

Conclusion

The hygiene hypothesis suggests that a newborn baby's immune system must be educated so it will function properly during infancy and the rest of life. One of the key elements of this education is a switch on T cells called TLR4. The bacterial protein LPS normally plays a key role by flipping that switch into the "on" position.

Prior researches suggested that since RSV flips the TLR4 switch, RSV should "educate" the child's immune system to defend against infections just like LPS does.

But it turns out that RSV does not flip the TLR switch in the same way as LPS. This difference in switching on TLR, combined with other characteristics of RSV, can prevent proper education of the immune system.

One difference in the way that RSV flips the TLR4 switch may be through the release of interferons, which suppresses the proliferation of T-cells.

Section 2.4

Air Pollution and Asthma

Text in this section is excerpted from "Respiratory Diseases," U.S. Environmental Protection Agency (EPA), October 2015.

Respiratory Diseases

Respiratory diseases and illness, such as asthma, bronchitis, pneumonia, allergic rhinitis, and sinusitis, can greatly impair a child's ability to function and are an important cause of missed school days and limitations of activities. Symptoms associated with both mild and more severe manifestations of these respiratory conditions, such as cough, wheeze, congestion, chest pain, shortness of breath, respiratory distress, and death in the most extreme cases, are responsible for substantial morbidity and a large cost burden to families and society.

Outdoor and indoor air pollution can adversely affect children's respiratory health. Studies have shown that air pollution can exacerbate existing respiratory conditions such as asthma and upper airway allergies. Increasing evidence suggests that exposure to certain air pollutants may contribute to the onset of asthma in children, although studies relating to the exacerbation of pre existing asthma are more prevalent because they are easier to conduct. Air pollution also increases a child's risk of developing respiratory infections, most likely by causing inflammation and/or impaired immune response.

EPA sets health-based National Ambient Air Quality Standards for six air pollutants. These pollutants, referred to as criteria air pollutants, are particulate matter (PM), ground-level ozone, nitrogen oxides, sulfur oxides, carbon monoxide (CO), and lead. Four of these pollutants have extensive evidence linking them to respiratory diseases in children (PM, ground-level ozone, nitrogen oxides, and sulfur oxides). The evidence for respiratory effects is weaker for CO, and lead has not been linked to adverse respiratory outcomes.

PM is associated with significant respiratory problems in children, including aggravated asthma; exacerbation of allergic symptoms; reduced growth of lung function; and increased hospital admissions, emergency room visits, and doctor visits for respiratory diseases, especially in children with lung diseases such as asthma. Particulate air pollution has also been associated with respiratory-related infant mortality, even at relatively low PM levels that are commonly experienced in the United States.

Short-term exposure to ground-level ozone can cause a variety of respiratory health effects, including airway inflammation; reduced lung function; increased susceptibility to respiratory infection; and respiratory symptoms such as cough, wheezing, chest pain, and shortness of breath. Ozone exposure can decrease the capacity to perform exercise and has been associated with the aggravation of respiratory illnesses such as asthma and bronchitis, leading to increased use of medication, absences from school, doctor and emergency department visits, and hospital admissions.

Studies have also found that long-term ozone exposure may contribute to the development of asthma, especially among children with certain genetic susceptibilities and children who frequently exercise outdoors.

Nitrogen dioxide (NO_2) is an odorless gas that can irritate the eyes, nose, and throat, and can cause shortness of breath. EPA has concluded that exposure to NO_2 can lead to increased respiratory illnesses and symptoms, more severe asthma symptoms, and an increase in the number of emergency department visits and hospital admissions for respiratory causes, especially asthma.

Short-term exposures of persons with asthma to elevated levels of sulfur dioxide (SO_2) while exercising at a moderate level may result in breathing difficulties, accompanied by symptoms such as wheezing, chest tightness, or shortness of breath. Studies also provide consistent evidence of an association between short-term SO_2 exposure and increased respiratory symptoms in children, especially those with asthma or chronic respiratory symptoms. Short term exposures to SO_2 have also been associated with respiratory-related emergency department visits and hospital admissions, particularly for children.

Exposure to CO reduces the capacity of the blood to carry oxygen, thereby decreasing the supply of oxygen to tissues and organs such as the heart. Research suggests correlations between CO exposure and the exacerbation of asthma; however, CO levels are highly correlated with other combustion-related pollutants, especially in locations near roads. Few analyses clearly distinguish the contributions of CO from those of the larger traffic-related air pollutant mixture, thus it is uncertain whether the observed health effects are truly attributable to CO or whether they are due to other co-occurring air pollutants.

In addition to the criteria air pollutants, EPA regulates 187 hazardous air pollutants (HAPs) that are known or suspected to cause serious health effects or adverse environmental effects. For many of these pollutants, information on health effects is scarce. HAPs that may be of particular concern for the induction and exacerbation of asthma include acrolein, formaldehyde, nickel, and chromium. Acrolein has been identified as a HAP of particular concern for possible respiratory effects at levels commonly found in outdoor air in the United States. Acrolein can cause respiratory irritation in individuals who do not have asthma.

Pollution from traffic-related sources, a mix of criteria air pollutants and HAPs, appears to pose particular threats to a child's respiratory system. Many studies have found a correlation between proximity to traffic (or to traffic-related pollutants) and occurrence of new asthma cases or exacerbation of existing asthma and other respiratory symptoms, including reduced growth of lung function during childhood. A report by the Health Effects Institute concluded that living close to busy roads appears to be an independent risk factor for the onset of childhood asthma.

The same report also concluded that the evidence was "sufficient" to infer a causal association between exposure to traffic-related pollution and exacerbations of asthma in children. Some studies have suggested that traffic-related pollutants may contribute to the development of allergic disease, either by affecting the immune response directly or by increasing the concentration or biological activity of the allergens themselves.

Children can also be exposed to air pollution inside homes, schools, and other buildings. Indoor air pollutants from biological sources such as mold; dust mites; pet dander (skin flakes); and droppings and body parts from cockroaches, rodents, and other pests or insects, can lead to allergic reactions, exacerbate existing asthma, and have been associated with the development of respiratory symptoms. Furthermore, the Institute of Medicine concluded that exposure to dust mites can cause asthma in susceptible children, and exposure to cockroaches may cause asthma in young children.

PM and NO_2, discussed previously as outdoor air pollutants, also pollute indoor air when they are emitted from gas stoves, gas or oil furnaces, fireplaces, wood stoves, and kerosene or gas space heaters. Indoor concentrations of these combustion byproducts can reach very high levels in developing countries where solid fuels are used extensively for cooking and home heating, but may also affect the respiratory health of children in developed countries, especially during the winter when use of fireplaces and space heaters is more common. Environmental tobacco smoke (ETS), also known as secondhand smoke, is an air pollutant mixture that includes particles and NO_2 as well as thousands of other chemicals. Exposure to ETS causes sudden infant death syndrome (SIDS), acute lower respiratory infection, ear problems, and more severe asthma in children. Smoking by parents causes respiratory symptoms and slows lung growth in their children.

A number of air pollutants emitted indoors by a variety of household items such as building materials and home furnishings, recently dry-cleaned clothes, cleaning supplies, and room deodorizers, have been associated with respiratory symptoms and may play a role in the exacerbation or development of childhood asthma. A recent systematic review of seven studies concluded that there is a significant association between exposure to formaldehyde—a chemical released from particle board, insulation, carpet, and furniture—and self-reported or diagnosed asthma in children.

Air pollutants can enter the bloodstream of pregnant women and cross the placenta to reach the developing fetus; thus the period of fetal development may be a window of special vulnerability for respiratory effects of some air pollutants. Studies indicate that prenatal exposure to ETS may increase the risk of developing asthma during childhood and/or lead to impaired lung function, especially among children with asthma.

Studies have also found that prenatal exposure to polycyclic aromatic hydrocarbons (hazardous air pollutants found in diesel exhaust, ETS, and smoke from burning organic materials) is associated with childhood respiratory illnesses and the development of asthma, particularly when in combination with prenatal or postnatal exposure to ETS. Limited studies of prenatal exposure to criteria air pollutants have found that exposure to PM, CO, and oxides of nitrogen and sulfur may increase the risk of developing asthma as well as worsen respiratory outcomes among those children who do develop asthma.

However, it is difficult to distinguish the effects of prenatal and early childhood exposure because exposure to air pollutants is often very similar during both periods.

Chapter 3

Asthma Triggers

Chapter Contents

Section 3.1

Common Allergic and Non-Allergic Asthma Triggers

This section includes excerpts from "Common Asthma Triggers," Centers for Disease Control and Prevention (CDC), August 20, 2012; text from "Household Mold Linked to Asthma in Children," *NIH News*, National Institutes of Health, September 2012; and text from "Indoor Asthma Triggers: Secondhand Smoke and Molds," U.S. Environmental Protection Agency (EPA), October 26, 2015.

Common Asthma Triggers

If you have asthma, an asthma attack can happen when you are exposed to "asthma triggers." Your triggers can be very different from those of someone else with asthma. Know your triggers and learn how to avoid them. Watch out for an attack when you can't avoid the triggers. Some of the most common triggers are below:

Cockroach Allergen

Cockroaches and their droppings can trigger an asthma attack. Get rid of cockroaches in your home by removing as many water and food sources as you can. Cockroaches are often found where food is eaten and crumbs are left behind. At least every 2 to 3 days, vacuum or sweep areas that might attract cockroaches. Use roach traps or gels to cut down on the number of cockroaches in your home.

Dust Mites

Dust mites are tiny bugs that are in almost every home. If you have asthma, dust mites can trigger an asthma attack. To prevent attacks, use mattress covers and pillowcase covers to make a barrier between dust mites and yourself. Don't use down-filled pillows, quilts, or comforters. Remove stuffed animals and clutter from your bedroom. Wash your bedding on the hottest water setting.

Mold

Molds create tiny spores to reproduce, just as plants produce seeds. Mold spores float through the indoor and outdoor air continually. When mold spores land on damp places indoors, they may begin growing. Molds are microscopic fungi that live on plant and animal matter. Molds can be found almost anywhere when moisture is present.

For people sensitive to molds, inhaling mold spores can trigger an asthma attack.

Breathing in mold can trigger an asthma attack. Get rid of mold in your home to help control your attacks. Humidity, the amount of moisture in the air, can make mold grow. An air conditioner or dehumidifier will help you keep the humidity level low. Get a small tool called a hygrometer to check humidity levels and keep them as low as you can—no higher than 50%. Humidity levels change over the course of a day, so check the humidity levels more than once a day. Fix water leaks, which let mold grow behind walls and under floors.

Household Mold Linked to Asthma in Children

Three types of mold were more common in the homes of babies who later developed asthma. The finding highlights how important it is to prevent water damage and mold growth in homes with infants.

Previous studies have linked childhood asthma to indoor mold, which can thrive in homes with moisture problems. The connection between mold and asthma, however, is complicated and not fully understood. Asthma is often associated with allergies, and molds release tiny particles into the air that can cause allergic reactions.

To learn more about the link between mold and childhood asthma, researchers visited the homes of nearly 300 infants who were about 8 months old. The scientists looked and smelled for evidence of mold. They also measured levels of 36 different types of mold in dust samples from each home.

Once the kids reached age 7, the researchers found, nearly 1 in 4 had developed asthma. The risk of asthma was greater for kids whose original homes had higher "mold scores."

Three particular species of mold were most associated with asthma. These species—*Aspergillus ochraceus, Aspergillus unguis* and *Penicillium variabile*—are common to water-damaged buildings.

Sometimes homes that at first seemed to have no mold had high mold scores according to the dust sample analyses. Other studies have found that many homes with high mold scores have undetected mold problems. Fixing these problems can improve asthma in children.

The link between the 3 molds and asthma doesn't prove that the molds cause asthma on their own. But it does provide evidence that indoor mold can contribute to the development of asthma.

Previous scientific studies have linked mold to worsening asthma symptoms, but the relevant mold species and their concentrations were unknown. Preventing home water damage and growth of these molds might help relieve some problems with asthma.

Actions You Can Take

- If mold is a problem in your home, you need to clean up the mold and eliminate sources of moisture.

- If you see mold on hard surfaces, clean it up with soap and water. Let the area dry completely.

- Use exhaust fans or open a window in the bathroom and kitchen when showering, cooking or washing dishes.

- Fix water leaks as soon as possible to keep mold from growing.

- Dry damp or wet things completely within one to two days to keep mold from growing.

- Maintain low indoor humidity, ideally between 30-50% relative humidity. Humidity levels can be measured by hygrometers, which are available at local hardware stores.

Pets

Furry pets can trigger an asthma attack. If you think a furry pet may be causing attacks, you may want to find the pet another home. If you can't or don't want to find a new home for the pet, keep it out of the person with asthma's bedroom.

Bathe pets every week and keep them outside as much as you can. People with asthma are not allergic to their pet's fur, so trimming the pet's fur will not help your asthma. If you have a furry pet, vacuum often. If your floors have a hard surface, such as wood or tile, damp mop them every week.

Smoke from Burning Wood or Grass

Smoke from burning wood or other plants is made up of a mix of harmful gases and small particles. Breathing in too much of this smoke can cause an asthma attack. If you can, avoid burning wood in your home. If a wildfire is causing poor air quality in your area pay attention to air quality forecasts on radio, television, and the Internet and check your newspaper to plan your activities for when air pollution levels will be low.

Tobacco Smoke

Tobacco smoke is unhealthy for everyone, especially people with asthma. If you have asthma and you smoke, quit smoking.

"Secondhand smoke" is smoke created by a smoker and breathed in by a second person. Secondhand smoke can trigger an asthma attack. If you have asthma, people should never smoke near you, in your home, in your car, or wherever you may spend a lot of time.

Outdoor Air Pollution

Outdoor air pollution can trigger an asthma attack. This pollution can come from factories, cars, and other sources. Pay attention to air quality forecasts on radio, television, and the Internet and check your newspaper to plan your activities for when air pollution levels will be low.

Other Triggers

Infections linked to influenza (flu), colds, and respiratory syncytial virus (RSV) can trigger an asthma attack. Sinus infections, allergies, breathing in some chemicals, and acid reflux can also trigger attacks.

Physical exercise; some medicines; bad weather, such as thunderstorms or high humidity; breathing in cold, dry air; and some foods, food additives, and fragrances can also trigger an asthma attack.

Strong emotions can lead to very fast breathing, called hyperventilation, that can also cause an asthma attack.

Section 3.2

Climate Change and Asthma

Text in this section is excerpted from "The Health Impacts of Climate
Change on Americans," WhiteHouse.gov, June 2014.

We know climate change will put vulnerable populations at greater
risk – including the elderly, our kids, and people already suffering from
burdensome allergies, asthma, and other illnesses. Pre-existing health
conditions make older adults susceptible to the cardiac and respiratory
impacts of air pollution. Higher rates of diabetes, obesity, or asthma in
some communities may place them at greater risk of climate-related
health impacts. Children, who breathe more air relative to their size
than adults, are also at higher risk of worsened asthma and respiratory
symptoms from air pollution.

Already, more than 8 percent of Americans are living with asthma,
including more than 9 percent of children. In fact, asthma is the third
leading cause of hospitalizations for children. It also hits some communities particularly hard. For instance, African Americans children
are twice as likely to be hospitalized for asthma as whites, and are
more likely to die from asthma. Latino children are 40 percent more
likely to die from asthma than white children.

Asthma is not just making people sick, it is costing taxpayers.
According to the Centers for Disease Control, the United States is
spending billions of dollars in Medicaid expenses related to asthma
each year.

In addition, climate change also increases the number and severity
of heat waves. Older individuals who have a higher risk of dying during
extreme heat events will bear a disproportionate share of the impacts.
Heat waves and other extreme weather events can also disproportionately affect low-income communities and some communities of color,
raising environmental justice concerns.

Section 3.3

Indoor Environmental Quality (IEQ)

This section includes excerpts from "Indoor Environmental Quality,"
Centers for Disease Control and Prevention (CDC),
May 17, 2013; text from "Isocyanates," Centers for Disease Control
and Prevention (CDC), April 23, 2014; and text from "Chemical
Irritants (Chloramines) & Indoor Pool Air Quality," Centers for
Disease Control and Prevention (CDC), July 12, 2013.

Overview

Indoor environmental quality (IEQ) refers to the quality of a building's environment in relation to the health and wellbeing of those who occupy space within it. IEQ is determined by many factors, including lighting, air quality, and damp conditions. Workers are often concerned that they have symptoms or health conditions from exposures to contaminants in the buildings where they work. One reason for this concern is that their symptoms often get better when they are not in the building. While research has shown that some respiratory symptoms and illnesses can be associated with damp buildings, it is still unclear what measurements of indoor contaminants show that workers are at risk for disease.

In most instances where a worker and his or her physician suspect that the building environment is causing a specific health condition, the information available from medical tests and tests of the environment is not sufficient to establish which contaminants are responsible. Despite uncertainty about what to measure and how to interpret what is measured, research shows that building-related symptoms are associated with building characteristics, including dampness, cleanliness, and ventilation characteristics.

Indoor environments are highly complex and building occupants may be exposed to a variety of contaminants (in the form of gases and particles) from office machines, cleaning products, construction activities, carpets and furnishings, perfumes, cigarette smoke, water-damaged building materials, microbial growth (fungal, mold, and bacterial), insects, and outdoor pollutants. Other factors such as indoor

45

temperatures, relative humidity, and ventilation levels can also affect how individuals respond to the indoor environment.

Understanding the sources of indoor environmental contaminants and controlling them can often help prevent or resolve building-related worker symptoms. Practical guidance for improving and maintaining the indoor environment is available.

Workers who have persistent or worsening symptoms should seek medical evaluation to establish a diagnosis and obtain recommendations for treatment of their condition.

Building Ventilation

Building ventilation is the circulation of air throughout a building. The ventilation or the heating, ventilating, and air-conditioning (HVAC) system of a building supplies and removes air either naturally (windows) and/or mechanically to and from a space. HVAC systems consist of mechanical parts which should provide air to building occupants at a comfortable temperature and humidity that is free of harmful concentrations of air pollutants. Building ventilation is one important factor affecting the relationship between airborne transmission of respiratory infections and the health and productivity of workers.

Why is the operation and maintenance of HVAC systems important?

Improper operation and maintenance of HVAC systems is one of the most common problems that impact workplace indoor environmental quality (IEQ). HVAC systems include all of the equipment used to ventilate, heat, and cool the building; to move the air around the building (ductwork); and to filter and clean the air. These systems can have a significant impact on how pollutants are distributed and removed. Maintaining good IEQ requires constant attention to the building's HVAC system, which includes the design, layout and pollutant source management or air filtration.

There are a variety of pollutants and sources of pollutants in a building such as:

- carbon dioxide and carbon monoxide
- tobacco smoke
- molds and bacteria
- cleaning products
- copy machines and printers

- pesticides
- vehicle exhaust

Construction and Renovation

Construction and renovation projects in office settings can adversely affect building occupants by the release of airborne particulates, biological contaminants, and gases. Careful planning for IEQ and the prevention of exposure during these activities is essential.

Particulates

Particulate material such as dusts and fibers are likely to be produced during construction and renovation activities. Sources include drywall, plaster, concrete, soil, wood, masonry, flooring, roofing, and ductwork. Non toxic dusts are irritants and can exacerbate lung conditions such as asthma and chronic obstructive lung disease.

Materials that contain fibers such as fiberglass composite materials or insulation can irritate the skin, eyes and respiratory tract when disbursed in the air and/or inhaled. Toxic dusts containing asbestos, polychlorinated biphenyls (PCBs) or lead can cause serious long-term health effects.

For all construction and renovation dusts, a plan to minimize exposure should be implemented. Appropriate containment should be in place to prevent disbursement into occupied areas. Certified and licensed contractors are required to conduct renovation.

Biological Materials

Chronic dampness from water intrusion leads to increased bacteria, mold and other microbes in a building environment. Microbial-contaminated materials require special precautions prior to demolition to prevent biological dusts from dispersing in the occupied space. Another example of biological contamination is an accumulation of bird or rodent droppings. In both cases, uncontrolled disturbances could spread potentially allergenic or infectious dust to occupied building areas. It is therefore important to implement appropriate engineering controls and decontamination techniques to minimize all occupant exposure.

Volatile Organic Compounds (VOCs)

Some building materials release gases called VOCs. Common VOC sources include:

- Caulks, sealants, and coatings

- Adhesives

- Paints, varnishes and/or stains

- Wall coverings

- Cleaning agents

- Fuels and combustion products

- Carpeting

- Vinyl flooring

- Fabric materials and furnishings

Occupants with VOC exposure often report disagreeable odors, exacerbation of asthma, irritation to the eyes, nose and throat, headaches and drowsiness. Health symptoms associated with VOC exposure can be minimized by choosing low VOC emitting products.

Chemicals and Odors

Chemicals and related odors can be sources of IEQ problems in buildings. Odors are organic or inorganic compounds and can be both pleasant and unpleasant. Some odors can be health hazards and some are not. While most chemical contaminants originate from within the building, chemicals can be drawn into a building from the outdoors as well.

Reducing exposure to chemicals in the workplace is a preventative action that can lead to improved outcomes for both worker health and to the environment.

Chemical Contaminant Sources

There are a variety of chemical contaminants found in a variety of sources. Volatile organic compounds (VOCs) are common chemical contaminants found in office and home environments and are a source of odors. VOCs are organic (containing carbon) chemicals that can easily evaporate into the air. Many products found in the office environment may have the potential to release VOCs. Examples include:

- Caulks, sealants, and coatings

- Adhesives

- Paints, varnishes and/or stains

- Wall coverings

- Cleaning agents

- Fuels and combustion products

- Carpeting

- Vinyl flooring

- Fabric materials and furnishings

- Air fresheners and other scented products

- Personal products of employees like perfume, shampoos, etc.

If these and other chemical contaminant sources are not controlled, indoor environmental quality problems can arise, even if the building's ventilation system is properly designed and well maintained.

Some Common Chemicals and Their Effects

Isocyanates are a family of highly reactive, low molecular weight chemicals. They are widely used in the manufacture of flexible and rigid foams, fibers, coatings such as paints and varnishes, and elastomers, and are increasingly used in the automobile industry, autobody repair, and building insulation materials. Spray-on polyurethane products containing isocyanates have been developed for a wide range of retail, commercial, and industrial uses to protect cement, wood, fiberglass, steel and aluminum, including protective coatings for truck beds, trailers, boats, foundations, and decks.

Isocyanates are powerful irritants to the mucous membranes of the eyes and gastrointestinal and respiratory tracts. Direct skin contact can also cause marked inflammation. Isocyanates can also sensitize workers, making them subject to severe asthma attacks if they are exposed again.

There is evidence that both respiratory and dermal exposures can lead to sensitization. Death from severe asthma in some sensitized subjects has been reported. Workers potentially exposed to isocyanates who experience persistent or recurring eye irritation, nasal congestion, dry or sore throat, cold-like symptoms, cough, shortness of breath, wheezing, or chest tightness should see a physician knowledgeable in work-related health problems.

Preventing exposure to isocyanates is a critical step in eliminating the health hazard. Engineering controls such as closed systems and ventilation should be the principal method for minimizing isocyanate exposure in the workplace. Other controls, such as worker isolation and use of personal protective equipment such as respirators and personal protective clothing to prevent dermal exposures may also be necessary. Early recognition of sensitization and prompt and strict elimination of exposures is essential to reduce the risk of long-term or permanent respiratory problems for workers who have become sensitized.

The most widely used compounds are diisocyanates, which contain two isocyanate groups, and polyisocyanates, which are usually derived from diisocyanates and may contain several isocyanate groups. The most commonly used diisocyanates include methylenebis (phenyl isocyanate) (MDI), toluene diisocyanate (TDI), and hexamethylene diisocyanate (HDI). Other common diisocyanates include naphthalene diisocyanate (NDI), methylene bis-cyclohexylisocyanate (HMDI) (hydrogenated MDI), and isophorone diisocyanate (IPDI). Examples of widely used polyisocyanates include HDI biuret and HDI isocyanurate.

Ammonia and bleach (sodium hypochlorite) cause asthma in workers who breathe too much of it in their jobs. They can trigger asthma attacks in children or Early Care and and Education (ECE) providers who already have asthma. They can also irritate the skin, eyes, and respiratory tract.

Quaternary ammonium compounds (also known as QUATs, QACs, or QATs) are not volatile compounds, but using them as sprays can cause nose and throat irritation. Benzalkonium chloride is a severe eye irritant and causes and triggers asthma. Exposures to QUATs may cause allergic skin reactions. Use of QUATs has been associated with the growth of bacteria that are resistant to disinfection. Sometimes this resistance also transfers to antibiotics. In laboratory studies, QUATs were found to damage genetic material (genes).

Phthalates are used in fragrances that are found in air fresheners and cleaning and sanitizing products. They are endocrine disruptors. Research indicates that phthalates increase the risk of allergies and asthma and can affect children's neurodevelopment and thyroid function. Studies show links between phthalates in mothers to abnormal genital development in boys. Phthalates have been found in human urine, blood, semen, amniotic fluid, and breast milk.

Volatile organic compounds (VOCs) are chemicals that vaporize at room temperature. Many VOCs that are released by cleaning supplies have been linked to chronic respiratory problems such as asthma, allergic reactions, and headaches.

Fragrances are mixtures of many chemicals, including VOCs. They can contain up to 3,000 separate ingredients. There is no requirement that fragrance ingredients be listed on the product label.

Many of these chemicals:

- can trigger asthma and allergies

- may be hazardous to humans

Terpenes are chemicals found in pine, lemon, and orange oils that are used in many cleaning and disinfecting products as well as in fragrances. Terpenes react with ozone, especially on hot smoggy days, forming formaldehyde which

- causes cancer

- is a sensitizer that is linked to asthma and allergic reactions

- has damaged genes in lab tests

- is a central nervous system depressant (slows down brain activity)

- may cause joint pain, depression, headaches, chest pains, ear infections, chronic fatigue, dizziness, and loss of sleep

Aerosols use of spray bottles, aerosol cans, and machines such as carpet washers create a fine mist (aerosolization) of the cleaning product, increasing the amount of chemical suspended in the air. These suspended chemicals cause problems with breathing such as asthma. The small particles created by aerosolization can get deeper into the lung. These products should never be used around children.

Indoor Pool Air Quality

Pool operators may receive complaints from swimmers and pool staff about stinging eyes, nasal irritation, or difficulty breathing after being in the water or breathing the air at swimming pools, particularly indoor pools. New research indicates that these symptoms may be an indication of poor water and indoor air quality at the pool caused by a build-up of irritants, known as chloramines, in the water and air.

Irritants in the air at swimming pools are usually the combined chlorine by-products of disinfection. These by products are the result of chlorine binding with sweat, urine, and other waste from swimmers. As the concentration of by-products in the water increases, they move into the surrounding air as well. Breathing air loaded with irritants can cause a variety of symptoms depending on the concentration of irritants in the air and amount of time the air is breathed. The symptoms of irritant exposure in the air can range from mild symptoms, such as coughing, to severe symptoms, such as wheezing or aggravating asthma. It is also known that routine breathing of irritants may increase sensitivity to other types of irritants such as fungi and bacteria.

The buildup of these irritants in the air is partially due to poor air turnover. The poor movement of fresh air over the pool surface, combined with the use of air recycling devices to control heating costs, leads to poor air exchange. Recyclers remove the moisture from the air, but they do not necessarily take in much fresh air. This may save money on heating, but the health risks to patrons and staff associated with the excessive use of these devices outweigh the financial benefits.

Without adequate fresh air, the recycled air flowing over the pool becomes saturated with chlorination by-products so that it can no longer absorb or pick up new by-products coming from the pool water. Because recyclers do not remove all of the by-products in the air, they allow the irritants to accumulate and reach unhealthy levels. In addition, if the air is saturated with irritants, new irritants produced in the water will stay in the pool water causing further irritation for swimmers, such as stinging or red eyes.

Fresh air is important; super chlorination can be an effective way to rid the pool water of these by-products but will not work if the air is saturated with irritants and ventilation is not adequate.

The problem of poor indoor air quality can be fixed through a combination of preventive measures. Improving air movement over the pool and increasing the air turnover rate will reduce irritant levels in the air. One option is to open all of the doors and windows in the pool area or to use fans to boost airflow over the pool surface when many swimmers are using the pool. When super chlorinating, do the same. Also, ensure that the air recycling systems are bringing in enough fresh air.

Adequate disinfectant levels and constant monitoring of water quality can also help reduce irritant levels by decreasing combined chlorine formation in the water. Combined chlorine levels in the water may be reduced by adding secondary disinfection systems, such as ultraviolet light or ozone. In addition, good hygiene is needed. Getting swimmers to shower before getting in the pool and promoting regular bathroom use to reduce the amount of urine in the pool will decrease the formation of irritants.

For the health of pool staff and patrons, remember that all indoor pools need adequate fresh air exchange and all pools need good water quality. This will help make all pools a healthier and more enjoyable place to play and work.

Section 3.4

Ozone and Asthma

This section includes excerpts from "Air Quality Index – A Guide
to Air Quality and Your Health," U.S. Environmental Protection
Agency (EPA), October 03, 2014; text from "Health Effects of Ozone
in Patients with Asthma and Other Chronic Respiratory Disease,"
U.S. Environmental Protection Agency (EPA), September 9, 2015;
and text from "Air Quality Guide for Ozone," U.S. Environmental
Protection Agency (EPA), September 10, 2015.

Why is air quality important?

Local air quality affects how you live and breathe. Like the
weather, it can change from day to day or even hour to hour. The
U.S. Environmental Protection Agency (EPA) and your local air quality agency have been working to make information about outdoor
air quality as easy to find and understand as weather forecasts.
A key tool in this effort is the Air Quality Index, or AQI. EPA and
local officials use the AQI to provide simple information about your
local air quality, how unhealthy air may affect you, and how you can
protect your health.

What is ozone?

Ozone is a gas found in the air we breathe. Ozone can be good or
bad, depending where it occurs:

- **Good ozone** is present naturally in the Earth's upper atmosphere—approximately 6 to 30 miles above the Earth's surface.
  This natural ozone shields us from the sun's harmful ultraviolet
  rays.

- **Bad ozone** forms near the ground when pollutants (emitted by
  sources such as cars, power plants, industrial boilers, refineries,
  and chemical plants) react chemically in sunlight. Ozone pollution is more likely to form during warmer months. This is when
  the weather conditions normally needed to form ground-level
  ozone—lots of sun—occur.

How does ozone affect people with asthma?

There are two major mechanisms by which people with asthma might be more severely affected by ozone than those without asthma. The first is that those with asthma might be more responsive or sensitive to ozone and therefore experience the lung function changes and respiratory symptoms common to all, but either at lower concentrations or with greater magnitude. There is evidence from some controlled exposure studies and some epidemiologic studies that this may be true. By far, the greater individual and public health concern is that the injury, inflammation, and increased airway reactivity induced by ozone exposure may result in a worsening of a person's underlying asthma status, increasing the probability of an asthma exacerbation or a requirement for more treatment.

Some panel studies have found relationships of ambient ozone concentration with increased asthma symptoms and with increased medication use among children with asthma. Other epidemiologic studies have documented relationships between higher ozone levels and increased ER visits and hospital admissions for asthma in the warm season. In a camp for children with asthma in New York, it was observed that on days when ozone concentrations were high, children in camp used their asthma inhalers more frequently than on days when ozone levels were low.

Presumably this was due to a perception that their asthma was worse on those days. Measures of peak expiratory flow in these children were lower on days when ozone levels were high, supporting this hypothesis. Although results are somewhat inconsistent among panel studies of asthmatics, one of the largest with 846 asthmatic children from eight U.S. urban areas monitored during the course of a summer found evidence for lower values of peak expiratory flow and an increased prevalence of respiratory symptoms for several mornings after days when ozone levels were high.

Reductions in morning lung function and an increase in morning symptoms are an indication of worsening asthma status and are consistent with increased asthma exacerbations. There is some evidence that children with more severe asthma are more likely to experience these ozonerelated effects than those with mild asthma.

In Atlanta, GA, in Buffalo and New York City, NY, and in many other places throughout the United States, visits to the hospital emergency room for asthma were more frequent on days when ozone concentrations were high (generally above 110 ppb as a 1-hour average or 60 ppb as a 7-hour average) compared to low ozone days. Similarly, in some places, hospital admissions for asthma were higher following days when ozone levels were elevated with effects generally being larger in the warm season than in the cold season.

The validity of these epidemiologic observations has been supported by the results of controlled experimental ozone exposures in human volunteers in which markers of asthma status were measured after ozone and after clean air exposures. In these studies, ozone has been demonstrated to worsen airway inflammation, to increase the airway response to inhaled allergen, and to increase nonspecific airway responsiveness, each of which is likely to indicate worsening asthma.

In several studies, people with asthma exposed to ozone were observed to have a greater influx in polymorphonuclear leukocytes (PMNs) and larger changes in other markers of airway inflammation than individuals without asthma, suggesting a more intense inflammatory response. In one study ozone increased the numbers of eosinophils found in the bronchoalveolar lavage (BAL) fluid of people with asthma. In contrast, eosinophils are not found in the BAL of individuals without asthma as a result of ozone exposure.

In another study, house dust mite (HDM) sensitive individuals underwent airway challenge with HDM antigen after ozone exposure and after air exposure. After ozone exposure, the concentration of HDM needed to cause a 20% fall in FEV1 was reduced compared to the air exposure, suggesting that people with asthma would have a greater response to environmental levels of HDM following ozone exposure.

Many studies have demonstrated that nonspecific airway responsiveness is greater following ozone exposure. Overall, these experimental findings in humans and laboratory animals are consistent with ozone causing an increase in asthma severity and, taken together, provide a plausible biological mechanism for the epidemiological observations. This suggests that the observed relationships between ambient ozone exposure and the higher probability of experiencing an asthma attack and other manifestations of worsening asthma are causal.

Table 3.1. Air Quality Guide for Ozone

Air Quality Index (0–500)	Who Needs to be Concerned?	What Should I Do?
Good (0–50)	It's a great day to be active outside.	
Moderate (51–100)	Some people who may be unusually sensitive to ozone.	**Unusually sensitive people:** *Consider reducing* prolonged or heavy outdoor exertion. Watch for symptoms such as coughing or shortness of breath. These are signs to take it a little easier. **Everyone else:** It's a good day to be active outside.
Unhealthy for Sensitive Groups (101–150)	Sensitive groups include **people with lung disease such as asthma, older adults, children and teenagers, and people who are active outdoors.**	**Sensitive groups:** *Reduce* prolonged or heavy outdoor exertion. Take more breaks, do less intense activities. Watch for symptoms such as coughing or shortness of breath. Schedule outdoor activities in the morning when ozone is lower. **People with asthma** should follow their asthma action plans and keep quick relief medicine handy.
Unhealthy (151–200)	Everyone	**Sensitive groups:** *Avoid* prolonged or heavy outdoor exertion. Schedule outdoor activities in the morning when ozone is lower. Consider moving activities indoors. **People with asthma,** keep quick-relief medicine handy. **Everyone else:** *Reduce* prolonged or heavy outdoor exertion. Take more breaks, do less intense activities. Schedule outdoor activities in the morning when ozone is lower.
Very Unhealthy (201–300)	Everyone	**Sensitive groups:** *Avoid all* physical activity outdoors. Move activities indoors or reschedule to a time when air quality is better. **People with asthma,** keep quick-relief medicine handy. **Everyone else:** *Avoid* prolonged or heavy outdoor exertion. Schedule outdoor activities in the morning when ozone is lower. Consider moving activities indoors.

Table 3.1. Continued

Air Quality Index (0–500)	Who Needs to be Concerned?	What Should I Do?
Hazardous (301–500)	Everyone	**Everyone:** *Avoid all* physical activity outdoors.

Who is most at risk?

Several groups of people are particularly sensitive to ozone, especially when they are active outdoors. This is because ozone levels are higher outdoors, and physical activity causes faster and deeper breathing, drawing more ozone into the body.

- **People with lung diseases, such as asthma, chronic bronchitis, and emphysema,** can be particularly sensitive to ozone. They will generally experience more serious health effects at lower levels. Ozone can aggravate their diseases, leading to increased medication use, doctor and emergency room visits, and hospital admissions.

- **Children,** including teenagers, are at higher risk from ozone exposure because they often play outdoors in warmer weather when ozone levels are higher, they are more likely to have asthma (which may be aggravated by ozone exposure), and their lungs are still developing.

- **Older adults** may be more affected by ozone exposure, possibly because they are more likely to have pre-existing lung disease.

- **Active people** of all ages who exercise or work vigorously outdoors are at increased risk.

- **Some healthy people** are more sensitive to ozone. They may experience health effects at lower ozone levels than the average person even though they have none of the risk factors listed above. There may be a genetic basis for this increased sensitivity.

In general, as concentrations of ground-level ozone increase, more people begin to experience more serious health effects. When levels are very high, everyone should be concerned about ozone exposure.

What are the health effects?

Ozone affects the lungs and respiratory system in many ways. It can:

- **Irritate the respiratory system**, causing coughing, throat soreness, airway irritation, chest tightness, or chest pain when taking a deep breath.

- **Reduce lung function**, making it more difficult to breathe as deeply and vigorously as you normally would, especially when exercising. Breathing may start to feel uncomfortable, and you may notice that you are taking more rapid and shallow breaths than normal.

- **Inflame and damage the cells that line the lungs.** Within a few days, the damaged cells are replaced and the old cells are shed—much like the way your skin peels after sunburn. Studies suggest that if this type of inflammation happens repeatedly, lung tissue may become permanently scarred and lung function may be permanently reduced.

- **Make the lungs more susceptible to infection.** Ozone reduces the lung's defenses by damaging the cells that move particles and bacteria out of the airways and by reducing the number and effectiveness of white blood cells in the lungs.

- **Aggravate asthma.** When ozone levels are unhealthy, more people with asthma have symptoms that require a doctor's attention or the use of medication. Ozone makes people more sensitive to allergens—the most common triggers for asthma attacks. Also, asthmatics may be more severely affected by reduced lung function and airway inflammation. People with asthma should ask their doctor for an asthma action plan and follow it carefully when ozone levels are unhealthy.

- **Aggravate other chronic lung diseases** such as emphysema and bronchitis. As concentrations of ground-level ozone increase, more people with lung disease visit doctors or emergency rooms and are admitted to the hospital.

- **Cause permanent lung damage.** Repeated short-term ozone damage to children's developing lungs may lead to reduced lung function in adulthood. In adults, ozone exposure may accelerate the natural decline in lung function that occurs with age.

Section 3.5

Roadway Air Pollution and Asthma

Text in this section is excerpted from "Near Roadway Air
Pollution and Health," U.S. Environmental Protection
Agency (EPA), October 23, 2015.

Near Roadway Air Pollution and Health

With more than 45 million people in the United States living, working, or attending school within 300 feet of a major road, airport or
railroad there is growing concern about the health impacts of roadway
traffic. Below are frequent questions U.S. Environmental Protection
Agency (EPA) receives concerning near roadway air pollution and what
EPA is doing to address this important health issue.

Frequently Asked Questions

What are the concerns associated with living, working, or attending school near major roads?

Air pollutants from cars, trucks and other motor vehicles are found
in higher concentrations near major roads. People who live, work or
attend school near major roads appear to have an increased incidence
and severity of health problems associated with air pollution exposures
related to roadway traffic including higher rates of asthma onset and
aggravation, cardiovascular disease, impaired lung development in
children, preterm and lowbirthweight infants, childhood leukemia,
and premature death.

What is a "major road" and how close to a such a road do you have to live, work or attend school to be considered "near" it?

Research findings indicate that roadways generally influence air
quality within a few hundred meters – about 500–600 feet downwind
from the vicinity of heavily traveled roadways or along corridors with

significant trucking traffic or rail activities. This distance will vary by location and time of day or year, prevailing meteorology, topography, nearby land use, traffic patterns, as well as the individual pollutant.

What influences air quality near major roadways?

The type of vehicles and fuel used, traffic activity, and the wind speed and direction can all have big effects on pollutant levels near major roadways. Generally, the more traffic, the higher the emissions; however, certain activities like congestion, stopandgo movement or high-speed operations can increase emissions of certain pollutants. The combination of rush hour and calm winds in the morning often leads to the highest concentrations during this time of the day.

How many people live or spend time near major roads and other transportation facilities?

EPA estimated that in 2009, more than 45 million people in the United States lived within 300 feet of a highway with four or more lanes, a railroad, or an airport, and population trends suggest this number is increasing. Many schools and child care centers are located within a few hundred feet of highways, particularly in urban areas. Furthermore, every day, the average American spends more than an hour in travel, most of which takes place on major roadways.

Are some people at greater risk from being close to major roadways or high traffic areas?

Children, older adults, people with preexisting cardiopulmonary disease, and people of low socioeconomic status are among those at higher risk for health impacts from air pollution near roadways.

What is EPA doing to address near roadway air pollution?

Over the past three decades, the EPA has worked to reduce harmful roadwayrelated emissions in a number of important ways. EPA has reduced pollution from new cars and trucks by establishing more stringent emission standards and cleaner fuel requirements. EPA also has a number of programs designed to reduce emissions from inuse vehicles not subject to the newest emission standards.

In addition, EPA sets the healthbased National Ambient Air Quality Standards (NAAQS) for pollutants that are emitted from onroad mobile sources and has recently required that air quality monitors be placed near high-traffic roadways for determining compliance with the NAAQS for NO_2, CO, and PM2. Finally, EPA is conducting research to better understand the phenomenon of near roadway pollution, exposure and adverse health effects, and how to reduce air pollution near these hightraffic areas.

Are there other actions that may reduce air pollution concentrations and exposures near major roadways?

There are a number of approaches that appear promising for reducing the air pollution near roadways. In addition to reducing vehicle emissions, other approaches involve the design of transportation projects and designs of buildings and facilities near major roadways. For example, research suggests that sound walls, cut sections, and roadside vegetation can reduce trafficrelated air pollutants immediately downwind of a roadway, although the extent of this reduction can vary by the dimension and type of feature.

Research is still underway to quantify the specific impacts these features have in reducing air pollutants nearroadway areas. In addition, design and siting of new buildings, and the use of indoor air filtration, may also be a way to minimize exposures to pollutants while indoors.

What air pollution exposures occur in vehicles?

In vehicle, air quality is influenced by surrounding vehicles and sometimes emissions from the vehicle itself. Studies generally report higher concentrations of air pollutants in vehicles when following heavy duty trucks and cars with visible tailpipe emissions. Tailgating and stopping very close to the vehicle in front during a traffic jam or at an intersection can increase air pollution in the following vehicle. A key factor in determining driver and passenger exposure is the vehicle's ventilation. Older diesel-powered buses also can have elevated concentrations of exhaust components inside the cabin.

What is EPA doing about railyard and port emissions?

EPA has established emission standards that will reduce emissions from each engine, including those for locomotives and marine vessels. Reducing idling also prevents emissions and improves nearby air quality. Features such as walls and vegetation may also reduce concentrations of air pollutants near these facilities, but little direct research exists for these locations.

Chapter 4

Asthma Prevalence, Health Care Use, and Mortality in the United States

Asthma Prevalence

In 2010, there were 17.2 million (8.7%) adults with asthma and 4.6 million (8.5%) children with asthma living in NACP grantee states, the District of Columbia, and Puerto Rico. Current asthma prevalence among adults ranged from 6.7% in Louisiana to 11.1% in Vermont; among children, the prevalence ranged from 5.9% in California to 18% in the District of Columbia. Differences in current asthma prevalence exist between certain population subgroups.

Adults

Age

Current asthma prevalence was higher among adults aged 18–24 years (10.3%) compared with adults aged 25–34 years (8.7%), 35–44 years (8.1%), 45–54 years (8.5%), 55–64 years (9.4%), and 65 years and older (8.1%).

Text in this chapter is excerpted from "Asthma Facts," Centers for Disease Control and Prevention (CDC), July 2013.

Sex

Current asthma prevalence was higher among females (10.7%) compared with males (6.5%).

Race and Ethnicity

When compared with white adults (8.7%), multi-race (15.1 %), and black (10.8%) adults had the higher current asthma prevalence.

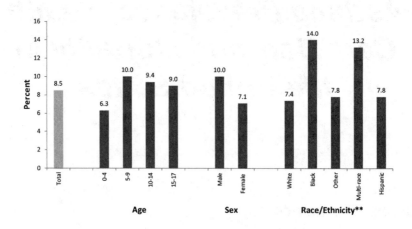

Figure 4.1. *Adult current asthma prevalence percent by age, sex, and race/ethnicity*

Source: Behavioral Risk Factor Surveillance System, Centers for Disease Control and Prevention
* 36 National Asthma Control Program Grantees
** White, black, other, and multi-race categories are non-Hispanic

Children

Age

Current asthma prevalence was lower among children aged 0–4 years (6.3%) compared with children aged 5-9 years (10.0%), 10–14 years (9.4%), and 15–17 years (9.0%).

Sex

Current asthma prevalence was higher among males (10.0%) compared with females (7.1%).

Race and Ethnicity

Current asthma prevalence was higher among black (14.0%) and multi-race (13.2%) children compared with white children (7.4%).

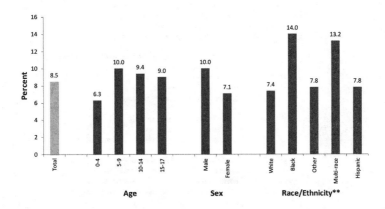

Figure 4.2. *Child current asthma prevalence percent by age, sex, and race/ ethnicity*

Source: Behavioral Risk Factor Surveillance System, Centers for Disease Control and Prevention
* 32 National Asthma Control Program Grantees
** White, black, other, and multi-race categories are non-Hispanic

Adult Education

Current asthma prevalence was higher among adults who did not graduate from high school (10.0%) compared with high school (8.8%) or college graduates (7.5%).

Household Income

Current asthma was more prevalent among adults who lived in households with an income less than $15,000 (13.3%), $15,000 to less than $25,000 (10.3%), $25,000 to less than $50,000 (8.3%), and $50,000 to less than $75,000 (8.0%) compared with adults who lived in households with an income of $75,000 or more (7.0%).

Adult Behavioral Risk Factors

Current asthma prevalence was higher among obese adults (12.0%) compared with not obese or overweight adults (7.2%) and overweight adults (7.5%).

Current asthma was more prevalent among current-daily (10.9%) and current-smoked some days (10.4%) smokers compared with never (9.0%) and former (8.0%) smokers.

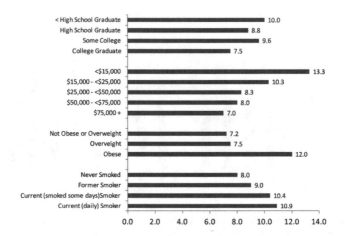

Figure 4.3. *Adult current asthma prevalence percent by education, income, and behavioral risk factors*

Source: Behavioral Risk Factor Surveillance System, Centers for Disease Control and Prevention
*36 National Asthma Control Program Grantees

Healthcare Utilization

Healthcare utilization measures may be used to assess morbidity and asthma control. Although routine office visits for asthma are highly recommended and are paramount for effective asthma management and control, asthma-related hospital stays, emergency department visits, and urgent care visits may indicate the existence of poorly controlled asthma and serve as markers for increased risk of future asthma exacerbations. Healthcare utilization differs significantly by age and by race and ethnicity.

Adult and Child Healthcare Utilization

Children were more likely to have one or more routine office visits, emergency department visits, and urgent care visits for asthma (75.7% vs. 55.2%, 22.2% vs. 13.8%, and 39.8% vs. 24.1%, respectively).

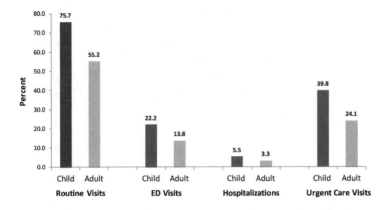

Figure 4.4. *Asthma healthcare utilization among children and adults with current asthma*

Source: Asthma Call-Back Survey (ACBS), Behavioral Risk Factor Surveillance System, Centers for Disease Control and Prevention
* 33 National Asthma Control Program Grantees completed the ACBS for adults and 16 National Asthma Control Program Grantees completed the ACBS for children
Source: Asthma Call-Back Survey (ACBS), Behavioral Risk Factor Surveillance System, Centers for Disease Control and Prevention
* 33 National Asthma Control Program Grantees completed the ACBS for adults and 16 National Asthma Control Program Grantees completed the ACBS for children

Adult and Child Healthcare Utilization by Race and Ethnicity

Children

Black children (88.9%) were more likely to have routine office visits for asthma reported compared with white children (73.0%).

Black children (38.3%) were more likely to have emergency department visits compared with white children (15.0%).

A similar proportion of black (5.7%), Hispanic (10.0%), and white (3.3%) children were hospitalized for asthma.

A similar proportion of black (39.8%), Hispanic (47.4%) and white (37.9%) children had urgent care visits for asthma.

Adults

A similar proportion of white (56.5%), black (53.2%), and Hispanic (50.7%) adults had routine office visits for asthma.

Black adults (22.1%) were nearly two times more likely to have emergency room visits for asthma compared with white adults (11.6%).

Black adults (6.2%) were more likely to have hospital stays for asthma compared with white adults (2.7%).

Hispanic (31.4%) and black (29.8%) adults were more likely to have urgent care visits for asthma compared with whites (22.5%).

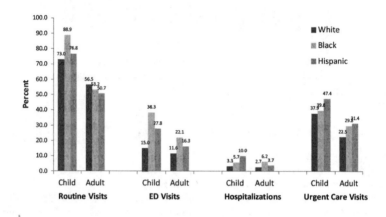

Figure 4.5. *Asthma healthcare utilization among children and adults with current asthma by race and ethnicity*

Source: Asthma Call-Back Survey (ACBS), Behavioral Risk Factor Surveillance System, Centers for Disease Control and Prevention
* White and black categories are non-Hispanic
**33 NACP Grantees completed ACBS for adults and 16 NACP Grantees completed the ACBS for children

Asthma Deaths

Asthma deaths are a rare event, particularly among children and young adults, with a majority of deaths occurring in persons aged 65 years and older. Asthma deaths are thought to be largely preventable with early treatment and special attention to patients who are at high risk of asthma-related deaths (e.g., using two or more canisters of short-acting beta agonist per month, hospitalization or ED visit for asthma in the past month, two or more hospitalizations or three or more ED visits for asthma in the past year), and other risk factors (e.g., low socioeconomic status, comorbidities such as cardiovascular disease, other chronic lung disease).

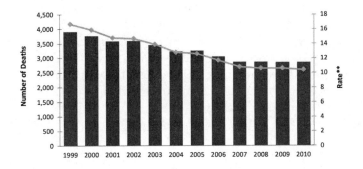

Figure 4.6. *Asthma death rates and number of deaths*

Source: National Vital Statistics System, National Center for Health Statistics, Centers for Disease Control and Prevention
* 35 National Asthma Control Program Grantees. (Puerto Rico is excluded)
**Age-adjusted rate per million population

Chapter 5

Reducing the Burden of Asthma

Populations Most at Risk for Asthma

- Children, women, black and multi-race Americans, and American Indians and Alaska Natives

Asthma by the Numbers

- Children who had asthma in 2011: 7.1 million

- Deaths from asthma in 2010: 3,404

- Visits to hospital outpatient departments with asthma as primary diagnosis in 2009: 1.2 million

- Visits to emergency departments with asthma as primary diagnosis in 2009: 2.1 million

- Yearly medical expenses per person with asthma from 2002 to 2007: $3,300

Evidence-Based Prevention Strategies

- Patient education

Text in this chapter is excerpted from "An Investment in America's Health," Centers for Disease Control and Prevention (CDC), 2013.

- Consistent and correct use of preventive medication
- Control of environmental factors (e.g., triggers) that affect asthma

Reducing the Burden of Asthma

The burden of asthma is characterized by the numbers of asthma-related hospitalizations, emergency room visits, deaths, school days missed, and other factors such as activity limitations. Because asthma has no known cure, the most effective way to manage it is by preventing the need for frequent, costly medical treatment due to uncontrolled symptoms and attacks. The National Asthma Control Program's (NACP) overarching goal is to provide people the tools to manage their asthma successfully, thereby reducing the collective burden of asthma.

Prevalence

Asthma continues to be a major public health concern. The number of reported cases has steadily increased since 1980, with the most rapid growth occurring from 1980–1996. In 2001, 20 million people (1 in 14) had asthma. By 2011, that number had grown to 26 million (1 in 12). The highest rates of asthma occur among children, women, multi-race and black Americans, and American Indians and Alaska Natives. In 2009 alone, there were over two million asthma-related emergency department visits and almost half a million hospitalizations; in 2010, 156 children and 3,248 adults died from asthma.

Economic Impact

From 2002-2007, medical expenditures due to asthma hospitalizations and emergency room visits increased from $48.6 billion to $50.1 billion or about $3,300 per person with asthma each year. When indirect costs due to days missed at school and work are factored in, that number climbs to $56 billion.

The Goal of National Asthma Control Program (NACP): Asthma Control and Management

Fortunately, asthma symptoms and costs can be controlled when people have the appropriate care, education, and guidance to manage their condition. Reducing exposure to triggers, treating patients with medications such as inhaled corticosteroids, and educating patients and caregivers can mitigate the severity of asthma symptoms and frequency of attacks. In 1999, CDC created the NACP to develop interventions based on these principles and reduce the societal and economic burden of asthma in the United States.

Progress in Controlling Asthma

The NACP has made significant progress in controlling asthma in the United States. Over the last 12 years, costs due to asthma illness and death have decreased by $23.1 billion, representing an estimated return on investment of $71 saved for each dollar spent. These savings reflect a shift from visits to more costly medical settings (hospitals and emergency rooms) to less expensive primary care settings (doctor offices and outpatient clinics). In addition, asthma death rates have decreased by 27% since 1999.

Part Two

Recognizing and Diagnosing Asthma

Chapter 6

Asthma Attacks

Chapter Contents

Section 6.1

What Is an Asthma Attack and What Triggers It?

Text in this section is excerpted from "Learn How to Control Asthma," Centers for Disease Control and Prevention (CDC), November 18, 2014; and text from "Prevent Allergy and Asthma Attacks at Home," U.S. Department of Health and Human Services (HHS), July 15, 2015.

What Is an Asthma Attack?

An asthma attack may include coughing, chest tightness, wheezing, and trouble breathing. The attack happens in your body's airways, which are the paths that carry air to your lungs. As the air moves through your lungs, the airways become smaller, like the branches of a tree are smaller than the tree trunk. During an asthma attack, the sides of the airways in your lungs swell and the airways shrink. Less air gets in and out of your lungs, and mucous that your body makes clogs up the airways even more.

You can control your asthma by knowing the warning signs of an asthma attack, staying away from things that cause an attack, and following your doctor's advice.

When you control your asthma:

- you won't have symptoms such as wheezing or coughing,

- you'll sleep better,

- you won't miss work or school,

- you can take part in all physical activities, and

- you won't have to go to the hospital.

What Causes an Asthma Attack?

An asthma attack can happen when you are exposed to "asthma triggers." Your triggers can be very different from those of someone else with asthma. Know your triggers and learn how to avoid them. Watch out for an attack when you can't avoid the triggers. Some of the most common triggers are tobacco smoke, dust mites, outdoor air pollution, cockroach allergen, pets, mold, and smoke from burning wood or grass.

What can cause an allergy or asthma attack?

Things that can cause an allergy or asthma attack are called allergens and irritants. Different people will react to different allergens and irritants.

Common causes of allergy and asthma attacks at home include:

- Mold or dampness
- Dust mites (tiny bugs that live in dust)
- Pets with fur, including cats and dogs
- Cockroaches (roaches and their droppings may cause asthma)
- Rodents (mice and rats)
- Secondhand smoke
- Wood smoke

Section 6.2

What Are the Signs and Symptoms of Asthma?

Text in this section is excerpted from "What Are the Signs and Symptoms of Asthma?" National Heart, Lung, and Blood Institute (NHLBI), August 4, 2014.

What Are the Signs and Symptoms of Asthma?

Common signs and symptoms of asthma include the following:

- **Coughing.** Coughing from asthma often is worse at night or early in the morning, making it hard to sleep.
- **Wheezing.** Wheezing is a whistling or squeaky sound that occurs when you breathe.

- **Chest tightness.** This may feel like something is squeezing or sitting on your chest.

- **Shortness of breath.** Some people who have asthma say they can't catch their breath or they feel out of breath. You may feel like you can't get air out of your lungs.

Not all people who have asthma have these symptoms. Likewise, having these symptoms doesn't always mean that you have asthma. The best way to diagnose asthma for certain is to use a lung function test, a medical history (including type and frequency of symptoms), and a physical exam.

The types of asthma symptoms you have, how often they occur, and how severe they are may vary over time. Sometimes your symptoms may just annoy you. Other times, they may be troublesome enough to limit your daily routine.

Severe symptoms can be fatal. It's important to treat symptoms when you first notice them so they don't become severe.

With proper treatment, most people who have asthma can expect to have few, if any, symptoms either during the day or at night.

What Causes Asthma Symptoms to Occur?

Many things can trigger or worsen asthma symptoms. Your doctor will help you find out which things (sometimes called triggers) may cause your asthma to flare up if you come in contact with them. Triggers may include:

- Allergens from dust, animal fur, cockroaches, mold, and pollens from trees, grasses, and flowers

- Irritants such as cigarette smoke, air pollution, chemicals or dust in the workplace, compounds in home décor products, and sprays (such as hairspray)

- Medicines such as aspirin or other nonsteroidal anti-inflammatory drugs and nonselective beta-blockers

- Sulfites in foods and drinks

- Viral upper respiratory infections, such as colds

- Physical activity, including exercise

Other health conditions can make asthma harder to manage. Examples of these conditions include a runny nose, sinus infections, reflux disease, psychological stress, and sleep apnea. These conditions need treatment as part of an overall asthma care plan.

Asthma is different for each person. Some of the triggers listed above may not affect you. Other triggers that do affect you may not be on the list. Talk with your doctor about the things that seem to make your asthma worse.

Section 6.3

What to Do During an Asthma Attack?

This section includes excerpts from "So You Have Asthma," National Heart, Lung, and Blood Institute (NHLBI), March 2013; and text from "Explore Asthma," National Heart, Lung, and Blood Institute (NHLBI), August 4, 2014.

Follow an Asthma Action Plan

You can work with your doctor to create a personal asthma action plan. The plan will describe your daily treatments, such as which medicines to take and when to take them. The plan also will explain when to call your doctor or go to the emergency room.

If your child has asthma, all of the people who care for him or her should know about the child's asthma action plan. This includes babysitters and workers at daycare centers, schools, and camps. These caretakers can help your child follow his or her action plan.

Go to the National Heart, Lung, and Blood Institute's (NHLBI's) "Asthma Action Plan" for a sample plan.

Avoid Things That Can Worsen Your Asthma

Many common things (called asthma triggers) can set off or worsen your asthma symptoms. Once you know what these things are, you can take steps to control many of them.

For example, exposure to pollens or air pollution might make your asthma worse. If so, try to limit time outdoors when the levels of these substances in the outdoor air are high. If animal fur triggers your asthma symptoms, keep pets with fur out of your home or bedroom.

One possible asthma trigger you shouldn't avoid is physical activity. Physical activity is an important part of a healthy lifestyle. Talk with your doctor about medicines that can help you stay active.

The NHLBI offers many useful tips for controlling asthma triggers.

If your asthma symptoms are clearly related to allergens, and you can't avoid exposure to those allergens, your doctor may advise you to get allergy shots.

You may need to see a specialist if you're thinking about getting allergy shots. These shots can lessen or prevent your asthma symptoms, but they can't cure your asthma.

Several health conditions can make asthma harder to manage. These conditions include runny nose, sinus infections, reflux disease, psychological stress, and sleep apnea. Your doctor will treat these conditions as well.

How to Manage an Asthma Attack

It's best to be prepared before symptoms get worse or an asthma attack happens. Review your asthma action plan so you know what to do if you have symptoms or an asthma attack. Keep your asthma action plan where you can easily find it. Follow your asthma action plan as soon as you begin to have symptoms, and follow it carefully. It can save your life.

Your asthma action plan tells you what to do if you have an asthma attack, including:

- What medicines to take and how much to take (based on your symptoms and peak flow number)
- How to know if the medicine is working
- What to do if the medicine does not stop the asthma attack symptoms
- When to call for emergency help and what number to call

Medicines

Your doctor will consider many things when deciding which asthma medicines are best for you. He or she will check to see how well a medicine works for you. Then, he or she will adjust the dose or medicine as needed.

Asthma medicines can be taken in pill form, but most are taken using a device called an inhaler. An inhaler allows the medicine to go directly to your lungs.

Not all inhalers are used the same way. Ask your doctor or another health care provider to show you the right way to use your inhaler. Review the way you use your inhaler at every medical visit.

Long-Term Control Medicines

Most people who have asthma need to take long-term control medicines daily to help prevent symptoms. The most effective long-term medicines reduce airway inflammation, which helps prevent symptoms from starting. These medicines don't give you quick relief from symptoms.

Long-term control medicines include:

- Inhaled corticosteroids

- Cromolyn

- Omalizumab (anti-IgE)

- Inhaled long-acting beta$_2$-agonists

- Leukotriene modifiers

- Theophylline

If your doctor prescribes a long-term control medicine, take it every day to control your asthma. Your asthma symptoms will likely return or get worse if you stop taking your medicine.

Long-term control medicines can have side effects. Talk with your doctor about these side effects and ways to reduce or avoid them.

Quick-Relief Medicines

All people who have asthma need quick-relief medicines to help relieve asthma symptoms that may flare up.

Quick-relief medicines include:

- Inhaled short-acting beta$_2$-agonists

These medicines act quickly to relax tight muscles around your airways when you're having a flareup. This allows the airways to open up so air can flow through them.

You shouldn't use quick-relief medicines in place of prescribed long-term control medicines. Quick-relief medicines don't reduce inflammation.

Chapter 7

Diagnosing Asthma

Chapter Contents

Section 7.1

Symptoms of Asthma

Text in this section is excerpted from "So You Have Asthma,"
National Heart, Lung, and Blood Institute (NHLBI), March 2013;
and text from "Living With Asthma," National Heart, Lung, and
Blood Institute (NHLBI), August 4, 2014.

Symptoms of Asthma

Most people who have asthma experience one or more of the following symptoms:

- **Coughing.** Coughing from asthma is often worse at night or early morning, making it hard to sleep. Sometimes coughing is your only symptom. Sometimes coughing brings up mucus, or phlegm.

- **Wheezing.** Wheezing is a whistling or squeaky sound when you breathe.

- **Chest tightness.** This can feel like something is squeezing or sitting on your chest.

- **Shortness of breath.** Some people say they can't catch their breath, or they feel breathless, or out of breath—like they can't get enough air out of their lungs.

The symptoms of asthma are different for different people. And symptoms for one person can change from one time to another. So can the frequency of symptoms.

How often you get symptoms will let you and your doctor know if you need to do more to control your asthma. Call your doctor if

- You have asthma symptoms more than 2 days a week.

- Your asthma wakes you up 2 or more times a month.

- You are using your quick-relief inhaler more than 2 days a week.

- Your asthma is getting in the way of your usual activities.

These are signs that your asthma is not well controlled and may be getting worse.

Asthma symptoms can sometimes be mild. At other times, they can be serious enough to make you stop what you are doing. And sometimes, symptoms can be so serious that they are life threatening.

In a severe asthma attack, your airways can narrow so much that not enough oxygen can get into the blood that goes to your vital organs. This condition is a medical emergency. People can die from severe asthma attacks.

With effective asthma management, however, most people who have asthma can expect to have few, if any, symptoms.

Watch for Signs That Your Asthma Is Getting Worse

Your asthma might be getting worse if:

- Your symptoms start to occur more often, are more severe, or bother you at night and cause you to lose sleep.

- You're limiting your normal activities and missing school or work because of your asthma.

- Your peak flow number is low compared to your personal best or varies a lot from day to day.

- Your asthma medicines don't seem to work well anymore.

- You have to use your quick-relief inhaler more often. If you're using quick-relief medicine more than 2 days a week, your asthma isn't well controlled.

- You have to go to the emergency room or doctor because of an asthma attack.

If you have any of these signs, see your doctor. He or she might need to change your medicines or take other steps to control your asthma.

Partner with your health care team and take an active role in your care. This can help you better control your asthma so it doesn't interfere with your activities and disrupt your life.

Section 7.2

How Asthma Is Diagnosed

Text in this section is excerpted from "How Asthma Is
Diagnosed," National Heart, Lung, and Blood Institute (NHLBI),
August 4, 2014; and text from "Handheld Device Diagnoses Asthma
with a Drop of Blood," National Institute of Biomedical Imaging and
Bioengineering (NIBIB), February 4, 2015.

Your primary care doctor will diagnose asthma based on your medical and family histories, a physical exam, and test results.

Your doctor also will figure out the severity of your asthma—that is, whether it's intermittent, mild, moderate, or severe. The level of severity will determine what treatment you'll start on.

You may need to see an asthma specialist if:

- You need special tests to help diagnose asthma

- You've had a life-threatening asthma attack

- You need more than one kind of medicine or higher doses of medicine to control your asthma, or if you have overall problems getting your asthma well controlled

- You're thinking about getting allergy treatments

Medical and Family Histories

Your doctor may ask about your family history of asthma and allergies. He or she also may ask whether you have asthma symptoms and when and how often they occur.

Let your doctor know whether your symptoms seem to happen only during certain times of the year or in certain places, or if they get worse at night.

Your doctor also may want to know what factors seem to trigger your symptoms or worsen them.

Your doctor may ask you about related health conditions that can interfere with asthma management. These conditions include a runny nose, sinus infections, reflux disease, psychological stress, and sleep apnea.

Physical Exam

Your doctor will listen to your breathing and look for signs of asthma or allergies. These signs include wheezing, a runny nose or swollen nasal passages, and allergic skin conditions (such as eczema).

Keep in mind that you can still have asthma even if you don't have these signs on the day that your doctor examines you.

Diagnostic Tests

Lung Function Test

Your doctor will use a test called spirometry to check how your lungs are working. This test measures how much air you can breathe in and out. It also measures how fast you can blow air out.

Your doctor also may give you medicine and then test you again to see whether the results have improved.

If the starting results are lower than normal and improve with the medicine, and if your medical history shows a pattern of asthma symptoms, your diagnosis will likely be asthma.

Other Tests

Your doctor may recommend other tests if he or she needs more information to make a diagnosis. Other tests may include:

- Allergy testing to find out which allergens affect you, if any.

- A test to measure how sensitive your airways are. This is called a bronchoprovocation test. Using spirometry, this test repeatedly measures your lung function during physical activity or after you receive increasing doses of cold air or a special chemical to breathe in.

- A test to show whether you have another condition with the same symptoms as asthma, such as reflux disease, vocal cord dysfunction, or sleep apnea.

- A chest X-ray or an EKG (electrocardiogram). These tests will help find out whether a foreign object or other disease may be causing your symptoms.

Diagnosing Asthma in Young Children

Most children who have asthma develop their first symptoms before 5 years of age. However, asthma in young children (aged 0 to 5 years) can be hard to diagnose.

Sometimes it's hard to tell whether a child has asthma or another childhood condition. This is because the symptoms of asthma also occur with other conditions.

Also, many young children who wheeze when they get colds or respiratory infections don't go on to have asthma after they're 6 years old.

A child may wheeze because he or she has small airways that become even narrower during colds or respiratory infections. The airways grow as the child grows older, so wheezing no longer occurs when the child gets colds.

A young child who has frequent wheezing with colds or respiratory infections is more likely to have asthma if:

- One or both parents have asthma

- The child has signs of allergies, including the allergic skin condition eczema

- The child has allergic reactions to pollens or other airborne allergens

- The child wheezes even when he or she doesn't have a cold or other infection

The most certain way to diagnose asthma is with a lung function test, a medical history, and a physical exam. However, it's hard to do lung function tests in children younger than 5 years. Thus, doctors must rely on children's medical histories, signs and symptoms, and physical exams to make a diagnosis.

Doctors also may use a 4–6 week trial of asthma medicines to see how well a child responds.

Handheld Device Diagnoses Asthma with a Drop of Blood

Despite its high prevalence, asthma is notoriously difficult to diagnose, characterize, and treat. Currently, there is no single test that doctors rely on to diagnose asthma. Instead, doctors take into account a patient's history, symptoms, triggers, and allergies along with results from several breathing tests. The most common of these tests uses a spirometer to record the amount and the rate of air that a patient breathes in and out over a period of time. Patients may also undergo a bronchial challenge, in which a doctor attempts to trigger asthma by having a patient inhale certain drugs that cause the bronchioles, or air passages in the lungs, to constrict; patients with asthma generally become symptomatic at a lower dose of the drug. This test can also be reversed by giving patients drugs that dilate the bronchioles, and important information can be gleaned based on how quickly the patient returns to a normal state.

Yet these breathing tests can be challenging to administer to children or the elderly, which make up a large population of asthmatic patients. In addition, many of the tests rely partially on patients to be symptomatic at the time of their doctor's visit, which, due to the intermittent nature of asthma, can easily result in a misdiagnosis. Furthermore, disease severity, expected clinical course, and risk of exacerbations are not easily determined with the tests that are currently available.

Section 7.3

Classification of Asthma based on Severity

Text in this section is excerpted from "Management of Asthma,"
Federal Bureau of Prisons (BOP), May 2013.

Severity

Severity is defined as the intensity of the disease process, and the level of severity is determined by assessing the disease burden in terms of impairment and risk of adverse events associated with asthma. Classifying asthma severity is useful for initial therapeutic decisions regarding appropriate medications and interventions.

- Although severity is more accurately assessed before a patient begins long-term asthma treatment, often a provider is faced with a patient who is already on a drug regimen for the treatment of their asthma. In these cases, it is useful to classify severity based on the minimum amount of drug therapy needed to achieve control. This method postulates that the patient is responsive to the current treatment and focuses on the importance of achieving a satisfactory level of asthma control.

- For patients not on long-term controller medications, severity is based on measurement of impairment and risk utilizing the most severe category in which any feature appears.

Impairment concerns the functional limitations of the patient, as well as the frequency and severity of symptoms. Impairment is usually assessed by spirometry and patient history. The evaluation of the inmate's symptoms over the previous four weeks include

- Need for a short-acting beta$_2$-agonist (SABA) for immediate relief
- Number of work/school days absent
- Ability to perform normal daily activities
- Night time awakenings
- Quality of life assessments.

Functional limitations should be assessed through spirometry by measuring FEV_1, FEV_6, and the ratio FEV_1/FEV_6. Peak flow is not reliable for assessing initial severity due to unique patient characteristics, but may be useful in assessing control on an ongoing basis. Validated self-assessment questionnaires—such as the Asthma Control Test, Asthma Control Questionnaire, and Asthma Therapy Assessment Questionnaire—can be helpful in evaluating impairment.

Risk is the likelihood that the patient will experience adverse events such as asthma exacerbations, progressive and irreversible loss of pulmonary function, or side effects to drug therapy. Risk can be hard to assess, but a comprehensive medical history can provide key information.

The test which should be most utilized when assessing the risk of future adverse events is spirometry—especially FEV_1 expressed as a percent of the predicted value or as a proportion of the FEV_6 (FEV_1/FEV_6). Other specific measures to assess risk in relation to severity include:

- Previous frequency and severity of exacerbation
- Oral corticosteroid use
- Urgent care visits
- Lung function

Table 7.1. Classifying Asthma Severity and Initiating Treatment

Components of Severity		Classification of Asthma Severity			
		Intermittent	Mild Persistent	Moderate Persistent	Persistent
Impairment	Symptoms	≤2 days/week	>2 days/week but not daily	Daily	Throughout the day
	Nighttime awakenings	≤2x/month	3–4x/month	>1x/week but not nightly	Often 7x/week
	Short-acting Beta$_2$-agonist use for symptom control (not prevention of EIB)	≤2 days/week	>2 days/week but not daily, and not more than 1x on any day	Daily	Several times per day
	Interference with normal activity	None	Minor limitation	Some limitation	Extremely limited
	Lung function Normal FEV1/FEV6: < 20 yr 85% 20–39 yr 80% 40–59 yr 75% 60–80 yr 70%	Normal FEV1 between xacerbations FEV1 >80% predicted FEV1/FEV6 Normal	FEV1 >80% predicted FEV1/FEV6 normal	FEV1 >60% but <80% predicted FEV1/FEV6 reduced 5%	FEV1 <60% Predicted FEV1/FEV6 reduced >5%
Risk	Exacerbations requiring oral systemic corticosteroids	0–1/year	≥2/year		
		Consider severity and interval since last exacerbation. Frequency and severity may fluctuate over time for patients in any severity category. Relative annual risk of exacerbations may be related to FEV1.			

Table 7.1. Continued

Components of Severity	Classification of Asthma Severity				
	Intermittent	Mild Persistent	Moderate Persistent	Persistent	
Recommended Step for Initiating Treatment	For intermittent: Step 1	For mild persistent: Step 2	For moderate persistent: Step 3	For severe Persistent: Step 4, 5, or 6	
			For Steps 3–6, consider adding short course of oral systemic corticosteroids.		
	In 2–6 weeks, evaluate the level of asthma control that has been achieved and adjust therapy accordingly.				

Table 7.2. Assessing Asthma Control and Adjusting Therapy

Components of Control		Classification of Asthma Control		
		Well-Controlled	**Not Well-controlled**	**Very Poorly Controlled**
Impairment	Symptoms	≤2 days/week	>2 days/week	Throughout the day
	Night-time awakenings	≤2x/month	1–3x/week	≥4x/week
	Interference with normal activity	None	Some limitation	Extremely limited
	Short-acting beta$_2$- agonist use for symptom control (not prevention of EIB)	≤2 days/week	>2 days/week	Several times per day
	FEV$_1$ or peak flow	>80% predicted/ personal best	60–80% predicted/ personal best	<60% predicted/ personal best
	Validated questionnaires: • ATAQ • ACQ • ACT	• 0 • ≤0.75 • ≥20	• 1–2 • ≥1.5 • 16–19	• 3–4 • N/A • ≤15
Risk	Exacerbations requiring oral systemic corticosteroids	0–1/year	≥2/year	
		Consider severity and interval since last exacerbation.		
	Progressive loss of lung function	Evaluation requires long-term follow-up care.		
	Treatment-related adverse effects	Medication side effects can vary in intensity from none to very troublesome and worrisome. The level of intensity does not correlate to specific levels of control, but should be considered in the overall assessment of risk.		

Table 7.2. Continued

Components of Control	Classification of Asthma Control		
	Well-Controlled	Not Well-controlled	Very Poorly Controlled
Recommended Action for Treatment	If well-controlled: Maintain current step. Regular follow-up at every 1–6 months to maintain control. Consider step down if well-controlled for at least 3 months	If not well-controlled: Step up 1 step. Re-evaluate in 2–6 weeks For side effects, consider alternative treatment options.	If very poorly controlled: Consider short course oforal systemic corticosteroids Step up 1–2 steps. Re-evaluate in 2 weeks. For side effects, consider alternative treatment options.

Chapter 8

Tests and Procedures Used to Diagnose Asthma

Chapter Contents

Section 8.1

Lung Function Test

Text in this section is excerpted from "What Are Lung Function Tests?" National Heart, Lung, and Blood Institute (NHLBI), September 17, 2012.

What Are Lung Function Tests?

Lung function tests, also called pulmonary function tests, measure how well your lungs work. These tests are used to look for the cause of breathing problems, such as shortness of breath.

Lung function tests measure:

- How much air you can take into your lungs. This amount is compared with that of other people your age, height, and sex. This allows your doctor to see whether you're in the normal range.

- How much air you can blow out of your lungs and how fast you can do it.

- How well your lungs deliver oxygen to your blood.

- The strength of your breathing muscles.

Doctors use lung function tests to help diagnose conditions such as asthma, pulmonary fibrosis (scarring of the lung tissue), and COPD (chronic obstructive pulmonary disease).

Lung function tests also are used to check the extent of damage caused by conditions such as pulmonary fibrosis and sarcoidosis. Also, these tests might be used to check how well treatments, such as asthma medicines, are working.

Overview

Lung function tests include breathing tests and tests that measure the oxygen level in your blood. The breathing tests most often used are:

- **Spirometry**. This test measures how much air you can breathe in and out. It also measures how fast you can blow air out.

- **Body plethysmography**. This test measures how much air is present in your lungs when you take a deep breath. It also measures how much air remains in your lungs after you breathe out fully.

- **Lung diffusion capacity**. This test measures how well oxygen passes from your lungs to your bloodstream.

These tests may not show what's causing breathing problems. So, you may have other tests as well, such as an exercise stress test. This test measures how well your lungs and heart work while you exercise on a treadmill or bicycle.

Two tests that measure the oxygen level in your blood are pulse oximetry and arterial blood gas tests. These tests also are called blood oxygen tests.

Pulse oximetry measures your blood oxygen level using a special light. For an arterial blood gas test, your doctor takes a sample of your blood, usually from an artery in your wrist. The sample is sent to a laboratory, where its oxygen level is measured.

Outlook

Lung function tests usually are painless and rarely cause side effects. You may feel some discomfort during an arterial blood gas test when the blood sample is taken.

Types of Lung Function Tests

Breathing Tests

Spirometry

Spirometry measures how much air you breathe in and out and how fast you blow it out. This is measured two ways: peak expiratory flow rate (PEFR) and forced expiratory volume in 1 second (FEV1).

PEFR is the fastest rate at which you can blow air out of your lungs. FEV1 refers to the amount of air you can blow out in 1 second.

During the test, a technician will ask you to take a deep breath in. Then, you'll blow as hard as you can into a tube connected to a small machine. The machine is called a spirometer.

Your doctor may have you inhale a medicine that helps open your airways. He or she will want to see whether the medicine changes or improves the test results.

Spirometry helps check for conditions that affect how much air you can breathe in, such as pulmonary fibrosis (scarring of the lung tissue). The test also helps detect diseases that affect how fast you can breathe air out, like asthma and COPD (chronic obstructive pulmonary disease).

Lung Volume Measurement

Body plethysmography is a test that measures how much air is present in your lungs when you take a deep breath. It also measures how much air remains in your lungs after you breathe out fully.

During the test, you sit inside a glass booth and breathe into a tube that's attached to a computer.

For other lung function tests, you might breathe in nitrogen or helium gas and then blow it out. The gas you breathe out is measured to show how much air your lungs can hold.

Lung volume measurement can help diagnose pulmonary fibrosis or a stiff or weak chest wall.

Lung Diffusion Capacity

This test measures how well oxygen passes from your lungs to your bloodstream. During this test, you breathe in a type of gas through a tube. You hold your breath for a brief moment and then blow out the gas.

Abnormal test results may suggest loss of lung tissue, emphysema (a type of COPD), very bad scarring of the lung tissue, or problems with blood flow through the body's arteries.

Tests to Measure Oxygen Level

Pulse oximetry and arterial blood gas tests show how much oxygen is in your blood. During pulse oximetry, a small sensor is attached to your finger or ear. The sensor uses light to estimate how much oxygen is in your blood. This test is painless and no needles are used.

For an arterial blood gas test, a blood sample is taken from an artery, usually in your wrist. The sample is sent to a laboratory, where its oxygen level is measured. You may feel some discomfort during an arterial blood gas test because a needle is used to take the blood sample.

Testing in Infants and Young Children

Spirometry and other measures of lung function usually can be done for children older than 6 years, if they can follow directions well.

Spirometry might be tried in children as young as 5 years. However, technicians who have special training with young children may need to do the testing.

Instead of spirometry, a growing number of medical centers measure respiratory system resistance. This is another way to test lung function in young children.

The child wears nose clips and has his or her cheeks supported with an adult's hands. The child breathes in and out quietly on a mouthpiece, while the technician measures changes in pressure at the mouth. During these lung function tests, parents can help comfort their children and encourage them to cooperate.

Very young children (younger than 2 years) may need an infant lung function test. This requires special equipment and medical staff. This type of test is available only at a few medical centers.

The doctor gives the child medicine to help him or her sleep through the test. A technician places a mask over the child's nose and mouth and a vest around the child's chest.

The mask and vest are attached to a lung function machine. The machine gently pushes air into the child's lungs through the mask. As the child exhales, the vest slightly squeezes his or her chest. This helps push more air out of the lungs. The exhaled air is then measured.

In children younger than 5 years, doctors likely will use signs and symptoms, medical history, and a physical exam to diagnose lung problems.

Doctors can use pulse oximetry and arterial blood gas tests for children of all ages.

Other Names for Lung Function Tests

- Lung diffusion testing; also called diffusing capacity and diffusing capacity of the lung for carbon monoxide, or DLCO

- Pulmonary function tests, or PFTs

- Arterial blood gas tests also are called blood gas analyses or ABGs.

Who Needs Lung Function Tests?

People who have breathing problems, such as shortness of breath, may need lung function tests. These tests help find the cause of breathing problems.

Doctors use lung function tests to help diagnose conditions such as asthma, pulmonary fibrosis (scarring of the lung tissue), and COPD (chronic obstructive pulmonary disease).

Lung function tests also are used to check the extent of damage caused by conditions such as pulmonary fibrosis and sarcoidosis. Also, these tests might be used to check how well treatments, such as asthma medicines, are working.

Diagnosing Lung Conditions

Your doctor will diagnose a lung condition based on your medical and family histories, a physical exam, and test results.

Medical and Family Histories

Your doctor will ask you questions, such as:

- Do you ever feel like you can't get enough air?
- Does your chest feel tight sometimes?
- Do you have periods of coughing or wheezing (a whistling sound when you breathe)?
- Do you ever have chest pain?
- Can you walk or run as fast as other people your age?

Your doctor also will ask whether you or anyone in your family has ever:

- Had asthma or allergies
- Had heart disease
- Smoked
- Traveled to places where they may have been exposed to tuberculosis
- Had a job that exposed them to dust, fumes, or particles (like asbestos)

Physical Exam

Your doctor will check your heart rate, breathing rate, and blood pressure. He or she also will listen to your heart and lungs with a stethoscope and feel your abdomen and limbs.

Your doctor will look for signs of heart or lung disease, or another disease that might be causing your symptoms.

Lung and Heart Tests

Based on your medical history and physical exam, your doctor will recommend tests. A chest X-ray usually is the first test done to find the cause of a breathing problem. This test takes pictures of the organs and structures inside your chest.

Your doctor may do lung function tests to find out even more about how well your lungs work.

Your doctor also may do tests to check your heart, such as an EKG (electrocardiogram) or an exercise stress test. An EKG detects and records your heart's electrical activity. A stress test shows how well your heart works during physical activity.

What to Expect before Lung Function Tests

If you take breathing medicines, your doctor may ask you to stop them for a short time before spirometry, lung volume measurement, or lung diffusion capacity tests.

No special preparation is needed before pulse oximetry and arterial blood gas tests. If you're getting oxygen therapy, your doctor may ask you to stop using it for a short time before the tests. This allows your doctor to check your blood oxygen level without the added oxygen.

What to Expect during Lung Function Tests

Breathing Tests

Spirometry might be done in your doctor's office or in a special lung function laboratory. Lung volume measurement and lung diffusion capacity tests are done in a special lab or clinic. For these tests, you sit in a chair next to a machine that measures your breathing. For spirometry, you sit or stand next to the machine.

Before the tests, a technician places soft clips on your nose. This allows you to breathe only through a tube that's attached to the testing machine. The technician will tell you how to breathe into the tube. For example, you might be asked to breathe normally, slowly, or rapidly.

Some tests require deep breathing, which might make you feel short of breath, dizzy, or light-headed, or it might make you cough.

Spirometry

For this test, you take a deep breath and then exhale as fast and as hard as you can into the tube. With spirometry, your doctor may give you medicine to help open your airways. Your doctor will want to see whether the medicine changes or improves the test results.

Lung Volume Measurement

For body plethysmography, you sit in a clear glass booth and breathe through the tube attached to the testing machine. The changes in pressure inside the booth are measured to show how much air you can breathe into your lungs.

For other tests, you breathe in nitrogen or helium gas and then exhale. The gas that you breathe out is measured.

Lung Diffusion Capacity

During this test, you breathe in gas through the tube, hold your breath for 10 seconds, and then rapidly blow it out. The gas contains a small amount of carbon monoxide, which won't harm you.

Tests to Measure Oxygen Level

Pulse oximetry is done in a doctor's office or hospital. An arterial blood gas test is done in a lab or hospital.

Pulse Oximetry

For this test, a small sensor is attached to your finger or ear using a clip or flexible tape. The sensor is then attached to a cable that leads to a small machine called an oximeter. The oximeter shows the amount of oxygen in your blood. This test is painless and no needles are used.

Arterial Blood Gas

During this test, your doctor or technician inserts a needle into an artery, usually in your wrist, and takes a sample of blood. You may feel some discomfort when the needle is inserted. The sample is then sent to a lab where its oxygen level is measured.

After the needle is removed, you may feel mild pressure or throbbing at the needle site. Applying pressure to the area for 5 to 10 minutes should stop the bleeding. You'll be given a small bandage to place on the area.

What to Expect after Lung Function Tests

You can return to your normal activities and restart your medicines after lung function tests. Talk with your doctor about when you'll get the test results.

What Do Lung Function Tests Show?

Breathing Tests

Spirometry

Spirometry can show whether you have:

- A blockage (obstruction) in your airways. This may be a sign of asthma, COPD (chronic obstructive pulmonary disease), or another obstructive lung disorder.

- Smaller than normal lungs (restriction). This may be a sign of heart failure, pulmonary fibrosis (scarring of the lung tissue), or another restrictive lung disorder.

Lung Volume Measurement

These tests measure how much air your lungs can hold when you breathe in and how much air is left in your lungs when you breathe out. Abnormal test results may show that you have pulmonary fibrosis or a stiff or weak chest wall.

Lung Diffusion Capacity

This test can show a problem with oxygen moving from your lungs into your bloodstream. This might be a sign of loss of lung tissue, emphysema (a type of COPD), or problems with blood flow through the body's arteries.

Tests to Measure Oxygen Level

Pulse oximetry and arterial blood gas tests measure the oxygen level in your blood. These tests show how well your lungs are taking in oxygen and moving it into the bloodstream. A low level of oxygen in the blood might be a sign of a lung or heart disorder.

What Are the Risks of Lung Function Tests?

Spirometry, lung volume measurement, and lung diffusion capacity tests usually are safe. These tests rarely cause problems.

Pulse oximetry has no risks. Side effects from arterial blood gas tests are rare.

Section 8.2

Nitric Oxide Test

"Nitric Oxide Test," © 2016 Omnigraphics, Inc.
Reviewed January 2016.

Definition

Exhaled nitric oxide (eNO) is a type of test used to measure the level of inflammation in the airways. Nitric oxide is a gas that is produced naturally in the lungs and other parts of the body as a response to inflammation. Since asthma is a disease that involves chronic inflammation, studies have found that the levels of eNO are significantly higher in the breath of people with asthma. Measuring and monitoring eNO levels thus helps doctors diagnose asthma and determine the effectiveness of different treatment approaches.

Why eNO Tests Are Recommended

Doctors typically diagnose asthma by evaluating the patient's medical history, conducting a physical examination, and performing various tests of pulmonary function, such as spirometry. Nitric oxide testing can be used in conjunction with these other diagnostic methods to confirm that a patient's symptoms are caused by asthma rather than other conditions that are not associated with airway inflammation, such as respiratory illness, pulmonary embolism, vocal cord dysfunction, or gastric reflux.

Nitric oxide testing can also help doctors evaluate potential treatment methods and assess the patient's response to medications. Inhaled anti-inflammatory medications, such as those found in steroid inhalers, are among the primary treatments for asthma. eNO testing can help doctors determine whether these medications are effectively controlling a patient's airway inflammation, or whether the dosages may need to be increased or decreased. Levels of eNO will be higher in patients whose asthma is untreated or poorly managed. Lowering eNO levels can lead to a reduction in asthma symptoms and an improvement in the patient's quality of life.

How eNO Tests Are Performed

Prior to taking an eNO test, patients are advised to avoid using an asthma inhaler, smoking, eating or drinking, using toothpaste or mouthwash, and exercising for at least two hours. The test itself is quite simple and generally only takes about five minutes. Patients will be seated and provided with a sterile mouthpiece. The mouthpiece is attached by a tube to an eNO measuring device. Patients will be asked to inhale deeply until their lungs are filled with air. Then they will be asked to exhale slowly and steadily. Most eNO devices are equipped with a computer screen that shows the rate of air flow to help patients regulate their exhalation. Patients may be asked to complete this process several times to ensure that the results are accurate. The entire test generally takes five minutes or less.

Doctors interpret the test results by comparing patients eNO levels to the levels that are typically found in the exhaled breath of people with healthy lungs. Normal nitric oxide levels are below 25 parts per billion in adults and below 20 parts per billion in children. Levels above 50 parts per billion in adults and 35 parts per billion in children are considered indications of airway inflammation related to asthma. It is important to note, however, that other factors may affect patientsnitric oxide levels, including medications, allergies, colds and other respiratory illnesses, smoking, age of the patient, asthma signs and symptoms, and past nitric oxide test results.

Exhaled nitric oxide testing is quick, easy, and noninvasive. It is considered particularly useful for young children who have trouble completing other types of pulmonary function tests. It may not provide beneficial information for all asthma patients, however, and it may not be available in all medical practices or covered by all types of health insurance.

References

1. Nelson, Jean. "Have You Heard about the New Test for Asthma?" Allergy Advice, June 27, 2011.

2. "Nitrous Oxide Test for Asthma." Mayo Clinic, 2015.

Section 8.3

Spirometry

Text in this section is excerpted from "Types of Lung Function Tests," National Heart, Lung, and Blood Institute (NHLBI), September 17, 2012.

Overview

Spirometry measures how much air you breathe in and out and how fast you blow it out. This is measured two ways: peak expiratory flow rate (PEFR) and forced expiratory volume in 1 second (FEV1).

PEFR is the fastest rate at which you can blow air out of your lungs. FEV1 refers to the amount of air you can blow out in 1 second.

During the test, a technician will ask you to take a deep breath in. Then, you'll blow as hard as you can into a tube connected to a small machine. The machine is called a spirometer.

The image shows how spirometry is done. The patient takes a deep breath and blows as hard as possible into a tube connected to a spirometer. The spirometer measures the amount of air breathed out. It also measures how fast the air was blown out.

Your doctor may have you inhale a medicine that helps open your airways. He or she will want to see whether the medicine changes or improves the test results.

Spirometry helps check for conditions that affect how much air you can breathe in, such as pulmonary fibrosis (scarring of the lung

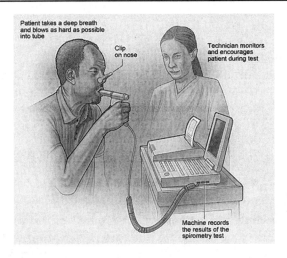

Figure 8.1. *Spirometry*

tissue). The test also helps detect diseases that affect how fast you can breathe air out, like asthma and COPD (chronic obstructive pulmonary disease).

The image shows how spirometry is done. The patient takes a deep breath and blows as hard as possible into a tube connected to a spirometer. The spirometer measures the amount of air breathed out. It also measures how fast the air was blown out.

Section 8.4

Chest X-Ray

Text in this section is excerpted from "What Is a Chest X-ray?"
National Heart, Lung, and Blood Institute (NHLBI), August 1, 2010.
Reviewed January 2016.

What Is a Chest X-Ray?

A chest X-ray is a painless, noninvasive test that creates pictures of the structures inside your chest, such as your heart, lungs, blood vessels, and thoracic cage bones. "Noninvasive" means that no surgery is done and no instruments are inserted into your body.

This test is done to find the cause of symptoms such as shortness of breath, chest pain, chronic cough (a cough that lasts a long time), fever, lung pathology, foreign bodies in the trachea, etc.

Overview

X-rays are electromagnetic waves. They use ionizing radiation to create pictures of the inside of your body. The mean radiation dose to is around 0.02 mSv (2 mrem) for PA view and 0.08 mSv (8 mrem) for a side view.

A chest X-ray takes pictures of the inside of your chest. The different tissues in your chest absorb different amounts of radiation.

Your ribs and spine are bony and absorb radiation well. They normally appear light on a chest X-ray. Your lungs, which are filled with air, normally appear dark. A disease in the chest that changes how radiation is absorbed also will appear on a chest X-ray.

Chest X-rays help doctors diagnose conditions such as pneumonia, heart failure, lung cancer, lung tissue scarring, sarcoidosis, bone fracture, hiatal hernia, plannned effusion, lung collapse etc. Doctors also may use chest X-rays to see how well treatments for certain conditions are working. Also, doctors often use chest X-rays before surgery to look at the structures in the chest.

Chest X-rays are the most common X-ray test used to diagnose health problems.

Outlook

Chest X-rays have few risks. The amount of radiation used in a chest X-ray is very small. A lead apron is used to protect certain parts of your body from the radiation.

A chest X-ray gives out a radiation dose similar to the amount of radiation you're naturally exposed to over 10 days.

Other Names for a Chest X-Ray

- Chest radiography
- CXR

Who Needs a Chest X-Ray?

Doctors may recommend chest X-rays for people who have symptoms such as shortness of breath, chest pain, chronic cough (a cough that lasts a long time), or fever. The test can help find the cause of these symptoms.

Chest X-rays look for conditions such as pneumonia, heart failure, lung cancer, lung tissue scarring, or sarcoidosis. The test also is used to check how well treatments for certain conditions are working.

Chest X-rays also are used to evaluate people who test positive for tuberculosis exposure on skin tests.

Sometimes, doctors recommend more chest X-rays within hours, days, or months of an earlier chest X-ray. This allows them to follow up on a condition.

People who are having certain types of surgery also may need chest X-rays. Doctors often use the test before surgery to look at the structures inside the chest.

What to Expect before a Chest X-Ray

You don't have to do anything special to prepare for a chest X-ray. However, you may want to wear a shirt that's easy to take off. Before the test, you'll be asked to undress from the waist up and wear a gown.

You also may want to avoid wearing jewelry and other metal objects. You'll be asked to take off any jewelry, eyeglasses, and metal objects that might interfere with the X-ray picture. Let the X-ray technician know if you have any body piercings on your chest.

Let your doctor know if you're pregnant or may be pregnant. In general, women should avoid all X-ray tests during pregnancy. Sometimes, though, having an X-ray is important to the health of the mother and fetus. If an X-ray is needed, the technician will take extra steps to protect the fetus from radiation.

What to Expect during a Chest X-Ray

Chest X-rays are done at doctors' offices, clinics, hospitals, and other health care facilities. The location depends on the situation. An X-ray technician oversees the test.

The entire test usually takes about 15 minutes.

During the Test

Depending on your doctor's request, you'll stand, sit, or lie for the chest X-ray. The technician will help position you correctly. He or she may cover you with a heavy lead apron to protect certain parts of your body from the radiation.

The X-ray equipment usually consists of two parts. One part, a box-like machine, holds the X-ray film or a special plate that records the picture digitally. You'll sit or stand next to this machine. The second part is the X-ray tube, which is located about 6 feet away.

Before the pictures are taken, the technician will walk behind a wall or into the next room to turn on the X-ray machine. This helps reduce his or her exposure to the radiation.

Usually, two views of the chest are taken. The first is a view from the back. The second is a view from the side.

For a view from the back, you'll sit or stand so that your chest rests against the image plate. The X-ray tube will be behind you. For the side view, you'll turn to your side and raise your arms above your head.

If you need to lie down for the test, you'll lie on a table that contains the X-ray film or plate. The X-ray tube will be over the table.

You'll need to hold very still while the pictures are taken. The technician may ask you to hold your breath for a few seconds. These steps help prevent a blurry picture.

Although the test is painless, you may feel some discomfort from the coolness of the exam room and the X-ray plate. If you have arthritis or injuries to the chest wall, shoulders, or arms, you may feel discomfort holding a position during the test. The technician may be able to help you find a more comfortable position.

When the test is done, you'll need to wait while the technician checks the quality of the X-ray pictures. He or she needs to make sure that the pictures are good enough for the doctor to use.

What to Expect after a Chest X-Ray

You usually can go back to your normal routine right after a chest X-ray.

A radiologist will analyze, or "read," your X-ray images. This doctor is specially trained to supervise X-ray tests and look at the X-ray pictures.

The radiologist will send a report to your doctor (who requested the X-ray test). Your doctor will discuss the results with you.

In an emergency, you'll get the X-ray results right away. Otherwise, it may take 24 hours or more. Talk with your doctor about when you should expect the results.

What Does a Chest X-Ray Show?

Chest X-rays show the structures in and around the chest. The test is used to look for and track conditions of the heart, lungs, bones, and chest cavity. For example, chest X-ray pictures may show signs of pneumonia, heart failure, lung cancer, lung tissue scarring, or sarcoidosis.

Chest X-rays do have limits. They only show conditions that change the size of tissues in the chest or how the tissues absorb radiation. Also, chest X-rays create two-dimensional pictures. This means that denser structures, like bone or the heart, may hide some signs of disease. Very small areas of cancer and blood clots in the lungs usually don't show up on chest X-rays.

For these reasons, your doctor may recommend other tests to confirm a diagnosis.

What Are the Risks of a Chest X-Ray?

Chest X-rays have few risks. The amount of radiation used in a chest X-ray is very small. A lead apron may be used to protect certain parts of your body from the radiation.

The test gives out a radiation dose similar to the amount of radiation you're naturally exposed to over 10 days.

Section 8.5

Allergy Tests for Asthma

Text in this section is excerpted from "Diagnosis of Environmental Allergies," National Institute of Allergy and Infectious Diseases (NIAID), May 12, 2015; and text from "Allergens & Irritants?" National Institute of Environmental Health Sciences (NIEHS), December 1, 2015.

Allergens and Irritants

Asthma is one of America's most common chronic health conditions. Many substances can aggravate allergies or increase the severity of asthma symptoms in individuals who are sensitive to these allergens or irritants.

Skin Tests

A skin prick test can detect if a person is sensitive to a specific allergen. Being "sensitive" means that the immune system produces a type of antibody called IgE against that allergen. IgE attaches to specialized cells called mast cells. This happens throughout the body, including the lining of the nose and the airways, as well as the skin.

During a skin prick test, a healthcare professional uses a piece of plastic to prick the skin on the arm or back and place a tiny amount of allergen extract just below the skin's surface. In sensitive people, the allergen binds to IgE on mast cells in the skin and causes them to release histamine and other chemicals that produce itching, redness, and minor swelling.

A positive skin test to a particular allergen does not necessarily indicate that a person has allergic rhinitis or asthma caused by that allergen. Up to 50 percent of the U.S. population may have at least one positive skin test to a common allergen, but less than half of those people have allergic rhinitis or asthma. Therefore, healthcare professionals often will try to match skin test results with the kind of allergen exposures person may have had.

Blood Tests

Instead of performing a skin test, doctors may take a blood sample to measure levels of allergen-specific IgE antibodies. Most people who are sensitive to a particular allergen will have IgE antibodies detectable by both skin and blood tests.

As with skin testing, a positive blood test to an allergen does not necessarily mean that a person's symptoms are caused by that allergen.

Allergy Component Tests

One reason why a positive skin or blood test does not always indicate that a person's symptoms are caused by a particular allergen is that allergens comprise many different components, some of which are more likely to cause symptoms than others. For example, birch tree pollen contains proteins, sugars, and fats. IgE antibodies to birch pollen proteins are likely to cause allergic reactions, but IgE antibodies to the sugars in birch pollen, although common, are less likely to cause allergic reactions. Allergy component tests are blood tests that can determine exactly which component of an allergen the IgE in a person's blood recognizes. This can help a health professional determine whether the allergen is likely to cause symptoms.

Chapter 9

Types of Asthma

Chapter Contents

Section 9.1

Allergic Asthma

Text in this section is excerpted from "Asthma and Its
Environmental Triggers," National Institute of Environmental
Health Sciences (NIEHS), February 2012.
Reviewed January 2016.

Are Allergies Related To Asthma?

Asthma can be triggered by substances in the environment called allergens. Indoor allergens from dust mites, cockroaches, dogs, cats, rodents, molds, and fungi and outdoor allergens called air pollutants such as sulphur dioxide (SO_2), nitrogen dioxide (NO_2), ozone (O_3) and particulate matter are among the most important environmental triggers for asthma.

National Institute of Environmental Health Sciences (NIEHS) scientists, along with researchers from the U.S. Department of Housing and Urban Development (HUD), conducted an extensive survey known as the National Survey of Lead Hazards and Allergens in Housing, which showed that 46 percent of the homes had dust mite allergens high enough to produce allergic reactions, while nearly 25 percent of the homes had allergen levels high enough to trigger asthma symptoms in genetically susceptible individuals. The survey also showed that nearly two-thirds of American homes have cockroach allergens.

What Can I Do to Reduce Allergens and Asthma Attacks?

NIEHS scientists identified several strategies that reduce indoor allergens and asthma symptoms—cockroach extermination, thorough professional cleaning, and in-home visits to educate the occupants about asthma management. Using these strategies, cockroach allergens were reduced by 84 percent, well below the threshold for producing asthma symptoms.

Other research showed that some simple steps—washing bedding in hot water; putting allergen-impermeable covers on pillows, box springs, and mattresses; and vacuuming and steam cleaning carpets and upholstered furniture—can significantly reduce dust mite allergen levels.

NIEHS has also collaborated with the National Institute of Allergy and Infectious Diseases to conduct the National Cooperative Inner-City Asthma Study aimed at reducing asthma among children in the inner city.

The program targeted six allergens that trigger asthma symptoms—dust mites, cockroaches, pet dander, rodents, secondhand smoke, and mold. Allergen-impermeable covers were placed on the mattress and box spring of the child's bed, and families were given vacuum cleaners equipped with high-efficiency particulate air (HEPA) filters. A HEPA air purifier was set up in the child's bedroom to remove tobacco smoke, dog and cat allergens, and mold. Children who received the help had 19 percent fewer clinic visits, a 13 percent reduction in the use of albuterol inhalers, and 38 more symptom-free days than those in the control group.

Simple steps for decreasing indoor allergens:

- Vacuum carpets and upholstered furniture every week
- Wash sheets and blankets in hot water every week
- Encase mattresses, pillows, and box springs in allergen-impermeable covers
- Steam clean carpets and floor mats every 8 weeks
- Replace carpeting with smooth surfaces such as hardwood or vinyl

Section 9.2

Exercise-Induced Asthma

This section includes excerpts from "Asthma & Physical Activity in the School," National Heart, Lung, and Blood Institute (NHLBI), April 2012; and text from "Exercise-Induced Bronchoconstriction (EIB) With or Without Chronic Asthma," Agency for Healthcare Research and Quality (AHRQ), July 31, 2012.

Exercise-induced asthma (also called exercise-induced broncho-spasm) is asthma that is triggered by physical activity. Vigorous exercise will cause symptoms for most students who have asthma if their asthma is not well-controlled. Some students experience asthma symptoms only when they exercise. Asthma varies from student to student and often from season to season or even hour by hour. At times, programs for students who have asthma may need to be temporarily modified, such as by varying the type, intensity, duration, and/or frequency of activity. At all times, students who have asthma should be included in activities as much as possible. Remaining behind in the gym or library or frequently sitting on the bench can set the stage for teasing, loss of self-esteem, unnecessary restriction of activity, and low levels of physical fitness.

Definition and Overview

- Exercise-induced bronchospasm (EIB) is defined as the transient narrowing of the lower airways that occurs after vigorous exercise. It may appear with or without asthma. The term exercise-induced asthma (EIA) should not be used because exercise does not induce asthma but rather is a trigger of bronchoconstriction.

- EIB occurs in response to heating and humidifying large volumes of air during a short period. The most important determinants of expression of EIB response and severity are the water content of the inspired air and/or the level of ventilation achieved and sustained during exercise.

- Respiratory water loss at high ventilation is associated with airway cooling and dehydration and an increase in osmolarity of the airway surface. The predominant theory of EIB is the osmotic theory, although the thermal theory may also play a role.

- Exercise itself is not necessary to cause airways to narrow; voluntary hyperpnea of dry air may induce bronchoconstriction similar to exercise. Eucapnic voluntary hyperpnea is used as a surrogate for exercise in the diagnosis of EIB, particularly in athletes.

- People who have EIB without asthma associated with airway inflammation and the presence of eosinophils are likely to be responsive to corticosteroids.

- EIB is accompanied by release of mediators such as prostaglandins (PGs), leukotrienes (LTs), and histamine.

- In approximately half of patients who have EIB, there is an interval of refractoriness lasting approximately 2 to 3 hours immediately after an episode of EIB during which additional exercise produces little or no bronchoconstriction.

Genetics and Environment

- Gene expression and environmental interaction may be relevant to the EIB phenotype.
- Oxidative stress caused by environmental pollutants that are inhaled during exercise may play an important role in the development and exaggeration of EIB.
- The pathogenesis of EIB in elite athletes may relate to effects on the airways arising from humidifying large volumes of dry air over months of training with or without exposure to environmental irritants, allergens, and viral agents.

Prevalence

- EIB is reported in most asthmatic patients.
- Patients with more severe or less well-controlled asthma are more likely to manifest EIB than patients with less severe or better controlled disease.
- The true prevalence of EIB in the general population is poorly defined because epidemiologic studies of EIB have not differentiated asthmatic vs. nonasthmatic populations. In addition, there is no consensus for the end point indicative of a positive response, and the conditions under which exercise is performed frequently differ.
- The prevalence of EIB in elite athletes appears to be higher than in the general population and depends on the type of sport, the maximum exercise level, and environmental conditions.
- The prevalence of EIB varies with history, type of challenge, and conditions under which the challenge is performed.
- The prevalence of EIB with and without asthma may be influenced by age, sex, and ethnicity.

Diagnosis

- Self-reported symptoms alone are not reliable for diagnosis of EIB.

- Optimal EIB management may require confirmation of the diagnosis using objective methods.

- Self-reported symptom-based diagnosis of EIB in the elite athlete lacks sensitivity and specificity and establishes the necessity for standardized, objective challenges using spirometry.

- The indirect challenge (e.g., exercise or surrogate such as eucapnic voluntary hyperpnea (EVH)) is preferred over a direct challenge (e.g., methacholine) for assessing EIB in the elite athlete.

- EVH is the preferred surrogate challenge for the elite athlete participating in competitive sports.

- The intensity of the exercise challenge for the elite athlete should be 95% or greater than actual or estimated maximal heart rate (HR max), and dry medical-grade air should be used in performing the challenge.

- Hyperosmolar aerosols may also be used as surrogates to exercise.

Differential Diagnosis

- Exercise-induced laryngeal dysfunction (EILD), primarily VCD and other glottic abnormalities, may be elicited by exercise and mimic EIB. Inspiratory stridor is a differentiating hallmark sign with EILD and not with EIB alone. Flattening of the inspiratory curve on spirometric maneuver may be seen concomitant with symptoms. EILD may occur alone or with EIB. Failure to respond to asthma management is a key historical feature suggesting EILD.

- Exercise-induced dyspnea and hyperventilation can masquerade as asthma, especially in children and adolescents.

- Shortness of breath with exercise may be associated with underlying conditions due to obstructive lung disease, such as chronic obstructive pulmonary disease (COPD), or restrictive lung physiology, such as obesity, skeletal defects (e.g., pectus excavatum), diaphragmatic paralysis, and interstitial fibrosis.

- Shortness of breath accompanied by pruritus and urticaria, with varying other systemic symptoms, suggests exercise-induced anaphylaxis (EIAna) rather than EIB.

- In the absence of objective evidence of EIB, breathlessness with exercise, with or without chest pain, may be caused by cardio-vascular, pulmonary, or gastroenterologic mechanisms other than asthma. Appropriate cardiopulmonary testing and/or referral to a cardiologist, pulmonologist, or gastroenterologist may be necessary.

- Exercise-induced dyspnea is seen as a physiologic limitation in otherwise healthy active individuals without bronchospasm.

- The association between EIB and gastroesophageal reflux disease (GERD) is controversial, and probably there is no relationship.

- Psychological factors need to be considered in the differential diagnosis of EIB.

- Dyspnea on exertion, which is prevalent in otherwise healthy, obese individuals, is not associated with EIB.

- Mitochondrial enzyme deficiency with myopathy is a rare cause of exercise limitation.

Section 9.3

Cough-Variant Asthma

"Cough-Variant Asthma," © 2016 Omnigraphics, Inc.
Reviewed January 2016.

A severe, persistent cough that does not produce any mucus can be a sign of cough-variant asthma. In fact, around 25 percent of people who seek medical attention for a chronic cough have cough-variant asthma. This type of asthma is often misdiagnosed because patients do not always have the classic symptoms of asthma, such as wheezing and shortness of breath. In children, however, cough-variant asthma often leads to the development of classic asthma symptoms.

Although the exact causes of cough-variant asthma are unknown, it often seems to develop following respiratory infections, vigorous exercise, or exposure to allergy triggers like strong fragrances or dust. Some people develop cough-variant asthma after they start taking beta-blockers, a class of drugs used to treat high blood pressure, heart disease, migraines, and eye problems like glaucoma. Cough-variant asthma also tends to appear in people with aspirin sensitivity.

Cough-variant asthma is tricky to diagnose because there are many other possible causes of a cough, including bronchitis, sinusitis, postnasal drip, chronic rhinitis, or acid reflux (heartburn). In addition, people with cough-variant asthma often have normal physical examinations and chest X-rays. To determine whether a persistent cough is related to asthma, doctors will likely perform a series of lung function tests.

One test that is typically used in the diagnosis of asthma is spirometry, which uses a device to measure the amount of air and the rate at which the patient can exhale. If this test does not indicate any impairment in lung function, the next option is a methacholine challenge. In this test, the patient inhales an aerosol mist containing methacholine, a drug that causes the airways to narrow and spasm. Although even healthy lungs will react to methacholine, a lower dosage is needed to trigger symptoms in people with asthma. A decline in lung function of 20 percent or more generally indicates that asthma is present.

Reference

"Cough-Variant Asthma." WebMD Asthma Health Center, 2015.

Section 9.4

Health Conditions That May Mimic Asthma

"Health Conditions That May Mimic Asthma,"
© 2016 Omnigraphics, Inc.
Reviewed January 2016.

The most common symptoms of asthma—such as wheezing, coughing, and shortness of breath—can also be caused by other health conditions. Some of the illnesses with symptoms that may mimic asthma include:

- **Respiratory Illnesses:** Many common respiratory illnesses can cause coughing, wheezing, and difficulty breathing, from the common cold to influenza. Sinusitis, or inflammation of the sinuses related to a viral or bacterial infection, often coexists with asthma. Other possible culprits include respiratory syncytial virus (RSV), which can cause pneumonia in children, and pulmonary aspergillosis, a fungal infection of the lungs.

- **Lung Diseases:** A variety of lung conditions may present symptoms similar to asthma, including accidental aspiration of food, water, or other matter into the lungs; obstruction of the airway by an esophageal tumor or enlarged thyroid gland; injury to the lungs or airways; or lung cancer (bronchogenic carcinoma). Chronic obstructive pulmonary disease (COPD) refers to several lung diseases that are often related to cigarette smoking, such as emphysema and chronic bronchitis. COPD is characterized by wheezing and difficulty breathing.

- **Heart Conditions:** Shortness of breath can also be an indication of heart disease. Congestive heart failure occurs when the heart does not circulate blood properly, leading to a buildup of fluid in the lungs. Myocardial ischemia occurs when the heart muscle does not receive adequate oxygen, usually because of a blockage in a coronary artery. Chest pain is the most common symptom, but shortness of breath with exercise may also occur.

- **Vocal Cord Dysfunction:** Vocal cord dysfunction is a condition in which the muscles of the larynx tighten and close, which can cause wheezing and difficulty breathing. This condition is most common among young women. The most extreme case is vocal cord paralysis, which involves a total loss of function in those muscles.

- **GERD:** The heartburn associated with gastroesophageal reflux disease can irritate the airways and cause symptoms that mimic asthma.

Diagnosing Asthma

Since so many other health conditions present similar symptoms, diagnosing asthma can be difficult. Doctors will typically begin by reviewing the patient's medical history and family history, including

123

any history of breathing problems, allergies, or lung conditions. They will also inquire whether the patient has ever smoked, as smoking is a significant risk factor in many of the heart and lung diseases that can mimic asthma. Doctors will also ask for a detailed description of the patient's symptoms, including when and how often they usually occur. In addition to conducting a physical examination, doctors will likely perform a number of different tests to confirm or rule out various conditions, such as allergy tests, blood tests, chest and sinus X-rays, and lung function tests. If the diagnosis is asthma, determining the specific type is necessary in order to treat it effectively.

Reference

"Health Conditions That Mimic Asthma." WebMD Asthma Health Center, 2015.

Section 9.5

Night-Time (Nocturnal) Asthma

"Night-Time (Nocturnal) Asthma," © 2016 Omnigraphics, Inc.
Reviewed January 2016.

Night-time or nocturnal asthma is a common type of the disease characterized by symptoms that worsen at night. People with nocturnal asthma may be awakened from sleep by wheezing, shortness of breath, coughing, and a feeling of tightness in the chest. When experienced at night, these symptoms are potentially dangerous. In fact, studies have shown that a majority of asthma-related deaths occur at night. People with nocturnal asthma also tend to have more severe daytime asthma symptoms.

Night-time asthma sufferers may also experience health problems stemming from sleep disturbances. People who are unable to get adequate, quality sleep often feel tired and irritable during the day. They may also have trouble concentrating at work or at school. In fact, sleep disturbances due to asthma are one of the leading causes of children missing school. Studies have shown that children with nocturnal asthma may experience decreased mental function that affects their performance in school. When nocturnal asthma is treated effectively, however, sleep disturbance is reduced and mental function improves.

Causes of Nocturnal Asthma

Researchers have identified a number of factors that may contribute to the worsening of asthma symptoms at night.

Sleep-Related Airway Changes

Airways tend to narrow during sleep, which increases airflow resistance. As a result, airway function decreases gradually through the night. Although healthy people may not notice this effect, it can trigger symptoms in people with asthma. In fact, research has shown that people with asthma are more likely to experience breathing problems during sleep no matter when the sleep period occurs. Lung function test results tend to be worst around five hours after falling asleep, even for people who sleep during the daytime hours.

Sleep-Related Hormone Changes

The levels of certain hormones in the bloodstream tend to fluctuate according to a general pattern throughout the day and night. The changing hormone levels create the natural sleep-wake cycle, or circadian rhythms, and can also exert a powerful effect on asthma symptoms. The hormone epinephrine, for instance, reaches its lowest level in most people around 4:00 A.M. This hormone helps keep airways open by relaxing muscles surrounding the bronchial tubes. In addition, epinephrine suppresses histamines and other substances that cause the body to produce mucus.

Mucus Drainage or Sinusitis

The increased production of mucus in the sinuses at night, combined with the narrowing of airways during sleep, can cause coughing and breathing problems in people with asthma. Sinusitis due to a viral or bacterial infection can also irritate sensitive airways and increase nocturnal asthma symptoms.

Reclining Position

Lying down may also contribute to night-time asthma symptoms. Reclining allows mucus secretions to drain from the sinuses and accumulate in the airways. In addition, it increases the volume of blood and decreases the volume of air in the lungs, which contributes to airway resistance.

Exposure to Allergens

About half of people who have an asthma attack immediately following exposure to an allergen will experience a second airway obstruction three to eight hours later. Known as a late phase response, this second episode can be more severe and prolonged than the initial one. Research indicates that exposure to allergens in the evening increases a patient's susceptibility to a late phase response at night.

Cooling of the Airways

Whether from sleeping in an air-conditioned bedroom in summer or turning the thermostat down in winter, breathing cold, dry air can result in the loss of heat from the airways. The cooling of the airways at night is considered a contributing factor to nocturnal asthma.

Heartburn

Gastroesophageal reflux disease (GERD), commonly known as acid reflux or heartburn, occurs when stomach acid flows back into the esophagus and larynx. In people with frequent heartburn, stomach acid can irritate the lower esophagus and lead to bronchial spasm and airway constriction. Stomach acid that reaches the throat can also drip down into the lungs, causing airway irritation and increased mucus production. Since lying down often makes heartburn worse, it can be related to nocturnal asthma.

Treatment of Nocturnal Asthma

Night-time asthma can interfere with sleep and create serious health risks. The keys to managing asthma symptoms that worsen at night include finding the right asthma medications and determining when to use them to ensure quality sleep. Daily medications, such as inhaled corticosteroids, can help reduce inflammation of the airways and thus prevent night-time symptoms. But some short-term medications cannot cover a long enough time period to allow patients to sleep through the night. In such cases, a long-acting inhaled corticosteroid or bronchodilator may help alleviate symptoms.

For people whose nocturnal asthma may be triggered by allergens, it is important to avoid exposure to common allergens like dust mites or animal dander, especially in the evening hours. Regulating the temperature and humidity of the bedroom and elevating the head of the bed may also be helpful. Finally, people with GERD can often get relief from nocturnal asthma symptoms by taking medication that reduces acid production in the stomach.

Section 9.6

Occupational Asthma

This section includes excerpts from "Do You Have Work-Related Asthma?" Occupational Safety and Health Administration (OSHA), March 2014; and text from "Respiratory Diseases," Centers for Disease Control and Prevention (CDC), December 21, 2012.

What Is Work-Related Asthma?

Work-related asthma is a lung disease caused or made worse by exposures to substances in the workplace. Common exposures include chemicals, dust, mold, animals, and plants. Exposure can occur from both inhalation (breathing) and skin contact. Asthma symptoms may start at work or within several hours after leaving work and may occur with no clear pattern. People who never had asthma can develop asthma due to workplace exposures. People who have had asthma for years may find that their condition worsens due to workplace exposures. Both of these situations are considered work-related asthma.

Work-related asthma was recognized by Hippocrates (460–370 B.C.) and it was associated with occupations involving work with metals, textiles, and animals including fish. Today work-related asthma is commonly encountered in isocyanate production, in healthcare workers who use natural rubber latex gloves (although this is becoming less of a problem due to the substitution of other materials), and among office workers due to poor indoor environmental quality.

A group of chemicals called isocyanates are one of the most common chemical causes of work-related asthma. OSHA is working to reduce exposures to isocyanates and has identified their use in numerous workplaces. It is estimated that between 15 and 30 percent of asthmatics have new-onset adult asthma or work-exacerbated asthma. Thus, over two million workers in the United States suffer from work-related asthma.

Why You Should Care about Work-Related Asthma

Work-related asthma may result in long-term lung damage, loss of work days, disability, or even death. The good news is that early diagnosis and treatment of work-related asthma can lead to a better health outcome.

Work-Related Asthma Quick Facts

- Work-related asthma can develop over any period of time (days to years).

- Work-related asthma may occur with changes in work exposures, jobs, or processes.

- It is possible to develop work-related asthma even if your workplace has protective equipment, such as exhaust ventilation or respirators.

- Work-related asthma can continue to cause symptoms even when the exposure stops.

- Before working with isocyanates or any other asthma-causing substances, ask your employer for training, as required under OSHA's Hazard Communication standard.

Chronic Obstructive Pulmonary Disease (COPD)

Chronic obstructive pulmonary disease refers to chronic bronchitis, emphysema, and combined presentations of these two diseases. Chronic obstructive pulmonary disease is a leading cause of morbidity and mortality in the United States and world-wide. Although often thought of as a disease caused by cigarette smoking, it is well-recognized that COPD is also caused by occupational exposures. It has been estimated that 15% of COPD is attributable to occupation. Coal mine dust and crystalline silica encountered in industries such as mining and construction are known risks. A study of participants in the Third

National Health and Nutrition Examination Survey found increased risk for COPD in a number of industries including rubber, plastics, and leather manufacturing; utilities; building services; textile manufacturing; and construction.

Risk of Interstitial Lung Diseases

Coal mine dust

As already noted, coal mine dust exposure can cause COPD. However, it is best known for causing coal workers' pneumoconiosis (CWP), a type of lung disease affecting the tissues and gas-exchange surface of the lung (interstitial lung disease). CWP usually develops slowly, taking 10 years or more from initial exposure to onset of disease. It causes changes in the chest radiograph and, in more serious cases, can cause shortness of breath, loss of pulmonary function, and even death. In the United States, the Coal Mine Health and Safety Act of 1969 (42 CFR Part 37) mandated a comprehensive set of measures to prevent CWP. Enactment was followed by a marked reduction in the prevalence of CWP in long-term coal miners. In addition, advanced cases have recently been detected in miners in their 30s and 40s. Especially in view of the increasing use of coal as an energy source and the predicted growth of coal mining, protecting coal miners from respiratory disease continues to be an important and ongoing priority.

Silica

Silica, also known as silicon dioxide, is the most common mineral on earth. Inhaling dusts that contain crystalline forms of silica can cause a fibrosing interstitial lung disease called silicosis. Silicosis usually takes at least 10 years after exposure to develop. However, it can develop more quickly, especially after large exposures.

Quartz is a common type of crystalline silica and is a large component of many types of rock. Inhalation exposure can occur in many kinds of work, including tunneling, quarrying, mining, construction, roadway repair and demolition, sandblasting or any type of work that breaks up quartz-containing rock. Cristobalite exposure can occur in foundry work as a result of heating amorphous silica. In addition to causing silicosis, crystalline silica exposure has been associated with pulmonary function impairment and COPD.

Silica has also been classified by the International Agency for Research on Cancer (IARC) as a known human carcinogen. Crystalline silica is thought to damage lung tissue in large part as a result of oxidant mechanisms, with freshly fractured crystalline silica is being more potent than aged materials. Silica-induced diseases can be prevented by reducing exposures.

Asbestos

Asbestos is a commercial term that refers to six types of fibrous minerals, including one serpentine (chrysotile) and five amphiboles [crocidolite (riebeckite asbestos), amosite (cummingtonite-grunerite asbestos), anthophyllite asbestos, tremolite asbestos, and actinolite asbestos]. Asbestos mineral fibers are flame and heat resistant, pliable, strong, refractory to corrosive chemicals, and provide insulation. Because of its ability to insulate from heat and protect against fire, asbestos has been widely used as a building material. It has been especially important in the shipbuilding industry.

It has also been woven into fabric to make fireproof, protective textile products, such as fireproof blankets and suits, It has been used as a brake liner (e.g., in automobiles and railroad rolling stock) and for engine gaskets and has been used to make filters (e.g., in the chemical industry). Although known and used for its fire resistant properties as early as 3000 B.C., asbestos, use of the material grew markedly in the United States. during the 20th century, peaking from the 1950s through the 1980s.

Although its use in the United States has largely disappeared, exposure continues to occur due to renovation or demolition of existing building stock or through exposure to asbestos-containing products such as brake linings or asbestos-containing cement products that continue to be imported. Inhalation of asbestos fibers can have many adverse health effects. Because these develop slowly, usually presenting a decade or more after exposure, asbestos-caused diseases remain an important problem.

Asbestos fibers can cause asbestosis, a fibrosing interstitial lung disease. They can also penetrate through the lung tissue to the pleura, which are the tissues lining the lungs and chest cavity. In the pleura, they can cause conditions including pleural effusions (fluid collections), pleural plaques, and diffuse pleural fibrosis. Asbestos fibers are also a cause of lung cancer. Risk increases multiplicatively if an exposed person also smokes.

Flock

Flock consists of short fibers that are cut from long filaments and glued to backing material such as cloth to provide a fuzzy, carpet-like surface texture. They are usually prepared from synthetic materials such as nylon, rayon, or polypropylene. The cutting process results in formation of airborne particles or fibers in the respirable range. Inhalation of flock dust has been associated with an interstitial lung disease called flock workers' lung. NIOSH has made recommendations to companies that manufacture flock and make flock containing products that aim to reduce workers' exposure to flock dust. These include: engineering controls and alternative methods to cleaning the workplace with compressed air, which re-aerosolizes settled dust.

Beryllium

Beryllium (Be): It has been estimated that more than 134,000 workers in the United States are involved in the manufacture, machining or manipulation of beryllium or beryllium-containing materials. Downstream from manufacture and primary machining jobs are a wide variety of occupations that include: dental technicians, jewelers, precious metal reclamation workers, welders, plumbers, electricians, and others.

Beryllium exposure can result in immune sensitization; it is thought that continuing exposure in the face of sensitization can cause chronic beryllium disease (CBD). In CBD, immune responses to inhaled beryllium lead to lung damage. Beryllium has also been classified by IARC as a known human carcinogen.

Part Three

Medications and Asthma Management

Chapter 10

Treating Asthma Symptoms

Chapter Contents

Section 10.1

Basic Principles for Asthma Control

This section includes excerpts from "How Is Asthma Treated and Controlled?" National Heart, Lung, and Blood Institute (NHLBI), August 4, 2014; and text from "Managing Exacerbations," National Heart, Lung, and Blood Institute (NHLBI), September 2012.

How Is Asthma Treated and Controlled?

Asthma is a long-term disease that has no cure. The goal of asthma treatment is to control the disease. Good asthma control will:

- Prevent chronic and troublesome symptoms, such as coughing and shortness of breath

- Reduce your need for quick-relief medicines (see below)

- Help you maintain good lung function

- Let you maintain your normal activity level and sleep through the night

- Prevent asthma attacks that could result in an emergency room visit or hospital stay

To control asthma, partner with your doctor to manage your asthma or your child's asthma. Children aged 10 or older—and younger children who are able—should take an active role in their asthma care.

Taking an active role to control your asthma involves:

- Working with your doctor to treat other conditions that can interfere with asthma management.

- Avoiding things that worsen your asthma (asthma triggers). However, one trigger you should not avoid is physical activity. Physical activity is an important part of a healthy lifestyle. Talk with your doctor about medicines that can help you stay active.

- Working with your doctor and other health care providers to create and follow an asthma action plan.

An asthma action plan gives guidance on taking your medicines properly, avoiding asthma triggers (except physical activity), tracking your level of asthma control, responding to worsening symptoms, and seeking emergency care when needed.

Record Your Symptoms

You can record your asthma symptoms in a diary to see how well your treatments are controlling your asthma.

Asthma is well controlled if:

- You have symptoms no more than 2 days a week, and these symptoms don't wake you from sleep more than 1 or 2 nights a month.

- You can do all your normal activities.

- You take quick-relief medicines no more than 2 days a week.

- You have no more than one asthma attack a year that requires you to take corticosteroids by mouth.

- Your peak flow doesn't drop below 80 percent of your personal best number.

If your asthma isn't well controlled, contact your doctor. He or she may need to change your asthma action plan.

Home Care

Develop a written asthma action plan.

- Recognize early signs, symptoms, and peak expiratory flow (PEF) measures that indicate worsening asthma.

- Adjust medications (increase SABA [short–acting beta$_2$–agonist] and, in some cases, add oral systemic corticosteroids) and remove or withdraw from environmental factors contributing to the exacerbation.

- Monitor response.

- Seek medical care if there is serious deterioration or lack of response to treatment. Give specific instructions on who and when to call.

Use a Peak Flow Meter

This small, hand-held device shows how well air moves out of your lungs. You blow into the device and it gives you a score, or peak flow number. Your score shows how well your lungs are working at the time of the test.

Your doctor will tell you how and when to use your peak flow meter. He or she also will teach you how to take your medicines based on your score.

Your doctor and other health care providers may ask you to use your peak flow meter each morning and keep a record of your results. You may find it very useful to record peak flow scores for a couple of weeks before each medical visit and take the results with you.

When you're first diagnosed with asthma, it's important to find your "personal best" peak flow number. To do this, you record your score each day for a 2- to 3-week period when your asthma is well-controlled. The highest number you get during that time is your personal best. You can compare this number to future numbers to make sure your asthma is controlled.

Your peak flow meter can help warn you of an asthma attack, even before you notice symptoms. If your score shows that your breathing is getting worse, you should take your quick-relief medicines the way your asthma action plan directs. Then you can use the peak flow meter to check how well the medicine worked.

Get Asthma Checkups

When you first begin treatment, you'll see your doctor about every 2 to 6 weeks. Once your asthma is controlled, your doctor may want to see you from once a month to twice a year.

During these checkups, your doctor may ask whether you've had an asthma attack since the last visit or any changes in symptoms or peak flow measurements. He or she also may ask about your daily activities. This information will help your doctor assess your level of asthma control.

Your doctor also may ask whether you have any problems or concerns with taking your medicines or following your asthma action plan. Based on your answers to these questions, your doctor may change the dose of your medicine or give you a new medicine.

If your control is very good, you might be able to take less medicine. The goal is to use the least amount of medicine needed to control your asthma.

Emergency Care

Most people who have asthma, including many children, can safely manage their symptoms by following their asthma action plans. However, you might need medical attention at times.

Call your doctor for advice if:

- Your medicines don't relieve an asthma attack.

- Your peak flow is less than half of your personal best peak flow number.

Call 9–1–1 for emergency care if:

- You have trouble walking and talking because you're out of breath.

- You have blue lips or fingernails.

At the hospital, you'll be closely watched and given oxygen and more medicines, as well as medicines at higher doses than you take at home. Such treatment can save your life.

Urgent or Emergency Care

Assess severity by lung function measures (for ages 5 years and up), physical examination, and signs and symptoms.

Treat to relieve hypoxemia and airflow obstruction; reduce airway inflammation.

- Use supplemental oxygen as appropriate to correct hypoxemia.

- Treat with repetitive or continuous SABA (short–acting beta$_2$–agonist), with the addition of inhaled ipratropium bromide in severe exacerbations.

- Give oral systemic corticosteroids in moderate or severe exacerbations or for patients who fail to respond promptly and completely to SABA.

- Consider adjunctive treatments, such as intravenous magnesium sulfate or heliox, in severe exacerbations unresponsive to treatment.

Monitor response with repeat assessment of lung function measures, physical examination, and signs and symptoms, and, in emergency department, pulse oximetry.

139

Discharge with medication and patient education:

- Medications: SABA, oral systemic corticosteroids; consider starting ICS (inhaled corticosteroids)

- Referral to follow–up care

- Asthma discharge plan

- Review of inhaler technique and, whenever possible, environmental control measures

Asthma Treatment for Special Groups

The treatments described above generally apply to all people who have asthma. However, some aspects of treatment differ for people in certain age groups and those who have special needs.

Children

It's hard to diagnose asthma in children younger than 5 years. Thus, it's hard to know whether young children who wheeze or have other asthma symptoms will benefit from long-term control medicines. (Quick-relief medicines tend to relieve wheezing in young children whether they have asthma or not.)

Doctors will treat infants and young children who have asthma symptoms with long-term control medicines if, after assessing a child, they feel that the symptoms are persistent and likely to continue after 6 years of age.

Inhaled corticosteroids are the preferred treatment for young children. Montelukast and cromolyn are other options. Treatment might be given for a trial period of 1 month to 6 weeks. Treatment usually is stopped if benefits aren't seen during that time and the doctor and parents are confident the medicine was used properly.

Inhaled corticosteroids can possibly slow the growth of children of all ages. Slowed growth usually is apparent in the first several months of treatment, is generally small, and doesn't get worse over time. Poorly controlled asthma also may reduce a child's growth rate.

Many experts think the benefits of inhaled corticosteroids for children who need them to control their asthma far outweigh the risk of slowed growth.

Older Adults

Doctors may need to adjust asthma treatment for older adults who take certain other medicines, such as beta blockers, aspirin and other pain relievers, and anti-inflammatory medicines. These medicines can prevent asthma medicines from working well and may worsen asthma symptoms.

Be sure to tell your doctor about all of the medicines you take, including over-the-counter medicines.

Older adults may develop weak bones from using inhaled corticosteroids, especially at high doses. Talk with your doctor about taking calcium and vitamin D pills, as well as other ways to help keep your bones strong.

Pregnant Women

Pregnant women who have asthma need to control the disease to ensure a good supply of oxygen to their babies. Poor asthma control increases the risk of preeclampsia, a condition in which a pregnant woman develops high blood pressure and protein in the urine. Poor asthma control also increases the risk that a baby will be born early and have a low birth weight.

Studies show that it's safer to take asthma medicines while pregnant than to risk having an asthma attack.

Talk with your doctor if you have asthma and are pregnant or planning a pregnancy. Your level of asthma control may get better or it may get worse while you're pregnant. Your health care team will check your asthma control often and adjust your treatment as needed.

People Whose Asthma Symptoms Occur with Physical Activity

Physical activity is an important part of a healthy lifestyle. Adults need physical activity to maintain good health. Children need it for growth and development.

In some people, however, physical activity can trigger asthma symptoms. If this happens to you or your child, talk with your doctor about the best ways to control asthma so you can stay active.

The following medicines may help prevent asthma symptoms caused by physical activity:

- Short-acting beta$_2$-agonists (quick-relief medicine) taken shortly before physical activity can last 2 to 3 hours and prevent exercise-related symptoms in most people who take them.

141

- Long-acting beta$_2$-agonists can be protective for up to 12 hours. However, with daily use, they'll no longer give up to 12 hours of protection. Also, frequent use of these medicines for physical activity might be a sign that asthma is poorly controlled.

- Leukotriene modifiers. These pills are taken several hours before physical activity. They can help relieve asthma symptoms brought on by physical activity.

- Long-term control medicines. Frequent or severe symptoms due to physical activity may suggest poorly controlled asthma and the need to either start or increase long-term control medicines that reduce inflammation. This will help prevent exercise-related symptoms.

Easing into physical activity with a warmup period may be helpful. You also may want to wear a mask or scarf over your mouth when exercising in cold weather.

If you use your asthma medicines as your doctor directs, you should be able to take part in any physical activity or sport you choose.

People Having Surgery

Asthma may add to the risk of having problems during and after surgery. For instance, having a tube put into your throat may cause an asthma attack.

Tell your surgeon about your asthma when you first talk with him or her. The surgeon can take steps to lower your risk, such as giving you asthma medicines before or during surgery.

Section 10.2

Stepwise Approach to Treatment

Text in this section is excerpted from "Management of Asthma,"
Federal Bureau of Prisons (BOP), May 2013.

Step Therapy for Asthma

Since the course of the disease is variable, once asthma control is achieved, monitoring is essential. At times it may be necessary to step up or down therapy. Stepping therapy down is necessary for identifying the minimum medication necessary to maintain control and minimizing the risk of adverse events.

- Once the provider assesses the patient's impairment and risk, the provider should refer to to determine the level of care for the corresponding treatment level. This can be accomplished both at initiation of therapy and during follow-up care.

Inhalers play a significant role in the treatment of asthma. When patients start using any new inhaler device, they should be educated on proper technique. This education should be performed with the device present.

After the initiation of the treatment plan, a follow-up appointment in 2–6 weeks is recommended to assess their response to the therapy. If the patient is not well-controlled, the asthma education and self-care behaviors need to be assessed before advancing to the next step. At times, a course of oral systemic steroids may be necessary to regain control of their asthma more quickly. After they have been well-controlled on a drug therapy for at least 3 months, then a step-down in therapy can be considered. As part of the step-down consideration, the expert panel recommends an inhaled corticosteroid (ICS) reduction of 25–50% every 3 months to the lowest possible dose that is required to maintain asthma control.

STEP 1: Intermittent Asthma

At this stage in asthma therapy, a detailed asthma management plan should be in place. This plan should ensure that the patient understands when and how a medication should be taken, how much to take, how to evaluate the response to therapy, when to seek medical care, and what to do when the desired effect is not achieved or side effects are encountered.

A short-acting inhaled bronchodilator (beta$_2$-agonist) as needed for symptom control is usually sufficient treatment for intermittent asthma. Periodic monitoring is appropriate to assess whether a maintenance medication is necessary. If a short-acting beta$_2$-agonists (SABA) is required more than 2 times a week, then they should be considered for a possible step-up in therapy.

For certain persons with intermittent asthma, severe life-threatening exacerbations may occur, separated by lengthy periods of normal pulmonary function without symptoms. For an exacerbation that is precipitated by a viral respiratory infection, the following is recommended:

- Mild symptoms: SABA every 4-6 hours for 24 hours or longer (nebulizer or metered dose inhalers (MDI) may be used)

- Moderate-severe symptoms: Short course of a systemic corticosteroid

- History of severe exacerbations with viral respiratory infections: Systemic corticosteroids at the first sign of infection

Note that SABA usage for exercise induced bronchospasm (EIB) or viral infections should not factor into this assessment. A person who is excessively using a SABA due to deconditioning, and has a decreased ability to exercise, does not necessarily require a step-up in treatment. The preemptive use of a SABA shortly before exercise will benefit people that experience EIB.

STEP 2: Mild Persistent Asthma

Persistent asthma should be treated with a daily "maintenance" medication. The most effective medications and the mainstay of asthma therapy are the inhaled corticosteroids. At this stage of asthma severity, an ICS should be initiated at a low dose. Although some studies have looked at the usefulness of pro re nata (PRN) ICS use in mild persistent asthma, there is no clear evidence of positive long-term outcomes. Therefore the BOP does not recommend intermittent usage of an ICS in asthma treatment.

People with persistent asthma must have a quick-relief medication available to them. Alternative treatments include mast cell stabilizers, leukotriene modifiers (LTRAs), and sustained release theophylline.

Mast cell stabilizers (cromolyn and nedocromil) have a strong safety profile, but limited efficacy. LTRAs (e.g., montelukast) have been shown to prevent symptoms and provide long-term control, but studies have shown them to be inferior to ICSs on most outcome measures. Theophylline has a narrow therapeutic index, and thus needs to be monitored periodically. Given its modest clinical effectiveness, due primarily to being a bronchodilator, theophylline is not a preferred medication; however, it remains a therapeutic option for some people (e.g., patients needing a tablet/capsule).

Some may have persistent asthma symptoms during certain seasons and intermittent symptoms the rest of the year. Consideration should be given to treat them with maintenance therapy during the affected season and step them down the rest of the year.

STEP 3: Moderate Persistent Asthma

A person requiring a step-up in therapy should have their inhaler technique and compliance reviewed. Environmental factors, as well as comorbid conditions could attribute to their worsening asthma, and should be taken into account. Consultation with an asthma specialist may also be considered at this stage.

The ICS should be increased to a medium dose. For most patients, this increase should improve lung function, reduce symptoms, and significantly reduce their risk of exacerbations. While taking an ICS at a medium dose can cause systemic side effects, the risk is small, due to limited systemic absorption.

Alternative therapies include maintaining the low-dose ICS with the addition of either an LTRA or theophylline; however, as in Step 2, these medications are not preferred.

STEP 4: Severe Persistent Asthma

Step 4 of care requires adding a long-acting beta$_2$-agonists (LABA) to the patient's medication regimen. The addition of a LABA has been shown to improve spirometric measurements, decrease symptoms, and reduce exacerbations in most people. Providers should be aware of the black box warning for rare life-threatening or fatal exacerbations associated with LABAs. With the addition of a LABA, the provider may be able to slightly decrease the dose of the ICS.

An alternative therapy would be the use of a high-dose ICS regimen. While high doses of ICS have shown only minimal improvements in LFTs, they can decrease the frequency of severe exacerbations. High doses of ICS do have a significantly higher risk of adverse effects. However, a high-dose ICS regimen may prove beneficial for patients who do not show significant reversibility to a short-acting bronchodilator, thereby preventing the use of a LABA. Significant reversibility can be characterized by an increase in FEV1 of greater than 200 mL and greater than 12% from baseline.

Other alternative therapies include the addition to the low-dose ICS of either an LTRA or theophylline; however, as in Step 2, these medications are not preferred. If an add-on therapy does not result in an improvement of the patient's asthma control, then it should be discontinued and a trial of another add-on therapy should be initiated.

Step 4 therapy is also appropriate for people who experience recurrent severe exacerbations.

STEP 5: Severe Persistent Asthma

Consultation with an asthma specialist may be prudent if a patient requires this step of treatment. High-dose ICS together with a LABA is recommended. Although studies have shown a flattening in the dose-response curve as the amount of ICS is increased in patients with mild to moderate asthma, patients with severe asthma continue to receive improved benefit.

At this step, if a person has sensitivity to relevant perennial allergens, omalizumab may be considered as an adjunctive therapy. A positive skin test or in vitro reactivity to perennial allergens must be confirmed. Clinicians who administer omalizumab should be prepared and equipped to identify and treat anaphylaxis.

STEP 6: Severe Persistent Asthma

At this step, consult with a pulmonary specialist is advised. An oral corticosteroid should be added to high-dose ICS and LABA on a trial basis. This trial is to assess reversibility; hence the need for long-term corticosteroid therapy. If corticosteroids need to be used for a longer period of time, then the lowest possible dose (single dose daily or on alternate days) should be utilized. Once asthma control is achieved, attempts should be made to reduce the systemic corticosteroids. Alternatively, a trial of an LTRA, theophylline, or zileuton can be added to high-dose ICS and LABA.

Section 10.3

Understanding the Different Types of Asthma Medications

Text in this section is excerpted from "How Is Asthma Treated and Controlled?" National Heart, Lung, and Blood Institute (NHLBI), August 4, 2014.

Medications for Asthma

Asthma is treated with two types of medicines: long-term control and quick-relief medicines. Long-term control medicines help reduce airway inflammation and prevent asthma symptoms. Quick-relief, or "rescue," medicines relieve asthma symptoms that may flare up.

Your initial treatment will depend on the severity of your asthma. Followup asthma treatment will depend on how well your asthma action plan is controlling your symptoms and preventing asthma attacks.

Your level of asthma control can vary over time and with changes in your home, school, or work environments. These changes can alter how often you're exposed to the factors that can worsen your asthma.

Your doctor may need to increase your medicine if your asthma doesn't stay under control. On the other hand, if your asthma is well controlled for several months, your doctor may decrease your medicine. These adjustments to your medicine will help you maintain the best control possible with the least amount of medicine necessary.

Asthma treatment for certain groups of people—such as children, pregnant women, or those for whom exercise brings on asthma symptoms—will be adjusted to meet their special needs.

Follow an Asthma Action Plan

You can work with your doctor to create a personal asthma action plan. The plan will describe your daily treatments, such as which medicines to take and when to take them. The plan also will explain when to call your doctor or go to the emergency room.

147

If your child has asthma, all of the people who care for him or her should know about the child's asthma action plan. This includes babysitters and workers at daycare centers, schools, and camps. These caretakers can help your child follow his or her action plan.

Avoid Things That Can Worsen Your Asthma

Many common things (called asthma triggers) can set off or worsen your asthma symptoms. Once you know what these things are, you can take steps to control many of them.

For example, exposure to pollens or air pollution might make your asthma worse. If so, try to limit time outdoors when the levels of these substances in the outdoor air are high. If animal fur triggers your asthma symptoms, keep pets with fur out of your home or bedroom.

One possible asthma trigger you shouldn't avoid is physical activity. Physical activity is an important part of a healthy lifestyle. Talk with your doctor about medicines that can help you stay active.

If your asthma symptoms are clearly related to allergens, and you can't avoid exposure to those allergens, your doctor may advise you to get allergy shots.

You may need to see a specialist if you're thinking about getting allergy shots. These shots can lessen or prevent your asthma symptoms, but they can't cure your asthma.

Several health conditions can make asthma harder to manage. These conditions include runny nose, sinus infections, reflux disease, psychological stress, and sleep apnea. Your doctor will treat these conditions as well.

Therapy

Introduction

- Frequent EIB in asthmatic patients suggests inadequate asthma control and requires patient re-evaluation to determine the need for additional therapy.

- Failure of appropriate pharmacotherapeutic agents to prevent EIB indicates the need to re-evaluate the diagnosis.

- Several pharmacotherapeutic agents are effective when given for the prevention or attenuation of EIB. They differ in their mechanisms of action and overall effectiveness. In addition, there is both intrapatient and interpatient variability in responsiveness.

- Medications may differ in effectiveness over time because of variability of asthma, environmental conditions, intensity of the exercise stimulus, and tachyphylaxis.

β_2-Adrenergic Receptor Agonists

- Inhaled β_2-adrenergic receptor agonists are the most effective group of agents for short-term protection against EIB and for accelerating recovery of FEV1 to baseline when given after a decrease in FEV1 after exercise.

- When given as a single dose or on an intermittent basis, short-acting β_2-agonists (SABAs) and long-acting β_2-agonists (LABAs) may protect against or attenuate EIB; SABAs are usually effective for 2 to 4 hours and LABAs for up to 12 hours.

- Daily use of β_2-adrenergic agents alone or in combination with inhaled corticosteroids (ICS) usually will lead to tolerance manifested as a reduction in duration and/or magnitude of protection against EIB and a prolongation of recovery in response to SABA after exercise. Therefore, monotherapy with adrenergic agents is generally recommended for use only on an intermittent basis for prevention of EIB.

- Regular (i.e., daily) use of β_2-agonists for EIB leads to relative loss of efficacy of the agent.

Leukotriene (LT) Inhibitors

- Daily therapy with LT inhibitors does not lead to tolerance and can be used for intermittent or maintenance prophylaxis; however, it provides protection that may not be complete and has no use to reverse airway obstruction when it occurs.

Mast Cell Stabilizers

- Cromolyn sodium and nedocromil sodium (currently not available in the United States in an inhaled form) when inhaled shortly before exercise attenuate EIB but have a short duration of action. They do not have a bronchodilator activity. They may be effective alone or as added therapy with other drugs for EIB.

Inhaled Corticosteroids

- Although ICS therapy can decrease the frequency and severity of EIB, its use does not necessarily eliminate the need for additional acute therapy with β_2-adrenergic agonists or other agents.

- ICS therapy does not prevent the occurrence of tolerance from daily β_2-agonist use.

Anticholinergic Agents

- Although ipratropium bromide has been inconsistent in attenuating EIB, a few patients may be responsive to this agent.

Methylxanthines, Antihistamines, and Other Agents

- Drugs in several other pharmacotherapeutic classes, including theophylline, antihistamines, calcium channel blockers, β_2-adrenergic receptor antagonists, inhaled furosemide, heparin, and hyaluronic acid, have been examined for actions against EIB with inconsistent results.

Nonpharmacologic Therapy

- Preexercise warm-up may be helpful in reducing the severity of EIB.

- Reduction of sodium intake and ingestion of fish oil and ascorbic acid supplementation may be helpful in reducing the severity of EIB.

Competitive and Elite Athletes

- EIB alone in elite athletes may have different characteristics than EIB with asthma in elite athletes or EIB in the general population. These divergent characteristics may include pathogenesis, presentation, diagnosis, management, and the requirement by governing bodies to obtain permission to receive pharmaceutical agents.

- Airway inflammation in elite athletes may be related to the high intensity of physical training, high minute ventilation, and inhalation of airborne pollutants and allergens.

- The diagnosis of EIB, whether alone or with asthma, in elite athletes may be difficult because history and presentation are not reliable. Objective testing is necessary to diagnose the condition accurately.

- In general, the treatment of EIB in patients who have asthma is similar in both recreational and elite athletes. However, the efficacy of therapy for EIB alone in athletes at any level is not well established.

Section 10.4

Drug Treatments for Asthma that Do Not Use Chlorofluorocarbons

Text in this section is excerpted from "Drug Treatments for Asthma
and Chronic Obstructive Pulmonary Disease that Do Not Use
Chlorofluorocarbons," U.S. Food and Drug Administration (FDA),
April 8, 2015.

Avoiding Chlorofluorocarbons

Many inhalers that do not use chlorofluorocarbons (CFC) are
already available for the treatment of asthma and chronic obstructive pulmonary disease. These products aren't necessarily "official"
direct alternatives to CFC Metered Dose Inhalers, but may in many
patients serve as a useful medication that could replace the need for
a particular CFC Metered Dose Inhaler. FDA will determine official
alternatives by using the criteria established through notice-and-com-
ment rulemaking, as it has done with albuterol.

Drugs are listed in alphabetical order by active moiety, with specific
brands available listed under each active moiety. What is an active
moiety? An active moiety is the part of a drug that makes the drug
work the way it does. Many different drug products may be marketed
with the same active moiety.

Each drug name in the list below is linked to the drug's regulatory history

- Tudorza Pressair (aclidinium bromide)
- Proventil HFA (albuterol sulfate inhalation aerosol)
- Ventolin HFA (albuterol sulfate inhalation aerosol)
- ProAir HFA (albuterol sulfate inhalation aerosol)
- ProAir Respiclick (albuterol sulfate inhalation powder)

- Combivent Respimat (albuterol sulfate and ipratropium bromide)
- Duoneb (albuterol sulfate and ipratropium bromide) Inhalation Solution
- Brovana (arformoterol tartrate) Inhalation Solution
- QVAR (beclomethasone dipropionate inhalation aerosol)
- Pulmicort Turbohaler (budesonide inhalation powder)
- Pulmicort Flexhaler (budesonide inhalation powder)
- Symbicort (budesonide and formoterol fumarate) Inhalation Aerosol
- Alvesco (ciclesonide) Inhalation Aerosol
- Aerospan HFA (flunisolide)
- Breo Ellipta (fluticasone furoate and vilanterol trifenatate)
- Flovent HFA (fluticasone propionate HFA inhalation aerosol)
- Flovent Diskus (fluticasone propionate inhalation powder)
- Foradil Aerolizer (formoterol fumarate inhalation powder)
- Perforomist (formoterol fumarate) Inhalation Solution
- Arcapta Neohaler (indacaterol inhalation powder)
- Atrovent HFA (ipratropium bromide HFA inhalation aerosol
- Xopenex (levalbuterol sulfate HFA inhalation aerosol)
- Asmanex (mometasone furoate) Inhalation Aerosol HFA
- Asmanex Twisthaler (mometasone furoate inhalation pzwder)
- Dulera (mometasone furoate and formoterol fumarate) Inhalation Aerosol
- Striverdi Respimat (olodaterol) Inhalation Spray
- Serevent Diskus (salmeterol xinafoate powder for inhalation)
- ADVAIR Diskus (salmeterol xinafoate/fluticasone propionate powder for inhalation)
- ADVAIR HFA (salmeterol xinafoate/fluticasone propionate)
- Spiriva Respimat (tiotropium bromide) Inhalation Spray
- Spiriva Handihaler (tiotropium bromide inhalation powder)
- Incruse Ellipta (umeclidinium inhalation powder)
- Anoro Ellipta (umeclidinium and vilanterol inhalation powder)

Section 10.5

Asthma Medicines: How They Work and How to Take Them?

This section includes excerpts from "So You Have Asthma,"
National Heart, Lung, and Blood Institute (NHLBI), March
2013; and text from "Management of Asthma," Federal Bureau of
Prisons (BOP), May 2013.

Most people who have asthma need two kinds of medicines: long-term control medicines and quick-relief medicines.

Long-term control medicines

These are medicines that you take every day for a long time, to stop and control the inflammation in your airways and thereby prevent symptoms and attacks from coming on in the first place.

These medicines work slowly, and you may need to take them for several weeks or longer before you feel better. If your asthma is not well controlled, your doctor may increase the dose or add another medicine to your treatment. Once your asthma is under control, your doctor may be able to reduce some of these medicines.

The most effective long-term control medicines are anti-inflammatory medicines. They reduce the inflammation in your airways, making the airways less sensitive and less likely to react to your asthma triggers.

> Anti-inflammatory medicines are most effective when you take them every day, even when you don't have any symptoms.

The most effective anti-inflammatory medicines for most people who have asthma are inhaled corticosteroids.

Some people don't like the idea of taking steroids. But the inhaled corticosteroids used to treat asthma are very different from the illegal anabolic steroids taken by some athletes. They are not habit-forming—even if you take them every day for many years. And, because

153

they are inhaled, the medicine goes right to your lungs where it is needed. Also, they have been studied for many years in large groups of adults and children as young as 2 years old and, in general, have been found to be well tolerated and safe when taken as directed by your doctor.

> Like many other medicines, inhaled corticosteroids can have side effects. But most doctors agree that the benefits of taking them and preventing attacks far outweigh the risks of side effects. Take inhaled corticosteroids as your doctor prescribes and use a spacer or holding chamber with your inhaler to make sure the medicine goes directly to your lungs. Be sure to rinse your mouth out with water, and don't swallow the water, after taking these medicines. Rinsing helps prevent an infection in the mouth.

Other long-term control medicines used to treat asthma include:

- Inhaled long-acting beta$_2$-agonists— These bronchodilators can help prevent symptoms when taken *with* inhaled corticosteroids by helping to keep airway muscles relaxed.

  - These medicines should *not* be used alone. They also should not be used to treat symptoms or an attack.

  - Two-in-one medicines that contain both corticosteroids and long-acting beta$_2$-agonists are available.

- Cromolyn sodium—This nonsteroidal anti-inflammatory medicine can be used to treat mild persistent asthma, especially in children. It's not as effective as inhaled corticosteroids.

- Leukotriene modifiers—These anti- leukotriene medicines are a newer class of long-term control medicines that block the action of chemicals in your airways. If not blocked, these chemicals, called leukotrienes, increase the inflammation in your lungs during an asthma attack.

Anti-leukotriene medicines, which are available in pill form, are used alone to treat mild persistent asthma or with inhaled corticosteroids to treat moderate persistent asthma. They are not as effective as inhaled corticosteroids for most patients.

- Theophylline—This medicine, also available in pill form, acts as a bronchodilator to relax and open the airways. It can help prevent nighttime symptoms. It is sometimes used alone to treat mild persistent asthma, but most of the time it is used with inhaled corticosteroids. If you take theophylline, you need to have your blood levels checked regularly to make sure the dose is right for you. With long-term control medicines, it's important to take them every day, as your doctor prescribes.

> Inhaled corticosteroids are the most effective long-term control medicines for asthma, and, in general, they are well tolerated and safe for both children and adults when taken as directed by your doctor.

Quick-relief medicines

You take these medicines when you need immediate relief of your symptoms. Everyone who has asthma needs a quick-relief medicine—usually taken by inhaler—to stop asthma symptoms before they get worse.

> Carry a quick-relief inhaler with you at all times to stop asthma symptoms before they get worse.

The preferred quick-relief medicine is an inhaled short-acting beta$_2$-agonist. It acts quickly to relax tightened muscles around your airways so that your airways can open up and allow more air to flow through.

You should take your quick-relief medicine at the first sign of any asthma symptoms. Your doctor may recommend that you take this medicine at other times, as well— for example, before exercise.

Short-acting beta$_2$-agonists include albuterol, levalbuterol, and pirbuterol. They are also called by their brand names.

Other quick-relief medicines are:

- Anticholinergics—These medicines are used primarily in the emergency department, but if you have moderate to severe asthma, your doctor may recommend that you use them with a short-acting beta$_2$-agonist to relieve symptoms. Or, if you can't tolerate a short-acting beta$_2$-agonist, this may be the treatment of choice for you.

155

- Systemic corticosteroids—Usually taken in the form of a pill or syrup, systemic corticosteroids may be used to speed your recovery after an asthma attack and to prevent more attacks. You would take them for 3–10 days. People who have severe asthma may need to take systemic corticosteroids for longer periods of time.

> Quick-relief medicine is very good at stopping asthma symptoms, but it does nothing to control the inflammation in your airways that produces these symptoms. If you need to use your quick-relief inhaler more often than usual, or if you need to use it more than 2 days a week, it may be a sign that you also need to take a long-term control medicine to reduce the inflammation in your airways. Discuss this with your doctor as soon as possible.

Taking Your Medicines: How's Your Technique?

- **Inhalers**

  An inhaler is a hand-held device that delivers the medicine right to the airways in your lungs where it is needed. There are several kinds of inhalers:

  - metered dose inhaler (MDI)
  - dry powder inhaler

- **Spacers and valved holding chambers**

  A spacer or valved holding chamber can make using an MDI a lot easier. It can also decrease the amount of medicine that lands on your tongue or in the back of your mouth. There are many kinds of spacers that can be chosen to fit your needs.

  - Some have a mouthpiece.
  - Some have a facemask that comes in different sizes to fit infants, children, and adults.
  - Many spacers fit on the end of an inhaler; for some, the canister of medicine fits into the device.
  - Some MDIs come with built-in spacers.

- **Nebulizers**

A nebulizer is another device for taking inhaled medicines. It provides the medicine in a fine, steady mist.

What Medicines Do You Need?

Your doctor is likely to consider a number of factors when deciding which medicines and how much of each you need. Your medicines should:

- Prevent your ongoing symptoms (you should not need to use your quick-relief medicine more than 2 days a week)

- Help maintain your normal lung function

- Help you be as active as you want to be, whether at work or at school

- Prevent your having repeated asthma attacks

- Help do all of this without causing major side effects

Each time you see your doctor, he or she will weigh all these things before recommending any changes in your medicines.

Usually, if you have been doing well for several months, your doctor may consider reducing the number or doses of medicines you're taking. But if your asthma is still not under control, he or she may recommend adding some medicines or increasing the doses of some of those you're already taking.

The goal is to achieve the best asthma control possible with the least amount of medicine.

It may take several visits before the doctor finds exactly the right medicines and doses for you. This is why watching your asthma symptoms and seeing your doctor regularly are so important.

Your doctor may also recommend other treatments to help manage other conditions that can affect your asthma. These include:

- Allergy shots (immunotherapy) if your allergies aren't easily controlled by avoiding your triggers and taking medicine.

- Pneumococcal (pneumonia) vaccinations, for older adults.

- Antibiotics, if you have a bacterial infection, such as pneumonia or suspected bacterial sinusitis. Antibiotics are not recommended for routine or emergency treatment of asthma.

Ask your doctor to write on your asthma action plan:

- The name of each of your quick-relief and long-term control medicines

- How much of each medicine you should take

- When to take each of your medicines

Basic Facts about Asthma Medications

For optimal self-management, patients need to be educated about their medication, especially how and when to use them. Regardless of the delivery device selected, detailed education on the use and maintenance of the device is necessary. The package inserts provided with these products often include detailed diagrams explaining proper technique. The patient should be able to demonstrate good technique initially and with each follow-up visit. Reinforcement of proper technique ensures proper delivery of medication.

Although numerous patients utilize metered dose inhalers (MDI) each day, many do not operate them correctly. As a result, both the provider and the patient may be unaware of improper usage and incorrectly assume a medication is ineffective. This may lead prescribers to unnecessarily change or step up therapy.

In order to promote the effective use of an inhaler, providers should:

- At each routine encounter, have the patient demonstrate using the MDI by performing an actual inhalation

- Prescribe inhalers with valved holding chambers or require the use of a spacer with the prescribed MDI for those patients who cannot demonstrate adequate technique.

- Educate the patient on how many inhalations should be used at one time. For example, if the instructions say to utilize two puffs, how long should the patient wait after each puff?

- Educate the patient on the order in which inhalers should be used. For example, should the patient use a beta-agonist before using a corticosteroid?

Chapter 11

Medications to Treat Asthma

Asthma medications are divided into two categories: relievers and controllers. Relievers are used for asthma attacks and not for long-term treatment of the disease. Controllers are used to prevent asthma symptoms. For controllers to work properly, people with asthma have to use them consistently, even when feeling well.

Relievers

Short-Acting Beta-Adrenergic Agonists

Short-acting beta-agonists (SABAs) such as albuterol can provide immediate symptom relief that lasts four to six hours. They do not decrease allergic inflammation but instead relax the muscles around the airway that tighten when an allergic person is exposed to an allergen or other asthma trigger. For people who rarely experience asthma attacks, SABAs may be used as the only medicine on an as-needed basis. People who are taking controller medicines often use SABAs for symptom relief.

Oral Corticosteroids

Oral corticosteroids such as prednisone, methyl prednisolone, and dexamethasone are typically used to treat severe asthma attacks.

Text in this chapter is excerpted from "Treatments for Environmental Allergies," National Institute of Allergy and Infectious Diseases (NIAID), April 22, 2015.

People with very severe asthma may use corticosteroids as controller medications, taking them daily or every other day. When used long-term at high doses, oral corticosteroids can cause many side effects, including weight gain, high blood pressure, diabetes, brittle bones, thinning skin, muscle weakness, and cataracts. Doctors who treat people with severe asthma usually will use various combinations of medications to try to reduce the corticosteroid dose.

Controllers

Inhaled Corticosteroids

Inhaled corticosteroids are effective at improving quality of life and preventing severe asthma attacks in people with persistent asthma. These medications can sometimes cause yeast infections in the mouth. If given in very high doses for long periods, they may cause some of the side effects typical of oral corticosteroids, such as brittle bones and an increased risk of cataracts. People with moderate to severe asthma may take inhaled corticosteroids along with other drugs called long-acting beta-adrenergic agonists.

Leukotriene Receptor Antagonists and 5-Lipoxygenase Inhibitors

Leukotriene receptor antagonists (LTRAs) block the action of leukotrienes, chemical messengers involved in allergic reactions. They may be used alone to treat mild asthma or along with an inhaled corticosteroid to treat moderate asthma, as well as to treat allergic rhinitis. People who have both mild asthma and allergic rhinitis can take an LTRA to treat both conditions. A related medication, called zileuton, prevents leukotriene production by blocking an enzyme called 5-lipoxygenase. Zileuton is only used for severe asthma, and evidence suggests that it may be particularly useful for people with asthma who have reactions to aspirin, a syndrome called aspirin-exacerbated respiratory disease, or AERD.

Long-Acting Beta-Adrenergic Agonists

In combination with an inhaled corticosteroid, long-acting beta-agonists (LABAs) are effective for asthma control. LABAs, the effects of which last for 12 hours, typically are not used alone because some studies have suggested that LABAs can be harmful if used without an inhaled corticosteroid.

Omalizumab

The Food and Drug Administration has approved the injectable medicine omalizumab to treat allergic asthma. Omalizumab works by binding to IgE, the antibody responsible for allergies, and removing it from the body. Omalizumab can prevent severe episodes of asthma in people whose asthma is not adequately controlled by other medicines.

Cromolyn Sodium

Doctors may recommend cromolyn sodium to treat mild asthma in young children. Liquid cromolyn sodium is placed in a mist-generating machine called a nebulizer, and children breathe in the mist.

Chapter 12

Inhaled Corticosteroids

Chapter Contents

Section 12.1

What Are Inhaled Corticosteroids?

This section includes excerpts from "Inhaled Corticosteriods: Keep
Airways Open," National Heart, Lung, and Blood Institute (NHLBI),
January 2013; and text from "Management of Asthma," Federal
Bureau of Prisons (BOP), May 2013.

Inhaled corticosteroids are the most effective medications for long-
term management of persistent asthma and should be utilized by
patients and clinicians as is recommended in the guidelines for treatment of asthma.

Use Inhaled Corticosteroids for Better Asthma Control and Fewer Flare-ups

Because asthma is a chronic inflammatory disorder, persistent
asthma is most effectively controlled with daily long-term control medication directed towards suppressing inflammation. Inhaled corticosteroids (ICS) are the most effective long-term therapy available for mild,
moderate, or severe persistent asthma. ICS are anti-inflammatory
medications that reduce airway hyperresponsiveness, inhibit inflammatory cell migration and activation, and block late phase reaction
to allergen. In general, ICS are well tolerated and safe at the recommended dosages.

Generally, ICS improves asthma control more effectively, in both
children and adults, than any other single long-term control medication. However, alternative options for medications are available to
tailor treatment to individual patient circumstances, needs, and preferences. The benefits of ICS outweigh the concerns about the potential
risk of a small, non-progressive reduction in growth velocity in children, or other possible adverse effects.

Systemic Corticosteroids

Systemic corticosteroids are indicated for moderate-to-severe exacerbations to speed recovery and prevent recurrence of exacerbations.
During an asthma exacerbation, doubling the dose of an inhaled

corticosteroid is not effective. Hydrocortisone sodium succinate or dexamethasone, given either intramuscular or intravenously, are the most rapid-acting agents; however, their onset of action is several hours. Short-term therapy should continue until the inmate achieves 80% of his/her personal best objective measures, usually 3–10 days.

Note: *Tapering systemic steroids following clinical improvement after a short treatment course does not prevent relapse and is not recommended.*

Long-Term Control Medications

Corticosteroids

Inhaled corticosteroid (ICS) formulations such as beclomethasone, mometasone, budesonide, and fluticasone are used for long-term control of asthma; their regular use, when medically indicated for asthma, is associated with improved asthma control, reduced risk of exacerbations, and decreased risk of death. Although the benefits of ICSs outweigh the risk of systemic adverse effects, they should be titrated to as low a dose as needed to maintain control. The NAEPP Expert Panel reported that most patients were able to maintain asthma control

Table 12.1. Inhaled Corticosteroids Dosing Chart

Inhaled Steroid	Low Dose	Medium Dose	High Dose
Beclomethasone HFA 40mcg or 80mcg	80–240 mcg **Initial:** 80mcg BID	240–480 mcg **Initial:** 160mcg BID	>480mcg **Max:** 320mcg BID
Budesonide 90mcg or 180mcg	180–600 mcg **Initial:** 180mcg BID	600–1200 mcg **Initial:** 360mcg BID	>1200mcg **Max:** 720mcg BID
Fluticasone HFA 44mcg, 110mcg, or 220 mcg	88–264 mcg **Initial:** 88mcg BID	>264–440 mcg **Initail:**220mcg BID (110mcg 2 puffs BID)	>440mcg **Max:** 880mcg BID
Mometasone Furoate 110mcg or 220mcg	220 mcg **Initial:** 220mcg daily	440 mcg **Initial:** 440mcg daily or220mcg BID	>440mcg **Max:** 440mcg BID
Fluticasone/ Salmeterol 100/50mcg, 250/50mcg, or 500/50mcg	100–300 mcg* **Initial:** 100/50mcg BID	>300–500 mcg* **Initial:** 250/50mcg BID	>500mcg* **Max:** 500/50 mcg BID

Table 12.1. Continued

Inhaled Steroid	Low Dose	Medium Dose	High Dose
Budesonide/ Formoterol 80/4.5mcg or 160/4.5mcg		320–640 mcg** Initial: 80/4.5mcg two puffs BID	640mcg** Max: 160/4.5mcg two puffs BID
Flunisolide 250mcg	500–1000 mcg Initial: 500mcg BID	1000–2000 mcg	2000mcg Max: 1000mcg BID

Low, medium, and high dosing of fluticasone/salmeterol is determined by the dose of fluticasone administered.
** Medium, high, and max dosing of budesonide/formoterol is determined by the dose of budesonide administered.*

with a 50% reduction in dose of their ICS, if the patient had been well-controlled on a high dose of an ICS alone for at least 60 days. Systemic corticosteroids such as methylprednisolone, prednisolone, and prednisone may be used long-term for the prevention of symptoms associated with severe persistent asthma.

Section 12.2

Gene Variant Affects Response to Inhaled Corticosteroids

Text in this section is excerpted from "Gene Variant Affects Response to Asthma Drugs," National Institutes of Health (NIH), October 3, 2011. Reviewed December 2015.

Gene Variant and Asthma Drugs

A genetic variant may explain why some people with asthma don't respond well to inhaled corticosteroids, the most widely prescribed medicine for long-term asthma control. In the future, knowledge of such variants could help doctors develop more effective, personalized asthma treatments.

Asthma is a complex inflammatory disease and many factors can influence how severely the disease affects people and how well they respond to treatments.

A poor response to inhaled corticosteroids often runs in families, so scientists have suspected that genetics plays a role. To learn more, a team of researchers carried out a genome-wide association study of children with asthma and their parents. The scientists searched for genetic variants linked to a poor response to inhaled corticosteroids.

The investigators first ran a genome-wide scan of the DNA of 118 children with asthma and their parents. As reported, the researchers uncovered a variant in the gene called glucocorticoid-induced transcript 1 (GLCCI1) that appeared to be associated with a poor response to inhaled corticosteroids.

The scientists verified this association in 935 additional children and adults with asthma who had enrolled in 4 independent studies. About 1 in 6 study participants had 2 copies of the GLCCI1 variant. Compared to those with 2 copies of the regular GLCCI1 gene, patients carrying 2 copies of the variant were more than twice as likely to respond poorly to inhaled corticosteroids. Those with a poor response had an average of one-third the level of lung improvement from inhaler treatment as those with 2 regular copies of the gene.

In laboratory cultures, the scientists saw changes caused by the GLCCI1 variant that might explain why it leads to a decreased response to inhaled corticosteroids. However, more studies will be needed to better understand how the variant operates in the lungs.

The researchers estimate that the GLCCI1 variant accounts for about 6.6% of the overall variation to inhaled corticosteroids between people. Also, because most of the study participants were white, the results may not be applicable to people of other ethnicities. More studies will be needed to explore whether GLCCI1 contributes to corticosteroid response in other ethnic groups.

This finding helps to explain the genetic basis for the long-standing observation that some people do not respond well to what is a common asthma treatment. The study illustrates the importance of research examining the relationship between genetic makeup and response to therapy for asthma, and underscores the need for personalized treatment for those who have it. A genetic variant may explain why some people with asthma don't respond well to inhaled corticosteroids, the most widely prescribed medicine for long-term asthma control. In the future, knowledge of such variants could help doctors develop more effective, personalized asthma treatments.

Section 12.3

Pros and Cons of Inhaled Corticosteroids

This section includes excerpts from "Inhaled Corticosteriods: Keep Airways Open," National Heart, Lung, and Blood Institute (NHLBI), January 2013; text from "Corticosteroid Therapy," Centers for Disease Control and Prevention (CDC), February 18, 2015; and text from "Medications that Weaken Your Immune System and Fungal Infections," Centers for Disease Control and Prevention (CDC), February 24, 2014.

Educate patients on the role of ICS in long-term asthma management

Communicating the effectiveness, safety, and importance of ICS for asthma control and addressing concerns about their long-term use should occur at all levels of health care. It is also important for clinicians and educators to tailor their communications based on consideration of the patient's health literacy level. As well, it is crucial to develop a heightened awareness of health disparities and cultural barriers that facilitate more effective communication with minority (ethnic or racial) or economically disadvantaged patients regarding the use of asthma medications that may improve asthma outcomes.

Side Effects

Corticosteroids have both short-term and long-term side effects. Low doses of corticosteroids may be helpful with minimal side effects, but use of high dose corticosteroids for a long time can cause serious side effects. People taking steroids must be watched carefully for side effects. Other treatments, such as red cell transfusions, should be considered if a patient requires high corticosteroid doses or if serious side effects develop.

Inhaled corticosteroids used to treat asthma can increase your chance of developing oral candidiasis (thrush). Inhaled corticosteroids include the following:

- Beclomethasone (QVAR®)

168

- Budesonide (Pulmicort®, Symbicort®*)

- Ciclesonide (Alvesco®)

- Flunisolide (AeroBid®)

- Fluticasone (Flovent®, Advair®*)

- Mometasone (Asmanex Twisthaler®, Dulera®*)

- Triamcinolone (Azmacort®)

    *a combination medication that also includes a bronchodilator

Possible side effects of short-term corticosteroid use:

- Upset stomach

- Increased blood sugar

- Increased hunger

- Behavior changes, trouble sleeping, irritability

- Increased risk of pneumonia, thrush (white coating in the mouth), and other infections

- Weight gain, salt and water retention

- High blood pressure

- Increased fat on the face (rounded face), upper back, and belly

- Stretch marks on the skin, acne, poor wound healing, increased and unusual hair growth

Possible side effects of long-term use (3 months or longer):

- All short-term side effects

- Poor growth in children (can be severe)

- Brittle bones (bones break easily, problems with hips and shoulder joints)

- Muscle weakness

- Diabetes

- Eye problems

Tips for Success

- Take steroids exactly as prescribed by your doctor.

- Take steroids in the morning (if prescribed once a day), and take them with food to prevent an upset stomach.

- If you miss a dose of medicine, take it as soon as possible. If it is almost time for the next dose, skip the missed dose and return to the regular schedule. Do not take a double dose or extra doses.

- Tell your doctor if you get sick. Your blood count might drop from the stress of being sick, and you might need extra doses of medicine or other treatment.

- Always check with your doctor before changing the dose or stopping this medicine. It can be dangerous to stop corticosteroids suddenly. Your doctor may want to slowly reduce the amount you're taking until you stop completely.

- Talk with your doctor about any concerns. Make a list of your questions. Do your research so you can help make decisions about your treatment

Chapter 13

Long-Term Control Medications

Most people who have asthma need to take long-term control medicines daily to help prevent symptoms. The most effective long-term medicines reduce airway inflammation, which helps prevent symptoms from starting. These medicines don't give you quick relief from symptoms.

Inhaled corticosteroids. Inhaled corticosteroids are the preferred medicine for long-term control of asthma. They're the most effective option for long-term relief of the inflammation and swelling that makes your airways sensitive to certain inhaled substances.

Reducing inflammation helps prevent the chain reaction that causes asthma symptoms. Most people who take these medicines daily find they greatly reduce the severity of symptoms and how often they occur.

Inhaled corticosteroids generally are safe when taken as prescribed. These medicines are different from the illegal anabolic steroids taken by some athletes. Inhaled corticosteroids aren't habit-forming, even if you take them every day for many years.

Like many other medicines, though, inhaled corticosteroids can have side effects. Most doctors agree that the benefits of taking inhaled

Text in this Chapter is excerpted from "Asthma Care Quick Reference," National Heart, Lung, and Blood Institute (NHLBI), September 2012.

corticosteroids and preventing asthma attacks far outweigh the risk of side effects.

One common side effect from inhaled corticosteroids is a mouth infection called thrush. You might be able to use a spacer or holding chamber on your inhaler to avoid thrush. These devices attach to your inhaler. They help prevent the medicine from landing in your mouth or on the back of your throat.

Check with your doctor to see whether a spacer or holding chamber should be used with the inhaler you have. Also, work with your health care team if you have any questions about how to use a spacer or holding chamber. Rinsing your mouth out with water after taking inhaled corticosteroids also can lower your risk for thrush.

If you have severe asthma, you may have to take corticosteroid pills or liquid for short periods to get your asthma under control.

If taken for long periods, these medicines raise your risk for cataracts and osteoporosis. A cataract is the clouding of the lens in your eye. Osteoporosis is a disorder that makes your bones weak and more likely to break.

Your doctor may have you add another long-term asthma control medicine so he or she can lower your dose of corticosteroids. Or, your doctor may suggest you take calcium and vitamin D pills to protect your bones.

Other long-term control medicines. Other long-term control medicines include:

- Cromolyn. This medicine is taken using a device called a nebulizer. As you breathe in, the nebulizer sends a fine mist of medicine to your lungs. Cromolyn helps prevent airway inflammation.

- Omalizumab (anti-IgE). This medicine is given as a shot (injection) one or two times a month. It helps prevent your body from reacting to asthma triggers, such as pollen and dust mites. Anti-IgE might be used if other asthma medicines have not worked well.

A rare, but possibly life-threatening allergic reaction called anaphylaxis might occur when the Omalizumab (Xolair) injection is given. If you take this medication, work with your doctor to make sure you understand the signs and symptoms of anaphylaxis and what actions you should take. A severe allergic reaction called anaphylaxis can happen when you receive Xolair. The reaction can occur after the first dose, or after many doses. It may also occur right after a Xolair injection or days later. Anaphylaxis is a life-threatening condition and can lead to death. Go to the nearest emergency room right away if you have any of these symptoms of an allergic reaction:

- wheezing, shortness of breath, cough, chest tightness, or trouble breathing
- low blood pressure, dizziness, fainting, rapid or weak heartbeat, anxiety, or feeling of "impending doom"
- flushing, itching, hives or feeling warm
- swelling of the throat or tongue, throat tightness, hoarse voice, or trouble swallowing

Your healthcare provider will monitor you closely for symptoms of an allergic reaction while you are receiving Xolair and for a period of time after your injection. Your healthcare provider should talk to you about getting medical treatment if you have symptoms of an allergic reaction after leaving the healthcare provider's office or treatment center.

Before receiving Xolair, tell your healthcare provider about all of your medical conditions, including if you:

- have any other allergies (such as food allergy or seasonal allergies)
- have sudden breathing problems (bronchospasm)
- have ever had a severe allergic reaction called anaphylaxis
- have or have had a parasitic infection
- have or have had cancer
- are pregnant or plan to become pregnant. It is not known if Xolair may harm your unborn baby.
- are breastfeeding or plan to breastfeed.

Tell your healthcare provider about all the medicines you take, including prescription and over-the-counter medicines, vitamins, or herbal supplements.

The most common side effects of Xolair in people with asthma:

Pain especially in your arms and legs, dizziness, feeling tired, skin rash, bone fractures, and pain or discomfort of your ears.

- Inhaled long-acting beta$_2$-agonists. These medicines open the airways. They might be added to inhaled corticosteroids to improve asthma control. Inhaled long-acting beta$_2$-agonists should never be used on their own for long-term asthma control. They must used with inhaled corticosteroids.

- Leukotriene modifiers. These medicines are taken by mouth. They help block the chain reaction that increases inflammation in your airways.

- Theophylline. This medicine is taken by mouth. Theophylline helps open the airways.

If your doctor prescribes a long-term control medicine, take it every day to control your asthma. Your asthma symptoms will likely return or get worse if you stop taking your medicine.

Long-term control medicines can have side effects. Talk with your doctor about these side effects and ways to reduce or avoid them.

With some medicines, like theophylline, your doctor will check the level of medicine in your blood. This helps ensure that you're getting enough medicine to relieve your asthma symptoms, but not so much that it causes dangerous side effects.

Long-Term Asthma Management

Asthma Control

Reduce Impairment

- Prevent chronic symptoms.

- Require infrequent use of short-acting beta$_2$-agonist (SABA).

- Maintain (near) normal lung function and normal activity levels.

Reduce Risk

- Prevent exacerbations.

- Minimize need for emergency care, hospitalization.

- Prevent loss of lung function (or, for children, prevent reduced lung growth).

- Minimize adverse effects of therapy.

Assessment and Monitoring

Initial Visit: Assess asthma severity to initiate treatment.

Follow-Up Visits: Assess asthma control to determine if therapy should be adjusted.

- Assess at each visit: Asthma control, proper medication technique, written asthma action plan, patient adherence, patient concerns.

- Obtain lung function measures by spirometry at least every 1–2 years; more frequently for asthma that is not well controlled.

- Determine if therapy should be adjusted: Maintain treatment; step up, if needed; step down, if possible.

Schedule follow-up care.

- Asthma is highly variable over time. See patients:

  - Every 2–6 weeks while gaining control

  - Every 1–6 months to monitor control

  - Every 3 months if step down in therapy is anticipated

Use of Medications

Select medication and delivery devices that meet patient's needs and circumstances.

- Use stepwise approach to identify appropriate treatment options.

- Inhaled corticosteroids (ICSs) are the most effective long-term control therapy.

- When choosing treatment, consider domain of relevance to the patient (risk, impairment, or both), patient's history of response to the medication, and willingness and ability to use the medication.

Review medications, technique, and adherence at each follow-up visit.

Chapter 14

Asthma Medication Delivery Mechanisms

Chapter Contents

Section 14.1

Types of Inhalers

Text in this section is excerpted from "So You Have Asthma,"
National Heart, Lung, and Blood Institute (NHLBI), March 2013.

Inhalers

Many asthma medicines—both quick-relief and long-term control
medicines—come as sprays and powders in an inhaler. An inhaler is
a hand-held device that delivers the medicine right to the airways in
your lungs where it is needed. There are several kinds of inhalers.

The metered dose inhaler (MDI) is a small canister that delivers
a measured dose of medicine through your mouth to your airways.

A dry powder inhaler delivers a pre-set amount of asthma medicine
in powder form. Different types of inhalers require different ways to
use them. It is important for you to learn how to use your inhaler correctly. Read the instructions that come with it. Also, ask your doctor,
pharmacist, or other health care professional to show you how to use
it. Then try it yourself and ask him or her to make sure you are using
it the right way.

Spacers and Valved Holding Chambers

A spacer or valved holding chamber can make using a MDI a lot
easier. It can also decrease the amount of medicine that lands on your
tongue or in the back of your mouth. This reduces irritation to your
throat and increases the amount of medicine that gets down into your
lungs where it belongs.

There are many kinds of spacers that can be chosen to fit your
needs.

- Some have a mouthpiece.

- Some have a facemask that comes in different sizes to fit infants,
  children, and adults.

- Many spacers fit on the end of an inhaler; for some, the canister
  of medicine fits into the device.

- Some MDIs come with built-in spacers.

Spacers are not needed for dry powder devices.

Spacers also come with instructions on how to use them and keep them clean. It's important to ask your doctor, pharmacist, or other health care professional to show you how to use a spacer with your MDI. Then try it yourself and ask him or her to make sure you're doing it correctly.

Section 14.2

How to Use Your Dry Powder Inhaler?

Text in this section is excerpted from "How to Use Your Dry Powder Inhaler?" National Heart, Lung, and Blood Institute (NHLBI), March 2013.

Dry Powder Inhaler

A dry powder inhaler delivers pre-set doses of medicine in powder form. The medicine gets to your airways when you take a deep, fast breath in from the inhaler. To keep your asthma under control, it is important to take your medicine as prescribed by your doctor or other health care professional and to use the proper technique to deliver the medicine to your lungs. If you don't use your inhaler correctly, you won't get the medicine you need.

Here are general steps for how to use and clean a dry powder inhaler. Be sure to read the instructions that come with your inhaler. Ask your doctor, pharmacist, or other health care professional (such as nurse practitioner, physician assistant, nurse, respiratory therapist, or asthma educator) to show you how to use your inhaler. Review your technique at each follow-up visit.

1. Remove cap and hold inhaler upright (like a rocket). If the inhaler is a Diskus, hold it flat (like a ying saucer).

2. Load a dose of medicine according to manufacturer's instructions (each brand of inhaler is different; you may have to

prime the inhaler the first time you use it). Do not shake the inhaler.

3. Stand up or sit up straight.

4. Take a deep breath in and blow out completely to empty your lungs. Do not blow into the inhaler.

5. Place the mouthpiece of the inhaler in your mouth and close your lips around it to form a tight seal.

6. Take a fast, deep, forceful breath in through your mouth.

7. Hold your breath and count to 10.

8. Take the inhaler out of your mouth. Breathe out slowly, facing away from the inhaler.

9. If you are supposed to take more than 1 inhalation of medicine per dose, wait 1 minute and repeat steps 2 through 8.

10. When you finish, put the cover back on the inhaler or slide the cover closed. Store the inhaler in a cool, dry place (not in the bathroom).

11. If using an inhaled corticosteroid, rinse out your mouth with water and spit it out. Rinsing helps to prevent an infection in the mouth.

How to Clean a Dry Powder Inhaler

• Wipe the mouthpiece at least once a week with a dry cloth.

• Do not use water to clean the dry powder inhaler.

Section 14.3

How to Use Your Metered-Dose Inhaler?

Text in this section is excerpted from "How to Use Your
Metered-Dose Inhaler?" National Heart, Lung, and Blood
Institute (NHLBI), March 2013.

Metered-Dose Inhaler

A metered-dose inhaler is a device that sprays a pre-set amount
of medicine through the mouth to the airways. To keep your asthma
under control, it is important to take your medicine as prescribed by
your doctor or other health care professional and to use the proper
technique to deliver the medicine to your lungs. If you don't use your
inhaler correctly, you won't get the medicine you need.

Here are general steps for how to use and clean a metered-dose
inhaler. Be sure to read the instructions that come with your inhaler.
Ask your doctor, pharmacist, or other health care professional (such as
nurse practitioner, physician assistant, nurse, respiratory therapist,
or asthma educator) to show you how to use your inhaler. Review your
technique at each follow-up visit.

1. Take off cap. Shake the inhaler. Prime (spray or pump) the
    inhaler as needed according to manufacturer's instructions
    (each brand is different).

2. If you use a spacer or valved holding chamber (VHC), remove
    the cap and look into the mouthpiece to make sure nothing
    is in it. Place the inhaler in the rubber ring on the end of the
    spacer/VHC.

3. Stand up or sit up straight.

4. Take a deep breath in. Tilt head back slightly and blow out
    completely to empty your lungs.

5. Place the mouthpiece of the inhaler or spacer/VHC in your
    mouth and close your lips around it to form a tight seal.

6. As you start to breathe in, press down firmly on the top of the medicine canister to release one "puff" of medicine. Breathe in slowly (gently) and as deeply as you can for 3 to 5 seconds.

7. Hold your breath and count to 10.

8. Take the inhaler or spacer/VHC out of your mouth. Breathe out slowly.

9. If you are supposed to take 2 puffs of medicine per dose, wait 1 minute and repeat steps 3 through 8.

10. If using an inhaled corticosteroid, rinse out your mouth with water and spit it out. Rinsing will help to prevent an infection in the mouth.

How to Clean a Metered-Dose Inhaler and Spacer / VHC

Keep your inhaler and spacer/VHC clean so they can work properly. Read the manufacturer's instructions and talk to your doctor, pharmacist, or other health care professional about how to clean your inhaler and spacer/VHC (each brand is different). When cleaning your inhaler and spacer/VHC, remember:

- Never put the medicine canister in water.

- Never brush or wipe inside the spacer/VHC.

Section 14.4

How to Use Your Nebulizer?

Text in this section is excerpted from "How to Use a Metered-Dose Inhaler?" National Heart, Lung, and Blood Institute (NHLBI), March 2013.

Nebulizer

A nebulizer is a machine that delivers medicine in a fine, steady mist. To keep your asthma under control, it is important to take your medicine as prescribed by your doctor or other health care professional and to use the proper technique to deliver the medicine to your lungs. If you don't use your nebulizer correctly, you won't get the medicine you need.

Here are general steps for how to use and clean a nebulizer. Be sure to read the instructions that come with your nebulizer. Ask your doctor, pharmacist, or other health care professional (such as nurse practitioner, physician assistant, nurse, respiratory therapist, or asthma educator) to show you how to use your nebulizer. Review your technique at each follow-up visit.

1. Wash hands well.

2. Put together the nebulizer machine, tubing, medicine cup, and mouthpiece or mask according to manufacturer's instructions.

3. Put the prescribed amount of medicine into the medicine cup. If your medicine comes in a pre-measured capsule or vial, empty it into the cup.

4. Place the mouthpiece in your mouth and close your lips around it to form a tight seal. If your child uses a mask, make sure it fits snugly over your child's nose and mouth. Never hold the mouthpiece or mask away from the face.

5. Turn on the nebulizer machine. You should see a light mist coming from the back of the tube opposite the mouthpiece or from the mask.

6. Take normal breaths through the mouth while the machine is on. Continue treatment until the medicine cup is empty or the mist stops, about 10 minutes.

7. Take the mouthpiece out of your mouth (or remove mask) and turn off the machine.

8. If using an inhaled corticosteroid, rinse mouth with water and spit it out. If using a mask, also wash the face.

How to Clean and Store a Nebulizer

After Each Treatment:

- Wash hands well.

- Wash the medicine cup and mouthpiece or mask with warm water and mild soap. Do not wash the tubing.

- Rinse well and shake off excess water. Air dry parts on a paper towel.

Once a Week:

Disinfect nebulizer parts to help kill any germs. Follow instructions for each nebulizer part listed in the package insert.

Always remember:

- Do not wash or boil the tubing.

- Air dry parts on a paper towel.

Between uses:

- Store nebulizer parts in a dry, clean plastic storage bag. If the nebulizer is used by more than one person, keep each person's medicine cup, mouthpiece or mask, and tubing in a separate, labeled bag to prevent the spread of germs.

- Wipe surface with a clean, damp cloth as needed. Cover nebulizer machine with a clean, dry cloth and store as manufacturer instructs.

- Replace medicine cup, mouthpiece, mask, tubing, filter, and other parts according to manufacturer's instructions or when they appear worn or damaged.

Section 14.5

How to Use Your Peak Flow Meter?

This section includes excerpts from "How to Use a Metered-Dose Inhaler?" National Heart, Lung, and Blood Institute (NHLBI), March 2013; and text from "So You Have Asthma," National Heart, Lung, and Blood Institute (NHLBI), March 2013.

Peak Flow Meter

Peak flow meters are devices used to measure how well air is moving through your lungs.

Here are some general steps for how to use a peak flow meter. Be sure to read the instructions that come with your peak flow meter.

Ask your doctor, pharmacist, or other health care professional (such as nurse practitioner, physician assistant, nurse, respiratory therapist, or asthma educator) to show you how to use your peak flow meter. Review your technique at each follow-up visit. This page also tells you what the numbers on the meter mean and how they can help you and your doctor or other health care professional keep your asthma under control.

1. Always stand up. Remove any food or gum from your mouth.

2. Make sure the marker on the peak flow meter is at the bottom of the scale.

3. Breathe in slowly and deeply. Hold that breath.

4. Place mouthpiece on your tongue and close lips around it to form a tight seal (do not put tongue in the hole).

5. Blow out as hard and fast as possible.

6. Write down the number next to the marker. (If you cough or make a mistake, do not write down that number. Do it over again.)

7. Repeat steps 3 through 6 two more times.

8. Record the highest of these three numbers in a notebook, calendar, or asthma diary.

Compare the highest number with the peak flow numbers on your written asthma action plan. Check to see which zone the number falls under and follow the plan's instructions for that zone.

GREEN ZONE: 80%–100% of personal best. Take daily long-term control medication, if prescribed.

YELLOW ZONE: 50%–79% of personal best. Add quick-relief medication(s) as directed and continue daily long-term control medication, if prescribed. Continue to monitor.

RED ZONE: Less than 50% of personal best. Add quick-relief medication(s) as directed. Get medical help now.

How to Find Your Personal Best Peak Flow Number

Your personal best peak flow number is the highest peak flow number you can achieve over a 2-week period when your asthma is under good control—that is, when you feel good and have no symptoms.

- At least twice a day for 2 to 3 weeks

- When you wake up and in late afternoon or early evening

- 15–20 minutes after you take your quick-relief medicine

- Any other time your doctor suggests

Write down the number you get for each peak flow reading. Your doctor will use these numbers to determine your personal best peak flow. Then your doctor will use that number to create three peak flow zones. These zones are usually set up on your asthma action plan like a traffic light—in green, yellow, and red. What your doctor tells you to do in each zone will help you know what to do when your peak flow number changes.

Section 14.6

Spacers and Valved Holding Chambers

Text in this section is excerpted from "So You Have Asthma,"
National Heart, Lung, and Blood Institute (NHLBI), March 2013.

Spacers

A spacer or valved holding chamber can make using a metered dose inhaler (MDI) a lot easier. It can also decrease the amount of medicine that lands on your tongue or in the back of your mouth. This reduces irritation to your throat and increases the amount of medicine that gets down into your lungs where it belongs.

There are many kinds of spacers that can be chosen to fit your needs.

- Some have a mouthpiece.

- Some have a facemask that comes in different sizes to fit infants, children, and adults.

- Many spacers fit on the end of an inhaler; for some, the canister of medicine fits into the device.

- Some MDIs come with built-in spacers.

Spacers are not needed for dry powder devices.

Spacers also come with instructions on how to use them and keep them clean. It's important to ask your doctor, pharmacist, or other health care professional to show you how to use a spacer with your MDI. Then try it yourself and ask him or her to make sure you're doing it correctly.

Chapter 15

Adverse Effects Related to the Use of Asthma Medications

Chapter Contents

Section 15.1

Don't Let Asthma Medication Side Effects Interfere with Your Asthma Control

A side effect is an unwanted, and sometimes harmful, consequence of taking a medication that occurs in addition to its intended effect. All types of medications involve side effects, including those that are typically prescribed to treat asthma. Some of these side effects are common, occurring in more than 10 percent of patients, while others are extremely rare. Some side effects are local, or limited to the part of the body that comes in direct contact with the medication, and only last for a few minutes. Others are systemic, meaning that they affect the whole body through the absorption of the medication into the bloodstream, and appear gradually with long-term usage.

Most asthma medications are considered safe when used as directed, and they are well tolerated by most people. But it is important for people with asthma to be aware of the potential side effects associated with the medications they take and discuss any problems that they experience with their doctors. Most side effects are relatively minor and can be prevented or limited by adjusting dosages. Since uncontrolled asthma is likely to cause more serious health problems than the side effects of medications, patients should never stop taking a medication without consulting with their doctors.

Side Effects of Common Asthma Medications

Inhaled Corticosteroids

Inhaled corticosteroid preventers have proven effective in controlling asthma, improving lung function, reducing hospitalization rates, and increasing quality of life for many people. The most common side effects are hoarseness (dysphonia) and oral thrush (candidiasis). These localized side effects can often be avoided by using a device equipped with a spacer to deliver the medication, and by rinsing the mouth and spitting after using the medication.

Long-term usage of high doses of inhaled corticosteroids is associated with a few systemic side effects, including cataracts, glaucoma, growth suppression, and decreased bone density (osteoporosis). Oral steroid medications like prednisone, which are sometimes prescribed for asthma, have been associated with these side effects as well. Although the occurrence of these side effects is uncommon, it is important for people who use inhaled corticosteroids to undergo regular health screening for these conditions.

Short-Acting and Long-Acting Beta Agonists

Albuterol inhalers and other short-acting beta agonists (SABA) provide quick relief of acute asthma symptoms for many people. Long-acting beta agonists (LABA) are maintenance treatments that can decrease the frequency of asthma episodes and the severity of symptoms for people whose asthma is not well controlled with inhaled corticosteroids.

Both of these medications have some possible side effects, however, including nausea, vomiting, appetite changes, headache, sore throat, sinus pain, dizziness, nervousness, tremors, hyperactivity, and trouble sleeping. If any of these side effects occur frequently or become bothersome, patients should consult with their doctors.

SABA and LABA medications are also associated with some serious side effects that require immediate medical attention, such as allergic reactions (including skin rash, hives, swelling of the face or mouth, or difficulty breathing), chest pain, irregular heartbeat, earache, severe headache, dizziness, difficulty breathing, and blistered or peeling skin. In addition, the U.S. Food and Drug Administration (FDA) issued a warning that LABA treatment may increase the severity of asthma attacks when they occur, possibly resulting in fatal asthma episodes.

Leukotriene Modifiers

Singulair (montelukast) and other leukotriene modifiers are often prescribed in addition to inhaled corticosteroids to help control asthma. They have also proven effective in treating mild persistent asthma and exercise-induced asthma. Potential side effects associated with these medications include headaches, upset stomach, skin rashes, and abnormalities in liver tests. The FDA has also issued warnings concerning mental health effects that have occurred in some patients, such as anxiety, restlessness, irritability, aggression, insomnia, bad dreams, hallucinations, depression, and suicidal thoughts and behaviors. People who experience any mental health side effects while taking these medications should consult with their doctors.

Cromolyn Sodium and Nedocromil

Intal (cromolyn sodium) and Tilade (nedocromil) are considered alternative treatments for people who experience asthma symptoms related to allergies. Since they work by blocking part of the immune system response, they can be taken prior to exposure to an allergen to prevent asthma symptoms from occurring. These medications are well tolerated by most people, and the side effects tend to decrease over time with continued use. Some of the possible side effects include coughing, sneezing, stuffy nose, itchy or sore throat, headache, and a bad taste in the mouth. Patients who experience wheezing or shortness of breath should seek medical attention.

Immunomodulators

Xolair and other immunomodulators are considered secondary medications to aid in the management of allergy-induced asthma. They are typically given as an injection, so some people experience pain or swelling at the injection site. Some other possible side effects include headache, sore throat, sinus infection, and upper respiratory tract infection.

In addition, a very small percentage of patients experience a severe, potentially life-threatening allergic reaction called anaphylaxis following a Xolair injection. Symptoms of anaphylaxis include swelling of the tongue or throat, faintness or dizziness, and difficulty breathing. Finally, studies have found a slight increase in the risk of cancer among people using Xolair, although it remains unclear whether a causal relationship exists.

Section 15.2

Osteoporosis

Text in this section is excerpted from "Osteoporosis,"
National Institute of Arthritis and Musculoskeletal and
Skin Diseases (NIAMS), April 2015.

What Is Osteoporosis?

Osteoporosis is a condition in which the bones become less dense and more likely to fracture. Fractures from osteoporosis can result in pain and disability. In the United States, more than 53 million people either already have osteoporosis or are at high risk due to low bone mass.

The Connection between Asthma and Osteoporosis

People with asthma tend to be at increased risk for osteoporosis, especially in the spine, for several reasons. First, anti-inflammatory medications, known as glucocorticoids, are commonly prescribed for asthma. When taken by mouth, these medications can decrease calcium absorbed from food, increase calcium lost from the kidneys, and decrease bone formation. Doses of more than 7.5 mg (milligrams) each day can cause significant bone loss, particularly during the first year of use. Corticosteroids also interfere with the production of sex hormones in both women and men, which can contribute to bone loss, and they can cause muscle weakness, which can increase the risk of falling and related fractures.

Many people with asthma think that milk and other dairy products trigger asthma attacks, although the evidence shows that this is only likely to be true if they also have a dairy allergy. This unnecessary avoidance of calcium-rich dairy products can be especially damaging for children with asthma who need calcium to build strong bones.

Because exercise often can trigger an asthma attack, many people with asthma avoid weight bearing physical activities that are known to strengthen bone. Those people who remain physically active often choose swimming as their first exercise of choice because it is less likely than other activities to trigger an asthma attack. Unfortunately, swimming does not have the same beneficial impact on bone health as weight-bearing exercises, which work the body against gravity. Weight-bearing exercises include walking, jogging, racquet sports, basketball, volleyball, aerobics, dancing, and weight training.

Osteoporosis Management Strategies

Strategies to prevent and treat osteoporosis in people with asthma are not significantly different from those used to treat people who do not have asthma.

Nutrition. A well-balanced diet rich in calcium and vitamin D is important for healthy bones. Good sources of calcium include low-fat dairy products; dark green, leafy vegetables; and calcium-fortified foods and beverages. Supplements can help ensure that the calcium requirement is met each day, especially in those with a proven milk allergy. The Institute of Medicine recommends a daily calcium intake of 1,000 mg each day for men and women up to age 50. Women over age 50 and men over age 70 should increase their intake to 1,200 mg daily.

Vitamin D plays an important role in calcium absorption and bone health. Food sources of vitamin D include egg yolks, saltwater fish, and liver. Many people obtain enough vitamin D from eating fortified foods. Other individuals, especially those who are older, live in northern climates, or use sunscreen, may require vitamin D supplements to achieve the recommended intake of 600 to 800 International Units (IU) each day.

Exercise. Like muscle, bone is living tissue that responds to exercise by becoming stronger. The best kind of activity for your bones is weight-bearing exercise that forces you to work against gravity. Some examples include walking, climbing stairs, weight training, and dancing. Regular exercise, such as walking, may help prevent bone loss and provide many other health benefits.

People who experience exercise induced asthma should exercise in an environmentally controlled facility and participate in activities that fall within their limitations. They may also use medication when necessary to enable them to exercise.

Healthy lifestyle. Smoking is bad for bones as well as the heart and lungs. Women who smoke tend to go through menopause earlier, triggering earlier bone loss. In addition, people who smoke may absorb less calcium from their diets. Alcohol also can affect bone health negatively. Those who drink heavily are more prone to bone loss and fracture because of both poor nutrition and an increased risk of falling.

Reducing exposure to asthma triggers, such as irritants and allergens, can help lessen a person's reliance on glucocorticoid medication. Avoiding people with colds and other respiratory infections and minimizing emotional stress can also be important.

Bone density test. A bone mineral density (BMD) test measures bone density at various sites of the body. This safe and painless test can detect osteoporosis before a fracture occurs and can predict one's chances of future fracture. People with asthma, particularly those receiving glucocorticoid therapy for 2 months or more, should talk to their doctors about whether they might be candidates for a BMD test.

Medication. Like asthma, osteoporosis is a disease with no cure. However, there are medications available to prevent and treat osteoporosis, including: bisphosphonates; estrogen agonists/antagonists (also called selective estrogen receptor modulators or SERMS); calcitonin; parathyroid hormone; estrogen therapy; hormone therapy; and a recently approved RANK ligand (RANKL) inhibitor.

Because of their effectiveness in controlling asthma with fewer side effects, inhaled glucocorticoids are preferred to oral forms of the medication. Bone loss tends to increase with increased glucocorticoid doses and prolonged use; therefore, the lowest possible dose for the shortest period of time that controls asthma symptoms is recommended.

Section 15.3

Maternal Asthma Medication Use and Birth Defects

Text in this section is excerpted from "Key Findings: Maternal Asthma Medication Use and the Risk of Selected Birth Defects," Centers for Disease Control and Prevention (CDC), October 22, 2014.

Recently, researchers used data from the National Birth Defects Prevention Study (NBDPS) to examine maternal asthma medication use during pregnancy and the risk of certain birth defects.

Asthma—a disease that affects the lungs:

Asthma is a common disease during pregnancy, affecting about 4%–12% of pregnant women. About 3% of pregnant women use asthma medications, including bronchodilators or anti-inflammatory drugs. Currently, guidelines recommend that women with asthma continue to use medication to control their condition during pregnancy. However, the safety data on using asthma medications during pregnancy are limited.

Main findings from this study:

- Data from the study showed that using asthma medication during pregnancy

  - Did not increase the risk for most of the birth defects studied.

  - Might increase the risk for some birth defects, such as esophageal atresia (birth defect of the esophagus or food tube), anorectal atresia (birth defect of the anus), and omphalocele (birth defect of the abdominal wall).

- The most commonly reported asthma medications used during pregnancy were

  - Albuterol (2%–3% of women)

  - Fluticasone (About 1% of women)

196

- It was difficult to determine if asthma or other health problems related to having asthma increased the risk for these birth defects, or if the increased risk was from the medication use during pregnancy.

> Pregnant women should not stop or start taking any type of medication that they need without first talking with a doctor. Women who are planning to become pregnant should discuss the need for any medication with their doctor before becoming pregnant and ensure they are taking only medications that are necessary.

Chapter 16

Immunotherapy and Asthma

Background

The medical management of patients with allergic rhinitis and allergic asthma includes allergen avoidance, pharmacotherapy, and immunotherapy. Daily use of pharmacotherapies for allergic rhinitis symptoms raises issues related to adherence, safety, and cost. Long-term use of inhaled steroids, long-acting brainchild's, and leukotriene antagonists for asthma control have risks for moderate to severe adverse effects.

Allergen immunotherapy is typically used for patients whose allergic rhinoconjunctivitis and allergic asthma symptoms cannot be controlled by medication and environmental control, patients who cannot tolerate their medications, or patients who do not comply with chronic medication regimens. The U.S. Food and Drug Administration (FDA) has approved the use of allergen extracts for Subcutaneous immunotherapy (SCIT) for treating allergic rhinitis and allergic asthma.

In the United States, a patient with allergies undergoing immunotherapy receives subcutaneous injections—in increasing doses—of an allergen-containing extract comprised of the relevant allergens to which he or she is sensitive in an attempt to suppress or eliminate allergy-related symptoms.

This chapter includes excerpts from "Brain Basics: Know Your Brain," National Institute of Neurological Disorders and Stroke (NINDS), April 28, 2014; and text from "Alzheimer's Disease: Unraveling the Mystery," National Institutes on Aging (NIA), January 22, 2015.

Subcutaneous Immunotherapy Involves a series of shots containing small amounts of allergen into the fat under the skin.

SCIT includes two phases: a buildup phase and a maintenance phase. During the buildup phase, doctors administer injections containing gradually increasing amounts of allergen once or twice per week. This phase generally lasts from three to six months, depending on how often the shots are given and the body's response. The aim is to reach a target dose that has been shown to be effective. Once the target dose is reached, the maintenance phase begins. Shots are given less frequently during the maintenance phase, typically every two to four weeks.

Some people begin experiencing a decrease in symptoms during the buildup phase, but others may not notice an improvement until the maintenance phase. Maintenance therapy generally lasts three to five years. The decision about how long to continue SCIT is based on how well it is working and how well a person tolerates the shots. For example, if after one year of maintenance therapy there is no evidence of improvement, it is hard to justify continuing immunotherapy for another two to four years. On the other hand, if a person is entirely symptom-free, he or she may choose to stop after three years rather than complete five years of treatment.

Many people continue to experience benefits for several years after the shots are stopped, and the theoretical potential of "curing" allergy makes the concept of immunotherapy very attractive.

Side effects from SCIT are usually minor and may include swelling or redness at the injection site. However, there is a small risk of serious allergic reactions such as anaphylaxis. Because most severe reactions occur shortly after injection, it is recommended that patients remain under medical supervision for at least half an hour after receiving a shot. Patients whose asthma is not under control are recommended to postpone their shot until their asthma is stable.

An estimated 5 percent of people with environmental allergies receive SCIT for allergic rhinitis and asthma, and less than 20 percent of people who begin SCIT finish the entire treatment course. The time and cost commitments that SCIT requires likely discourage some people from starting or completing treatment. Development of new forms of immunotherapy that require shorter treatment duration may result in more patients being interested in receiving allergen immunotherapy.

NIAID funds research to investigate several approaches to improve the effectiveness and safety of SCIT and decrease the duration of treatment. Scientists are exploring the use of modified allergens that may elicit the same or better effects with fewer shots, while decreasing the risk of side effects. Scientists also are developing treatment approaches that combine SCIT with other medications. For example, researchers from the NIAID-sponsored Immune Tolerance Network are testing a combination of SCIT and an investigational allergy drug as a potential treatment for cat allergy.

Adverse Effects of SCIT

Adults

- Local reactions (such as redness, swelling, pruritus, or induration at injection site) were usually mild and occurred in 5 to 58 percent of patients and in 0.6 to 54 percent of injections and were more common than systemic reactions.

- The most common systemic reactions were respiratory reactions, occurring in up to 46 percent of patients and in up to 3 percent of injections.

- General symptoms (such as headache, fatigue, and arthritis) occurred in up to 44 percent of patients and were usually mild or unspecified.

- Gastrointestinal reactions were reported in only one study.

- Thirteen anaphylactic reactions were reported in four trials (n = 205 immunotherapy patients). No deaths were reported.

Pediatric Patients

- Local reactions were the most common adverse reactions in the pediatric population receiving SCIT.

- There were no reports of anaphylaxis or deaths.

Chapter 17

Alternative and Complementary Asthma Therapies

Chapter Contents

Section 17.1

Alternative and Complementary Therapies for Treating Asthma

Text in this section is excerpted from "Asthma and Complementary
Health Approaches," National Center for Complementary and
Integrative Health (NCCIH), October 20, 2015.

Complementary Health Approaches for Asthma

Most people are able to control their asthma with conventional therapies and by avoiding the substances that can set off asthma attacks.
Even so, some people turn to complementary health approaches in their
efforts to relieve symptoms. According to the 2002 National Health
Interview Survey (NHIS), which included a comprehensive survey on
the use of complementary health approaches by Americans, asthma
ranked 13th as a condition prompting use of complementary health
approaches by adults; 1.1 percent of respondents (an estimated 788,000
adults) said they had used a complementary approach for asthma in
the past year. In the 2007 NHIS survey, which included adults and
children, asthma ranked eighth among conditions prompting use of
complementary health approaches by children, but did not appear in
a similar ranking for adults.

What the Science Says about Complementary Health Approaches and Asthma

According to reviewers who have assessed the research, there is
not enough evidence to support the use of any complementary health
approaches for the relief of asthma.

- Several studies have looked at actual or true **acupuncture**—
  stimulation of specific points on the body with thin metal needles—for asthma. Although a few studies showed some reduction in medication use and improvements in symptoms and
  quality of life, the majority showed no difference between actual
  acupuncture and simulated or sham acupuncture on asthma

symptoms. At this point, there is little evidence that acupuncture is an effective treatment for asthma.

- There has been renewed patient interest in **breathing exercises** or **retraining** to reduce hyperventilation, regulate breathing, and achieve a better balance of carbon dioxide and oxygen in the blood. A review of seven randomized controlled trials found a trend toward improvement in symptoms with breathing techniques but not enough evidence for firm conclusions.

- A 2011 study examined the **placebo** response in patients with chronic asthma and found that patients receiving a placebo (placebo inhaler and simulated acupuncture) reported significant improvement in symptoms such as chest tightness and perception of difficulty breathing. However, lung function did not improve in these patients. This is an important distinction because although the patients felt better, their risk for becoming very sick from untreated asthma was not lessened.

If You Are Considering Complementary Health Approaches for Asthma

- Conventional medical treatments are very effective for managing asthma symptoms. See your health care provider to discuss a comprehensive medical treatment plan for your asthma.

- Do not use any complementary approaches to postpone seeing your health care provider about asthma-like symptoms or any health problem.

- Do not replace conventional treatments for asthma with unproven products or practices.

- Keep in mind that dietary supplements can act in the same way as drugs. They can cause health problems if not used correctly or if used in large amounts, and some may interact with medications you take. Your health care provider can advise you. If you are pregnant or nursing a child, or if you are considering giving a child a dietary supplement, it is especially important to consult your (or your child's) health care provider.

- Tell all your health care providers about any complementary health approaches you use. Give them a full picture of what you do to manage your health. This will help ensure coordinated and safe care.

Section 17.2

Magnesium Supplements for the Treatment of Asthma

Text in this section is excerpted from "Magnesium Supplements May
Benefit People With Asthma," National Center for Complementary
and Integrative Health (NCCIH), January 30, 2015.

Magnesium Supplements May Benefit People With Asthma

Some previous studies have reported associations between low magnesium consumption and the development of asthma. Now, recent
research supported by National Center for Complementary and Alternative Medicine (NCCAM) and published in the Journal of Asthma
provides additional evidence that adults with mild-to-moderate asthma
may benefit from taking magnesium supplements.

Researchers from Bastyr University in Kenmore, Washington, and
the University of California, Davis, enrolled 52 men and women aged
21 to 55 with mild-to-moderate asthma. The participants consumed
either 340 mg of magnesium citrate or placebo daily for 6.5 months.
The researchers examined clinical asthma symptoms and control using
tests to measure lung responsiveness and pulmonary function, inflammation markers, and magnesium levels at the beginning of the study
and every month thereafter.

The researchers found that those who took magnesium experienced
significant improvement in lung activity and the ability to move air in
and out of their lungs. Those taking magnesium also reported other
improvements in asthma control and quality of life compared with
people who received placebo. There were no significant changes for
objective measures of forced expiratory volume in 1 second (the volume
of air that can be exhaled in 1 second after taking a deep breath) or
inflammation and magnesium levels in either group.

During the study, the researchers indicated that members of both
groups had similar levels of magnesium in serum or within red blood
cells. Participants in both groups also had similar levels of C-reactive

protein (a marker of inflammation) throughout the study. Airway inflammation is an important component of asthma.

The researchers noted that this study adds to the body of research that shows subjective and objective benefits of magnesium supplements in people with mild-to-moderate asthma.

Section 17.3

Tiotropium Bromide Effective When Added to Low-Dose Inhaled Corticosteroids

Text in this section is excerpted from "Possible Alternate Therapy for Adults with Poorly Controlled Asthma," National Institutes of Health (NIH), September 19, 2010. Reviewed January 2016.

A drug commonly used for the treatment of chronic obstructive pulmonary disease (COPD) successfully treats adults whose asthma is not well-controlled on low doses of inhaled corticosteroids, according to researchers at National Heart, Lung, and Blood Institute (NHLBI), part of the National Institutes of Health.

"This study's results show that tiotropium bromide might provide an alternative to other asthma treatments, expanding options available to patients for controlling their asthma," said NHLBI Acting Director Susan B. Shurin, M.D. "The goal in managing asthma is to prevent symptoms so patients can pursue activities to the fullest."

According to the study, adding tiotropium bromide to low doses of inhaled corticosteroids is more effective at controlling asthma than doubling inhaled corticosteroids alone, and as effective as adding the long-acting beta agonist salmeterol. The results were published online in the New England Journal of Medicine and presented at the Annual Congress of the European Respiratory Society in Barcelona, Spain.

Increasing inhaled corticosteroids or supplementing them with long-acting beta agonists like salmeterol are the two preferred treatment options available for adults whose asthma is poorly controlled on low doses of inhaled corticosteroids. However, higher doses of corticosteroids do not improve symptoms for all patients and can have significant side effects, while long-acting beta agonists have come under scrutiny for their risk of worsening asthma symptoms that could result in hospitalization and, rarely, death.

"Tiotropium relaxes smooth muscle in the airways through a different mechanism than long-acting beta agonists, and thus may help people who do not respond well to currently recommended treatments," said study lead Stephen Peters, M.D., Ph.D., of Wake Forest University Baptist Medical Center, Winston-Salem, N.C. "Further analysis of the study data will help us better to understand which patients respond best to tiotropium. Then we will need to conduct longer-term studies to establish its safety for asthma patients and to determine its effect on the frequency and severity of asthma exacerbations."

Conducted by the NHLBI's Asthma Clinical Research Network, the study compared three treatment methods: doubling the dose of inhaled corticosteroids alone, supplementing a low dose of inhaled corticosteroids with a long-acting beta agonist (salmeterol), and supplementing a low dose of inhaled corticosteroids with a long-acting anticholinergic drug (tiotropium bromide). Anticholinergics block a part of the autonomic nervous system that can cause airway muscles to contract. The study followed 210 adults whose asthma was not well-controlled on low doses of inhaled corticosteroids alone. Participants received each treatment for 14 weeks with two-week breaks in between, for a total of 48 weeks.

Tiotropium bromide was shown to be effective using several asthma control measurements, including patients' day-to-day lung function as well as the number of days in which they had no asthma symptoms and did not need to use their albuterol rescue inhalers. When patients began the trial, their average number of such "asthma control days" was 77 per year (extrapolated from the treatment period). Doubling corticosteroids gave patients another 19 symptom-free days on average, while adding tiotropium to low-dose corticosteroids gave them another 48.

"Much research over the last century has explored the role of cholinergic mechanisms [which constrict the airways] and anticholinergic therapies in asthma. However, this is the first study to explore adding an anticholinergic inhaler to low-dose inhaled corticosteroids," said

James Kiley, Ph.D., director of the NHLBI's Division of Lung Diseases. "The Asthma Clinical Research Network is designed to address exactly these kinds of practical and important management questions, with the ultimate goal of helping asthma patients."

The NHLBI established the Asthma Clinical Research Network in 1993 to conduct multiple, well-designed clinical trials for rapid evaluation of new and existing therapeutic approaches to asthma and to disseminate laboratory and clinical findings to the healthcare community.

Section 17.4

Traditional Chinese Herbs May Benefit People with Asthma

Text in this section is excerpted from "Traditional Chinese
Herbs May Benefit People With Asthma," National Center for
Complementary and Integrative Health (NCCIH), January 30, 2015.

Asthma affects millions of adults and children in the United States. Its increasing prevalence, the absence of curative treatments, and concerns about side effects from long-term use of asthma drugs have prompted interest in complementary and alternative therapies such as traditional Chinese medicine (TCM) herbs.

In a recent article, NCCAM-supported scientists from the Mount Sinai School of Medicine reviewed research evidence on TCM herbs for asthma, focusing on studies reported since 2005:

- Preliminary clinical trials of formulas containing *Radix glycyr-rhizae* in combination with various other TCM herbs have had positive results. One study compared an herbal formula called ASHMI (antiasthma herbal medicine intervention) with the drug prednisone in adults; three others looked at herbal formulas as complementary therapies in children. All of the trials reported improvement in lung function with the herbal formulas and found them to be safe and well tolerated. Most of the trials showed significant improvements in asthma symptom scores, although one did not.

- A three-year followup of 14 patients with asthma taking an extract of *Sophora flavescens* Ait (a component of ASHMI) reported positive clinical results and no side effects.

- Laboratory findings on TCM herbal remedies suggest several possible mechanisms of action against asthma, including an anti-inflammatory effect, inhibition of smooth-muscle contraction in the airway, and modulation of immune system responses.

Chapter 18

New Developments in Asthma Treatment

Chapter Contents

Section 18.1

Bronchial Thermoplasty System

Text in this section is excerpted from "Alair Bronchial
Thermoplasty System," U.S. Food and Drug Administration (FDA),
September 6, 2013.

What is Bronchial Thermoplasty System?

The Bronchial Thermoplasty System is composed of a catheter with
an electrode that delivers radiofrequency energy (a form of electromagnetic energy) directly to the airways of the lungs. A controller unit
generates and controls the energy.

How does it work?

The Bronchial Thermoplasty System treats severe persistent
asthma by delivering thermal radiofrequency energy to the airway
wall to heat the tissue in a controlled manner in order to reduce airway smooth muscle mass (muscle thickness). Patients are treated in
multiple sessions, each targeting a different area of the lungs.

When is it used?

The Bronchial Thermoplasty System is indicated for the treatment
of severe persistent asthma in patients 18 years and older whose
asthma is not well-controlled with inhaled corticosteroids and long-acting beta-agonist medicines.

What will it accomplish?

The Bronchial Thermoplasty System reduces the number of severe
asthma attacks that require systemic corticosteroid medicines in
patients with severe, persistent asthma. Possible side-effects over
the course of the treatments include asthma attacks, wheezing, chest
discomfort, chest pain, partial collapse of the lungs (atelectasis), lower
airway bleeding (hemoptysis), anxiety, headaches, and nausea.

When should it not be used?

Patients with the following conditions should not be treated:

- Presence of a pacemaker, defibrillator, or other implantable electronic devices.

- Known sensitivity to medicines required to perform an internal examination of the airways (bronchoscopy), including lidocaine, atropine, and benzodiazepines.

- Patients previously treated with the Alair System should not be retreated in the same area(s). No clinical data are available studying the safety and/or effectiveness of repeat treatments.

Patients should not be treated while the following conditions are present:

- Active respiratory infection.

- Severe asthma attacks or changing dose of systemic corticosteroids for asthma (up or down) in the past 14 days.

- Known problems with blood coagulation (coagulopathy).

- As with other bronchoscopic procedures, patients should stop taking anticoagulants, antiplatelet agents, aspirin and non-steroidal anti-inflammatory drugs (NSAIDS) before the procedure with physician guidance.

Section 18.2

Exposure to Certain Bacteria May Protect Toddlers from Wheezing

Text in this section is excerpted from "Early Exposure to Certain Bacteria May Protect Toddlers from Wheezing," National Institute of Allergy and Infectious Diseases (NIAID), June 6, 2014.

Research funded by the National Institutes of Health (NIH) suggests that exposure to specific combinations of allergens and bacteria within the first year of life may protect children from wheezing and allergic disease. These observations come from the Urban Environment and Childhood Asthma (URECA) study, which aims to identify factors responsible for asthma development in children from inner-city settings, where the disease is more prevalent and severe. Since 2005, the URECA study has enrolled 560 children from four cities—Baltimore, Boston, New York and St. Louis. The children all have at least one parent with asthma or allergies, placing them at high risk for developing asthma. The study is following the children from birth, and the current publication evaluates the group through three years of age.

During early life, recurrent wheezing and sensitivity to common allergens are risk factors for developing asthma. In the current study, the researchers measured the frequency of wheezing episodes and levels of exposure to five common inner-city allergens—cat, cockroach, dog, dust mite and mouse. Surprisingly, they found that exposure to cockroach, mouse and cat during the first year of life was associated with a lower risk of recurrent wheezing by age three.

A smaller study within the URECA cohort tested whether bacteria, measured in house dust, influence asthma risk. Researchers sorted 104 children into four groups: no wheezing or sensitivity to allergens, wheezing only, sensitivity to allergens only, or both wheezing and sensitivity to allergens. They found that children with no wheezing or sensitivity to allergens at age three were more likely to have encountered high levels of allergens and a greater variety of bacteria, particularly those belonging to the *Bacteriodes* and *Firmicutes* groups, during their first year of life. These observations support the emerging concept that

214

early-life exposure to high bacterial diversity may protect kids from developing allergies. Most importantly, the findings show that this protection is even stronger when children also encounter high allergen levels during this time.

Section 18.3

Nucala to Treat Asthma

Text in this section is excerpted from "FDA Approves Nucala to Treat Severe Asthma," U.S. Food and Drug Administration (FDA), November 4, 2015.

The U.S. Food and Drug Administration (FDA) approved Nucala (mepolizumab) for use with other asthma medicines for the maintenance treatment of asthma in patients age 12 years and older. Nucala is approved for patients who have a history of severe asthma attacks (exacerbations) despite receiving their current asthma medicines.

Asthma is a chronic disease that causes inflammation in the airways of the lungs. During an asthma attack, airways become narrow making it hard to breathe. Severe asthma attacks can lead to asthma-related hospitalizations because these attacks can be serious and even life-threatening. According to the Centers for Disease Control and Prevention, as of 2013, more than 22 million people in the U.S. have asthma, and there are more than 400,000 asthma-related hospitalizations each year.

"This approval offers patients with severe asthma an additional therapy when current treatments cannot maintain adequate control of their asthma," said Badrul Chowdhury, M.D., Ph.D., director of the Division of Pulmonary, Allergy, and Rheumatology Products in the FDA's Center for Drug Evaluation and Research.

Nucala is administered once every four weeks by subcutaneous injection by a health care professional into the upper arm, thigh, or abdomen. Nucala is a humanized interleukin-5 antagonist monoclonal antibody produced by recombinant DNA technology in Chinese hamster ovary cells. Nucala reduces severe asthma attacks by reducing the levels of blood eosinophils—a type of white blood cell that contributes to the development of asthma.

The safety and efficacy of Nucala were established in three double-blind, randomized, placebo-controlled trials in patients with severe asthma on currently available therapies. Nucala or a placebo was administered to patients every four weeks as an add-on asthma treatment. Compared with placebo, patients with severe asthma receiving Nucala had fewer exacerbations requiring hospitalization and/or emergency department visits, and a longer time to the first exacerbation. In addition, patients with severe asthma receiving Nucala experienced greater reductions in their daily maintenance oral corticosteroid dose, while maintaining asthma control compared with patients receiving placebo. Treatment with mepolizumab did not result in a significant improvement in lung function, as measured by the volume of air exhaled by patients in one second.

The most common side effects of Nucala include headache, injection site reactions (pain, redness, swelling, itching, or a burning feeling at the injection site), back pain, and weakness (fatigue). Hypersensitivity reactions can occur within hours or days of being treated with Nucala, including swelling of the face, mouth, and tongue; fainting, dizziness, or lightheadedness; hives; breathing problems and rash. Herpes zoster infections have occurred in patients receiving Nucala. Herpes zoster is the virus that causes shingles.

Nucala is made by GlaxoSmithKline, in Research Triangle Park, North Carolina.

The FDA, an agency within the U.S. Department of Health and Human Services, protects the public health by assuring the safety, effectiveness, and security of human and veterinary drugs, vaccines and other biological products for human use, and medical devices. The agency also is responsible for the safety and security of our nation's food supply, cosmetics, dietary supplements, products that give off electronic radiation, and for regulating tobacco products.

Section 18.4

Scientists Identify Receptor for Asthma-Associated Virus

Text in this section is excerpted from "NIH-Funded Scientists Identify Receptor for Asthma-Associated Virus," National Institute of Allergy and Infectious Diseases (NIAID), April 06, 2015

Scientists Identify Receptor for Asthma-Associated Virus

Scientists funded by the National Institute of Allergy and Infectious Diseases (NIAID), have identified a cellular receptor for rhinovirus C, a cold-causing virus that is strongly associated with severe asthma attacks. A variant in the gene for this receptor previously had been linked to asthma in genetic studies, but the potential role of the receptor, called CDHR3, in asthma was unknown. The new findings help clarify the function of CDHR3 and point to a novel target for the development of prevention and treatment strategies against rhinovirus C-induced colds and asthma attacks.

Researchers at the University of Wisconsin-Madison, discovered that CDHR3 recognizes and binds rhinovirus C, enabling the virus to enter human cells. Like all viruses, rhinovirus C uses the molecular machinery of host cells to replicate and become infectious. While the cellular receptors for other rhinovirus types are known, the rhinovirus C receptor had remained elusive. The scientists identified CDHR3 as a potential candidate by analyzing cells that either were or were not susceptible to rhinovirus C infection. When engineered to produce CDHR3, cells that normally were not susceptible to rhinovirus C could bind the virus and support its replication.

Notably, cells bearing a specific CDHR3 gene variant showed greatly enhanced rhinovirus C binding and produced more progeny virus than cells with normal CDHR3. In previous genetic studies, this variant had been linked to a greater risk of wheezing illnesses and asthma hospitalizations during childhood. The new findings suggest that this gene variant could be a risk factor for childhood wheezing illnesses caused by rhinovirus C, which in turn may increase the risk of developing asthma. In the future, development of drugs that block CDHR3 potentially could help prevent and treat illnesses caused by rhinovirus C.

Chapter 19

Clinical Trials and Asthma

Chapter Contents

Section 19.1

What Are Clinical Trials?

Text in this section is excerpted from "Clinical Trials," National
Heart, Lung, and Blood Institute (NHLBI), July 15, 2015.

What Are Clinical Trials?

Clinical trials are research studies that explore whether a medical
strategy, treatment, or device is safe and effective for humans. These
studies also may show which medical approaches work best for certain illnesses or groups of people. Clinical trials produce the best data
available for health care decisionmaking.

The purpose of clinical trials is research, so the studies follow strict
scientific standards. These standards protect patients and help produce reliable study results.

Clinical trials are one of the final stages of a long and careful
research process. The process often begins in a laboratory (lab), where
scientists first develop and test new ideas.

If an approach seems promising, the next step may involve animal testing. This shows how the approach affects a living body and
whether it's harmful. However, an approach that works well in the
lab or animals doesn't always work well in people. Thus, research in
humans is needed.

For safety purposes, clinical trials start with small groups of
patients to find out whether a new approach causes any harm. In
later phases of clinical trials, researchers learn more about the new
approach's risks and benefits.

A clinical trial may find that a new strategy, treatment, or
device

- improves patient outcomes

- offers no benefit or

- causes unexpected harm

All of these results are important because they advance medical
knowledge and help improve patient care.

Why Are Clinical Trials Important?

Clinical trials are a key research tool for advancing medical knowledge and patient care. Clinical research is done only if doctors don't know

- whether a new approach works well in people and is safe and

- which treatments or strategies work best for certain illnesses or groups of people.

Some clinical trials show a positive result. The results from other clinical trials show what doesn't work or may cause harm.

Clinical trials, help improve and advance medical care. They also can help health care decisionmakers direct resources to the strategies and treatments that work best.

How Do Clinical Trials Work?

If you take part in a clinical trial, you may get tests or treatments in a hospital, clinic, or doctor's office. In some ways, taking part in a clinical trial is different from having regular care from your own doctor. For example, you may have more tests and medical exams than you would otherwise. The purpose of clinical trials is research, so the studies follow strict scientific standards. These standards protect patients and help produce reliable study results.

Clinical Trial Protocol

Each clinical trial has a master plan called a protocol. This plan explains how the trial will work. The trial is led by a principal investigator (PI), who often is a doctor. The PI prepares the protocol for the clinical trial.

The protocol outlines what will be done during the clinical trial and why. Each medical center that does the study uses the same protocol.

Key information in a protocol includes

- how many patients will take part in the clinical trial;

- who is eligible to take part in the clinical trial;

- what tests patients will get and how often they will get them;

- what type of data will be collected during the clinical trial; and

- detailed information about the treatment plan.

Eligibility Criteria

A clinical trial's protocol describes what types of patients are able to take part in the research—that is, who is eligible. Each trial must include only people who fit the patient traits for that study (the eligibility criteria).

Eligibility criteria differ from trial to trial. They include factors such as a patient's age and gender, the type and stage of disease, and whether the patient has had certain treatments or has other health problems.

Eligibility criteria ensure that new approaches are tested on similar groups of people. This makes it clear to whom a clinical trial's results apply. These criteria also are a safety measure. They ensure a trial excludes any people for whom the protocol has known risks that outweigh any possible benefits.

Clinical Trial Phases

Clinical trials of new medicines or medical devices are done in phases. These phases have different purposes and help researchers answer different questions.

For example, phase I clinical trials test new treatments in small groups of people for safety and side effects.

Phase II clinical trials look at how well treatments work and further review these treatments for safety.

Phase III clinical trials use larger groups of people to confirm how well treatments work, further examine side effects, and compare new treatments with other available treatments.

Who Can Participate in Clinical Trials?

Each clinical trial defines who is eligible to take part in the study. Each trial must include only people who fit the patient traits for that study (the eligibility criteria).

Some trials enroll people who have a specific disease or condition. Others enroll healthy people to test new approaches to prevention, diagnosis, or screening.

In the past, clinical trial participants often were White men. Researchers assumed that trial results were valid for other populations as well.

Researchers now realize that women and people in different ethnic groups sometimes respond differently than White men to the same medical approach. As a result, the National Institutes of Health and the National Heart, Lung, and Blood Institute (NHLBI) are committed to sponsoring clinical trials that include women and that are ethnically diverse.

Children also need clinical trials that focus on them, as medical treatments and approaches often differ for children. For example, children may need lower doses of certain medicines or smaller medical devices. Their stage of development also can affect how safe a treatment is or how well it works.

Children (aged 18 and younger) get special protection as research subjects. Almost always, parents must give legal consent for their child to take part in a clinical trial.

When researchers think that a trial's potential risks are greater than minimal, both parents must give permission for their child to enroll. Also, children aged 7 and older often must agree (assent) to take part in clinical trials. Clinical trials for children have the same scientific safeguards as clinical trials for adults. For more information about clinical trials for children, go to www.nhlbi.nih.gov/studies/children-and-clinical-studies.

What to Expect during a Clinical Trial

During a clinical trial, doctors, nurses, social workers, and other health care providers might be part of your treatment team. They will monitor your health closely. You may have more tests and medical exams than you would if you were not taking part in a clinical trial.

Your treatment team also may ask you to do other tasks. For example, you may have to keep a log about your health or fill out forms about how you feel.

Some people will need to travel or stay in hospitals to take part in clinical trials. Many clinical trials take place in medical centers and doctors' offices around the country.

What Are the Possible Benefits and Risks of Clinical Trials?

Possible Benefits

Taking part in a clinical trial can have many benefits. For example, you may gain access to new treatments before they're widely available. If a new treatment is proven to work and you're in the group getting it, you might be among the first to benefit.

223

If you're in a clinical trial and don't get the new strategy being tested, you may receive the current standard care for your condition. This treatment might be as good as, or better than, the new approach. You also will have the support of a team of health care providers, who will likely monitor your health closely.

In late-phase clinical trials, possible benefits or risks of a treatment can be identified earlier than they would be in general medical practice. This is because late-phase trials have large groups of similar patients taking the same treatment the same way. These patients are closely watched by Data and Safety Monitoring Boards.

Even if you don't directly benefit from the results of the clinical trial you take part in, the information gathered can help others and add to scientific knowledge. People who take part in clinical trials are vital to the process of improving medical care. Many people volunteer because they want to help others.

Possible Risks

Clinical trials do have risks and some downsides, such as the following.

The new strategies and treatments being studied aren't always better than current standard care.

Even if a new approach benefits some participants, it may not work for you.

A new treatment may have side effects or risks that doctors don't know about or expect. This is especially true during phase I and phase II clinical trials. The risk of side effects might be even greater for trials with cutting-edge approaches, such as gene therapy or new biological treatments.

Health insurance and health care providers don't always cover all patient care costs for clinical trials. If you're thinking about taking part in a clinical trial, find out ahead of time about costs and coverage.

You should learn about the risks and benefits of any clinical trial before you agree to take part in the trial. Talk with your doctor about specific trials you're interested in.Talk with your doctor about specific trials you're interested in. For a list of questions to ask your doctor and the research staff, go to www.nhlbi.nih.gov/studies/clinicaltrials/protect.

Section 19.2

Asthma Research Studies

Text in this section is excerpted from "Asthma Research Studies,"
National Heart, Lung, and Blood Institute (NHLBI), July 15, 2015.

Severe Asthma Pioglitazone Clinical Trial

The purpose of this study is to determine if a widely used agent for
diabetes can improve asthma.

Background

Individuals who have severe asthma that is not easily controlled by
current treatments are in need of new treatments to prevent potentially
life-threatening asthma attacks. Experiments in mice have found that
a medication called pioglitazone hydrochloride (Actos), which is used to
treat patients with diabetes, may be effective for treating severe asthma.
Researchers are interested in determining whether Actos is effective in
improving the quality of life in subjects with severe asthma who continue to have symptoms despite maximum standard medical therapy.

Objectives

To assess the effectiveness of pioglitazone hydrochloride as a treatment for patients with severe asthma that is not controlled by standard
treatments.

Eligibility

Individuals between 18 and 75 years of age who have been diagnosed with and treated for severe asthma for at least 1 year.

Design

- Potential participants will have a screening visit to determine
  eligibility for the study. The visit will involve breathing tests,
  chest X-rays, heart and lung monitoring, and blood tests.

- Eligible participants will have a full medical history and will answer a series of questionnaires about their quality of life with asthma.

- Phase 1: Patients will record lung function and asthma symptoms morning and evening for 4 weeks. At the end of this period, patients will be evaluated with breathing, allergy, and blood tests, as well as questionnaires. Patients will also provide a sputum sample.

- Phase 2: Patients will receive regular doses of either pioglitazone hydrochloride or a placebo for 16 weeks. Patients will return to the National Institutes of Health every 4 weeks for tests.

- Phase 3: Wash-out period without study drugs for 4 weeks, similar to Phase 1.

- Phase 4: Patients will receive regular doses of either pioglitazone hydrochloride or a placebo for 16 weeks. Patients who received placebo will be given the study drug, and vice versa. Patients will return to the National Institutes of Health every 4 weeks for tests.

- Phase 5: Medications will be stopped, and patients will return to the National Institutes of Health 4 weeks later for final tests.

Longitudinal Observational Study of Severe Asthma

The purpose of this study is to learn more about the factors that cause severe asthma.

Background

Asthma is a lung condition that causes difficulty breathing and decreased lung function. Some people with asthma have more severe disease symptoms. They may be less responsive to standard treatments such as steroids. Researchers want to compare severe asthmatics with mild or moderate asthmatics or people without asthma over a long period. This information may help identify new treatments for people whose asthma is not well controlled by standard medications.

Objectives

To compare severe asthmatics with mild or moderate asthmatics, and healthy volunteers, to study the progression and outcomes of the disease.

Eligibility

Individuals at least 18 years of age who have been diagnosed with asthma for at least 1 year.

Healthy volunteers at least 18 years of age.

Design

This study will involve an initial visit to the NIH Clinical Center for all participants. Selected participants may be asked to return for repeat visits over a number of years. The test results from participants with asthma will be compared with those from the healthy volunteers.

- All participants will be screened with a physical exam and medical history.

- Participants may (but will not necessarily) have the following tests at each visit:

  - Complete medical history and physical exam

  - Blood, urine, sputum, and nasal cell samples

  - Breath tests and heart and lung function tests

  - Six-minute walk test to measure ability to exercise

  - Imaging studies such as chest X-rays, bone density scans, and sinus scans

  - Allergy skin testing

  - Vocal cord exam

  - Overnight sleep study

- Participants may remain on the study for as long as they are willing to participate and do not develop health problems that will interfere with the study.

Genetics of Asthma Research Study

The purpose of this research is to identify genes that may be involved in the development or severity of asthma.

Background

Asthma is a lung condition that causes difficulty breathing and decreased lung function. Some people with asthma have more severe disease symptoms. They may be less responsive to standard treatments such as steroids. Researchers want to compare severe asthmatics with mild or moderate asthmatics or people without asthma over a long period. This information may help identify new treatments for people whose asthma is not well controlled by standard medications.

Objectives

To compare severe asthmatics with mild or moderate asthmatics, and healthy volunteers, to study the progression and outcomes of the disease.

Eligibility

- Individuals at least 18 years of age who have been diagnosed with asthma for at least 1 year.
- Healthy volunteers at least 18 years of age.

Design

- This study will involve an initial visit to the NIH Clinical Center for all participants. Selected participants may be asked to return for repeat visits over a number of years. The test results from participants with asthma will be compared with those from the healthy volunteers.
- All participants will be screened with a physical exam and medical history.
- Participants may (but will not necessarily) have the following tests at each visit:
  - Complete medical history and physical exam
  - Blood, urine, sputum, and nasal cell samples
  - Breath tests and heart and lung function tests
  - Six-minute walk test to measure ability to exercise
  - Imaging studies such as chest X-rays, bone density scans, and sinus scans
  - Allergy skin testing
  - Vocal cord exam
  - Overnight sleep study

- Participants may remain on the study for as long as they are willing to participate and do not develop health problems that will interfere with the study.

Sample Collections from the Airways of Asthmatic Patients

This study involves a procedure called a fiberoptic bronchoscopy in which cells and fluids are collected from the airways using a pencil-thin tube that is passed into the lungs. The purpose of this research is to identify factors that may cause airway inflammation in patients with asthma.

Purpose

Fiberoptic bronchoscopy is a procedure which involves passing a pencil-thin tube into the lung in order to collect fluid and cells from the airways. Fiberoptic bronchoscopy can collect cells from the walls of airways by gently brushing them (bronchial brushing). In addition, squirting small amounts of sterile water in to the airway and gently suctioning it back into the bronchoscope (bronchoalveolar lavage) collects cells.

In this study, researchers plan to perform these tests on patients with asthma and normal volunteers. This research may help to improve the understanding of the processes involved in airway inflammation and asthma.

Section 19.3

Ongoing Asthma-Related Clinical Trials

This chapter includes excerpts from "Researchers Refine How Immune Pathways Contribute to Asthma," National Institute of Allergy and Infectious Diseases (NIAID), August 19, 2015; text from "Common Fungus Promotes Airway Sensitivity in Asthma," National Institute of Allergy and Infectious Diseases (NIAID), April 10, 2015; and text from "Meet Chip: Lungs," National Center for Advancing Translational Sciences (NCATS), May 15, 2015.

Findings May Improve Clinical Trial Design for Experimental Therapies

A new study has shown that targeting two immune cells—Th2 and Th17—and their downstream, inflammatory effects is better than targeting just one pathway in the context of asthma. The researchers also show that blocking the Th2 pathway, which is a target of commonly-prescribed corticosteroid drugs, may unexpectedly boost conditions for Th17-driven inflammation. These results clarify how immune cells and their products contribute to asthma, and the work may enable researchers to design and test therapies that target both pathways.

Asthma Subtypes Lend Clue

Asthma affects the airways of the lungs, resulting in breathing difficulties, coughing, wheezing, and chest pain. Environmental triggers, such as pollen, mold, and viruses, cause inflammation and constrict the airways, resulting in an asthma attack. Researchers are studying why and how airways become inflamed, which occurs when the immune system overreacts.

Although people with asthma share similar symptoms, scientists are looking more closely at how patients differ, subgrouping based on the types of aberrant immune signals observed. Approximately 10 percent of people with asthma do not achieve disease control under conventional therapies and may benefit from more targeted therapies that address the specific immune problem.

In the new study, the researchers looked retrospectively at lung samples from 51 asthma patients who had a range of disease severity. The team found that the patients clustered into three groups based on the activity of immune cells associated with asthma—Th2 and Th17. Patients exhibited high Th2, high Th17, or low activity of both pathways. Interestingly, no patients had simultaneously high Th2 and Th17 activity, indicating that these pathways are somehow mutually exclusive.

Immune Cells Drive Inflammation

Th2 cells and their products, including signals called interleukin 4 (IL-4) and interleukin 13 (IL-13), are known drivers of asthma. Corticosteroids, which are prescribed for treating asthma attacks, lower Th2 activity, among other effects. More recently, Th17 cells and their products, including interleukin 17 (IL-17), have attracted more attention as researchers uncovered their role in inflammatory diseases.

However, how these pathways influence each other is less known, particularly in the context of asthma.

The study team used a mouse model of asthma to explore Th2 and Th17 activity, and they tested the effect of blocking Th2 activity alone or blocking both Th2 and Th17. Interestingly, mice that receive anti-Th2 therapy, which suppressed IL-4 and IL-13 signals, experienced enhanced Th17 responses. The findings suggest that Th2 may serve as a brake for Th17. When Th2 is blocked, conditions are unexpectedly primed for Th17 activity, which may influence the effectiveness of therapy over time. In line with this idea, the patients who exhibited high Th17 activity were all taking corticosteroids, with moderate to severe disease.

When Th2 and Th17 were simultaneously blocked in the mouse model of asthma, the researchers observed greater benefit than blocking one pathway alone. Dual treatment resulted in less airway inflammation, less mucus production, and importantly, no enhancement of Th17 activity; Th17 activity typically is associated with inflammation caused by neutrophils, a type of immune cell. The study highlights the need to explore both inflammatory pathways in asthma research.

Common Fungus Promotes Airway Sensitivity in Asthma

NIAID scientists have found that an allergy-causing substance, or allergen, from a common fungus triggers a sequence of molecular events that contribute to the airway sensitivity characteristic of asthma. Their findings, reported in the April 13, 2015, issue of *Nature Communications*, point to potential targets for new asthma treatments.

Background

More than 250 million people worldwide are living with asthma, a chronic disease that inflames and narrows the airways of the lungs. One of the hallmarks of asthma is airway hyper-responsiveness, a heightened tendency of the airways to tighten in response to allergens or other triggers. During an asthma attack, the smooth muscle lining the airways contracts, narrowing the airways. Inflammation and excess mucus production also contribute to the airway obstruction that results in asthma symptoms such as coughing, wheezing, and shortness of breath.

Nearly 10 percent of people with asthma have severe, treatment-resistant disease. Often, such people are sensitive to the common fungus *Aspergillus fumigatus*, which grows both outdoors and indoors. Its spores, which are widespread in the air, enter the body when inhaled. For most people, everyday exposure to *A. fumigatus* is rarely a problem. But people with chronic lung diseases or weakened immune systems are at higher risk of developing infections or allergic reactions to the fungus.

Results of Study

Working with mouse tissues and cultured human cells, NIAID scientists showed that a major *A. fumigatus* allergen called Alp 1 can promote airway hyper-responsiveness by disrupting interactions between airway smooth muscle cells and the extracellular matrix, a network of molecules that holds cells together in tissues and helps guide tissue function. The researchers found that Alp 1 degrades the extracellular matrix and sets off a chain of cell-signaling events that leads to tightening of the airways.

To examine the extent to which inhaled Alp 1 reaches the airway smooth muscle, the researchers examined lung sections from human volunteers. They detected high levels of Alp 1 in the smooth muscle of people with asthma, particularly those sensitive to *A. fumigatus*. In contrast, muscle tissues from healthy volunteers had little Alp 1. Their findings suggest that asthma-associated inflammation and damage to airway linings may help promote entry of allergens such as Alp 1 into the smooth muscle of the airways.

Significance

The scientists describe a process in which airway smooth muscle cells respond directly to an inhaled allergen to cause airway hyper-responsiveness, a hallmark of asthma. In the future, drugs that intervene in this process potentially could help reduce asthma symptoms.

Next Steps

Future studies of people with severe asthma may help determine whether the presence of Alp 1 in airway smooth muscle or possibly in mucus can serve as a marker of fungal-associated asthma. Eventually, development of agents that block the action of Alp 1 or other molecules involved in triggering airway hyper-responsiveness may lead to potential new asthma treatments.

Lungs on a Chip

Researchers at Harvard University are working to make an innovative model that incorporates lung smooth muscle cells to mimic complex lung conditions in the human body, something that is impossible in animals.

To test this new pulmonary model, the NIH-supported researchers are using chip technology to study asthma. The cells that line the airways are extremely sensitive in people who have asthma. During asthma symptoms, the muscles tighten too much and narrow the airways, making breathing difficult. Using a chip that integrates this muscle tissue, the researchers aim to measure how drugs targeted against one tissue, such as inhaled asthma drugs that target the lungs, affect the other tissues.

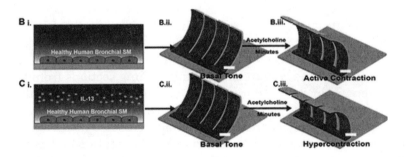

Figure 19.1. *Cells in a chip*

The top three images (B i–iii) show healthy muscle cells in a chip based on an airway. When the researchers add the drug acetylcholine, the cells contract just as they would in a healthy person. The bottom three images (C i–iii) show what happens to healthy muscle cells treated with a chemical (interleukin 13) that mimics asthma. When acetylcholine is added, the cells squeeze too much (hypercontraction), just as they would in a person with asthma.

Looking Ahead

Using this chip, scientists could screen potential new drugs quickly to test whether they are toxic to the lungs. Data from these tests could help speed the drug approval process and make new treatments available sooner.

The technology also could be part of a bigger, multi-organ system. Scientists could link this chip with other chips—for example, with chips representing the heart and liver—to test how drugs affect multiple organ systems at once.

Chapter 20

The Role of CDC in Asthma Management

The Centers for Disease Control and Prevention's (CDC's) National Asthma Control Program (NACP) helps millions of Americans understand, manage, and gain control over their asthma. CDC launched the NACP in 1999 to address the rising public health impact of asthma. The program leads national initiatives and provides state funding for a variety of activities focused on surveillance, intervention, partnerships, and evaluation. These activities have provided millions of people with asthma the essential tools for controlling their disease and helped them understand how to improve the quality of their lives through proper asthma management. NACP-funded activities have also educated families, providers, and school systems about preventing asthma attacks. Since 1999, the NACP has worked with partners to:

- Establish a coordinated national public health response to control asthma.
- Build and sustain asthma control programs in 34 states, the District of Columbia, and Puerto Rico.
- Support national and state asthma surveillance systems.
- Improve asthma management in schools across the country.
- Evaluate programs to identify and share best practices.
- Target interventions to populations and communities disproportionately affected by asthma.

Text in this chapter is excerpted from "An Investment in America's Health," Centers for Disease Control and Prevention (CDC), 2013.

- Share CDC expertise with state and local public health practitioners.

- Fund over 120 positions in health departments nationwide and support more than 160 contracts for asthma services created by the Program.

The NACP's return on investment is compelling: for every dollar spent on national and state-level programs, $71 in asthma-related expenditures is saved. This is a strong indication that the nation is on track to curb the burden of asthma. To sustain and build upon these efforts, the NACP must continue to lead the public health response to asthma control by helping millions of people with asthma gain control over their lives, thereby reducing the national burden of asthma.

Reducing the Burden of Asthma

The burden of asthma is characterized by the numbers of asthma-related hospitalizations, emergency room visits, deaths, school days missed, and other factors such as activity limitations. Because asthma has no known cure, the most effective way to manage it is by preventing the need for frequent, costly medical treatment due to uncontrolled symptoms and attacks. The NACP's overarching goal is to provide people the tools to manage their as thma successfully, thereby reducing the collective burden of asthma.

The Goal of NACP: Asthma Control and Management

Fortunately, asthma symptoms and costs can be controlled when people have the appropriate care, education, and guidance to manage their condition. Reducing exposure to triggers, treating patients with medications such as inhaled corticosteroids, and educating patients and caregivers can mitigate the severity of asthma symptoms and frequency of attacks. In 1999, CDC created the NACP to develop interventions based on these principles and reduce the societal and economic burden of asthma in the United States.

Progress in Controlling Asthma

The NACP has made significant progress in controlling asthma in the United States. Over the last 12 years, costs due to asthma illness and death have decreased by $23.1 billion, representing an estimated return on investment of $71 saved for each dollar spent. These savings reflect a shift from visits to more costly medical settings (hospitals and emergency rooms) to less expensive primary care settings (doctor offices and outpatient clinics). In addition, asthma death rates have decreased by 27% since 1999.

Leading a Coordinated Public Health Response

Before 1999 the lack of high quality asthma surveillance within populations limited public health practitioners' ability to implement effective asthma control measures. With only national-level statistics they could not answer these basic questions: Who has asthma? Who suffers from asthma attacks? Among which populations is asthma increasing the fastest? In response in 1999, CDC announced the availability of funds for a new cooperative agreement program, *Addressing Asthma from a Public Health Perspective*. The objectives of the program were to

1. Focus on asthma-related activity within the state health agency

2. Increase understanding of asthma-related data and their application to program planning by develop ing an ongoing surveillance system

3. Increase state and territory use of a public health approach to reduce the burden of asthma

4. Link the health agency to the many agencies and organizations addressing asthma in the population

5. Participate in intervention program activities

CDC initially awarded grants to four states—Illinois, Minnesota, Oregon, and Rhode Island—and established the NACP to administer the cooperative agreements and provide technical assistance as states implemented and grew their programs. Since then the program has expanded to support 34 states, the District of Columbia, and Puerto Rico

Measures of Success

Controlling asthma requires a multifaceted approach focusing on patient behaviors; home, work, and school environments; knowledge and skills of health care providers; and public health programs and policies that influence asthma management practices. Highly effective asthma control programs conduct activities that target these components and lead to a reduced burden of asthma. These activities include improving surveillance to track asthma more effectively, training health professionals using the best available science, and educating individuals with asthma and their families.

To measure the success of their efforts, asthma program evaluators assess a number of short- to long-term outcomes. These include increased patient awareness of asthma self-management skills, improved medical management of asthma, increased understanding of asthma disparities by state and local health departments, and changes in public health practice affecting asthma management. These outcomes ultimately lead to a reduced burden of asthma: fewer asthma-related hospitalizations and deaths, fewer school and work days missed, decreased disparities in asthma outcomes among various affected populations, and improved quality of life for people living with asthma

Since 2001, the NACP has provided $238 million to state and territorial asthma programs, national non-governmental organizations, and local communities to implement asthma activities. NACP also conducts national asthma activities and provides technical assistance to various partners and communities in the United States. Some state programs rely almost exclusively on NACP funding to sustain their programs, while others have successfully leveraged NACP funding to bring in additional funds from grants, tobacco and other tax revenue, and various federal and state public health programs.

Figure 20.1. *Example of short-, intermediate-, and long term outcomes associated with asthma control program activities supported by NACP.*

Success of State Asthma Control Programs

The key to NACP's success has been the integration of surveillance, partnerships, interventions, and evaluation, the building blocks of the Program. To receive funding, NACP requires states to conduct activities in these categories.

Epidemiologic Surveillance

Accurate, timely surveillance data are essential for understanding the nature and patterns of asthma to improve planning, targeting, and implementing interventions. State and local health departments rely on asthma surveillance data to direct and to evaluate their efforts to reduce the burden of asthma. In their five-year state asthma plans, CDC requires funded state asthma programs to identify and document the goals, objectives, and strategies needed to reduce the burden of asthma. CDC released the 2011 Asthma State Profiles (www.cdc.gov/asthma/nacp.htm) to provide an overview of the burden of asthma in 34 states, the District of Columbia, and Puerto Rico.

CDC's Asthma Call-Back Survey (ACBS) is one of the most important tools public health officials use to track surveillance goals, evaluate programs, direct policy, and plan future activities. After a series of pilot tests beginning in 2003, the NACP implemented the ACBS as a follow-up survey to the Behavioral Risk Factor Surveillance System (BRFSS). The BRFSS is a state-based system of health surveys that generate information about health risk behaviors, clinical preventive practices, and health care access and use. By 2010, the ACBS had expanded to 40 states, the District of Columbia, and Puerto Rico. States use ACBS data to measure state and local rates of asthma-related healthcare utilization, knowledge and skills in asthma self-management, number of lost days of work and school due to asthma, and other variables. Before the ACBS existed, none of this information was available at the state level.

The NACP also funds states to collect and analyze asthma surveillance data from hospitals, Medicaid records, and other sources, including records of hospitalizations, emergency department visits, and incidents of mortality.

This suite of asthma surveillance datasets forms a detailed picture of the burden of asthma at the state level. Coupled with CDC's national-level asthma data, public health practitioners can now characterize asthma patterns and trends in much greater detail and report the most up-to-date statistics on asthma.

- Eight percent of Americans had asthma in 2009.

- More than nine people die from asthma every day; black Americans are two to three times more likely to die from asthma than any other racial or ethnic group.

- In 2011, 52% of people with asthma reported having an asthma attack within the last year; Oregon had the highest rate of asthma attacks (63.1%) and North Carolina had the lowest (40.8%)

- About 1 in 11 children and 1 in 12 adults had asthma in 2010; black children are twice as likely to have asthma as white children.

- Low-income populations, minorities, and children living in inner cities visit the emergency department more often and are more likely to be hospitalized or die due to asthma.

- Nearly one in two children with asthma reports missing at least one day of school each year because of asthma.

- Three in five people with asthma must limit their physical activity due to their asthma.

Partnerships with Asthma Programs and Organizations

CDC promotes collaboration by actively recruiting and engaging both internal and external partners. Partners may include other programs within state health departments, state and local asthma coalitions, healthcare plans and providers, advocacy organizations, and other CDC-funded initiatives. State asthma control programs have significantly broadened the reach of their services by forming sustainable partnerships with other agencies and organizations committed to reducing the burden of asthma.

Evidence-based Interventions to Reduce the Burden of Asthma.

The NACP first incorporated interventions into its cooperative agreement structure in 2002. That year the program funded grantees to implement two scientifically-evaluated asthma interventions: the Asthma and Allergy Foundation of America's "Asthma Care Training for Kids" and the American Lung Association's "Open Airways for Schools." Surveillance data show that these interventions decrease acute care visits and hospitalizations and increase compliance with asthma care plans. By 2007, NACP funded all 36 grantees to develop and maintain a broad array of asthma interventions, including programs or campaigns for

- Adult-specific asthma education and prevention

- A sthma awareness, outreach, and communication

- Caregiver, school-and childcare center-based education and prevention

- Education and prevention targeted to underserved populations

- Trigger reduction and home visits

- Healthcare provider education and training

- Health plan coverage of asthma services
- Indoor air quality-based education and prevention
- Senior citizen-specific asthma education and prevention
- State systems-based change
- Tobacco use reduction

Evaluating Effectiveness and Impact of State Programs

CDC understands the value of evaluation to assess how well asthma programs are working and requires each grantee to have an experienced evaluator on staff to conduct and support evaluation. Each grantee must also develop a five-year strategic evaluation plan to measure progress toward program goals and objectives for the surveillance, partnerships, and interventions described in their state asthma plans. To support this effort and promote sound evaluation practice and consistency among grantees, the NACP developed the Learning & Growing through Evaluation: State Asthma Program Evaluation Guide (www.cdc.gov/asthma/program_eval/guide.htm). CDC, in partnership with the U.S. Environmental Protection Agency, also presented a series of webinars to guide asthma programs through the essential elements of evaluation.

Some NACP grantees' regular evaluations are beginning to show compelling results indicating a sound return on investment in the program.

NACP's National-Level Accomplishments

In addition to providing funding and technical support directly to state health departments, CDC partners with other federal and non-governmental agencies to promote national-level asthma control efforts in alignment with *Healthy People 2020* goals and objectives for asthma. The NACP supports collaborative projects and initiatives among CDC divisions, other programs within the U.S. Department of Health and Human Services (HHS), other federal agencies, and non-governmental organizations.

Healthy People 2020 Objectives

1. Reduce asthma deaths
2. Reduce hospitalizations for asthma

3. Reduce emergency room visits for asthma
4. Reduce activity limitations among persons with current asthma
5. Reduce the proportion of persons with asthma who miss school or work days
6. Increase the proportion of persons with current asthma who rec eive formal patient education
7. Increase the proportion of persons with current asthma who receive appropriate asthma care according to National Asthma Education and Prevention Program (NAEPP) G uidelines
8. Increase the number of States, Territories, and the District of Columbia with a comprehensive asthma surveillance system for tracking asthma cases, illness, and disability at the State level

HHS Partners

From inception, the NACP has provided financial and technical support as well as enhanced national-level surveillance. The NACP worked with CDC's National Center for Chronic Disease Prevention and Health Promotion to pilot two optional asthma prevalence questions to the BRFSS beginning in 1999. By 2000, the core questionnaire administered to all U.S. states and territories incorporated these questions. Around the same time, the NACP partnered with the National Center for Health Statistics to use the National Health Interview Survey to collect data on asthma attacks, asthma management, asthma-related absenteeism, emergency room visits, and hospitalizations.

Other Federal Partners

Experts from the NACP, the National Institutes of Health, and ot her governmental and non-governmental organizations contributed to the devel opment of the National Asthma Education and Prevention Program Guidelines, the nation's gold standard for asthma care and management. The Guidelines identify critical measures thought to have the biggest impact on asthma care and patient health. Those measures include the use of inhaled corticosteroids to control asthma, use of a written asthma action plan to guide patient self-management, regular follow-up visits with a primary care provider, and control of environmental triggers that worsen the patient's asthma. The NACP is also participating with other CDC partners, HHS agencies, the U.S. Environmental Protection Agency, and the U.S. Department of Housing and Urban Development on the President's Coordinated Federal Action Plan to Reduce Racial and Ethnic Asthma Disparities.

President's Coordinated Federal Action Plan to Reduce Racial and Ethnic Asthma Disparities: Strategies to Address Asthma Disparities

1. Reduce barriers to the implem entation of guidelines-based asthma management.
2. Enhance capacity to deliver integrated, comprehensive asthma care to children in communities with racial and ethnic asthma disparities.
3. Improve capacity to identify the children most impacted by asthma disp arities.
4. Accelerate efforts to identify and test interventions that may prevent the onset of asthma among ethnic and racial minority children.

Spurred by the federal focus on environmental justice and recent data showing substantial disparities among poor and minority children with asthma compared to other demographic groups with asthma, the *Plan* describes four key strategies to address disparities and plans for federal agency collaborations on each strategy during the next 3–5 years.

Cities and Local Health Departments

The NACP provided funding to the Controlling Asthma in American Cities Project (CAACP), a locally-based collaborative in seven cities: Chicago, Minneapolis/St. Paul, New York, Oakland, Philadelphia, Richmond, and St. Louis. CAACP's goal was to develop comprehensive, culturally appropriate, localized asthma control plans targeting children (0–18 years) in inner-city areas with large unmet asthma control needs. Since the project ended in 2008, several CAACP sites have secured their own funding to sustain the efforts launched in 2002.

Schools

The NACP plays a pivotal role in promoting "Asthma -Friendly Schools," which are schools that follow policies and procedures allowing children to manage their asthma and thrive in the learning environment. Throughout the 2000s, the NACP worked with CDC's Division of Adolescent and School Health to fund various asthma control strategies across several urban school districts and created tools to assist them with program planning and monitoring. Two of these tools were the "Creating an Asthma-Friendly School " video and "Strategies for Addressing Asthma Within a Coordinated School Health Program," a web-based guidance document for schools seeking to improve the health and attendance of students with asthma. Currently, most of the asthma work in school settings is supported by the states, based on local surveillance data and targeted interventions.

Non-Governmental Organizations

Since 2002 the NACP has partnered with non-governmental organizations to carry out or fund activities and initiatives aimed at reducing the burden of asthma.

- CDC collaborated with the Allergy and Asthma Network/Mothers of Asthmatics and the Asthma and Allergy Foundation of America to develop asthma tools and programs for CDC grantees. Large hospital systems, urban hospitals, city health departments, school systems, and local chapters of national asthma organizations are now implementing these tools.

- The NACP supported the work of the American Lung Association and other national asthma advocacy organizations to encourage all 50 states to pass "self-carry" laws for asthma medication.

- In partnership with the Task Force on Community Preventive Services, an independent, nonfederal body of public health and prevention experts, the NACP systematically reviewed the effectiveness of home-based, multi-trigger, multi-component educational and environmental interventions. The NACP is currently working with state and local asthma control programs to implement these interventions and evaluate their impact.

- With the National Institute of Environmental Health Sciences and the American Legion Child Welfare Foundation, the NACP funded development of *Environmental Management of Pediatric Asthma: Guidelines for Health Care Providers*, produced by the National Environmental Education Foundation. The Guidelines teach health care providers how to incorporate management of environmental asthma triggers into pediatric practice and how to communicate with patients about effective home-based interventions.

Plans for the Future

The last 30 years of asthma surveillance data tell an important story with potential implications for the future. Asthma prevalence rose sharply in the 1980s and 1990s, as did the incidence of adverse outcomes related to asthma. Hospitalization rates increased at an average rate of 2.9% per year from 1980 to 1984 and then slowed to 1.2% per year from 1984 to 2009. Death rates increased from 1980 to 1989, leveled off from 1989 to 1998, and then decreased from 1999 to 2009. This decline in deaths is the most important indicator of the success of the NACP's investment in reducing the burden of asthma.

Since 1999, CDC has worked to establish a network of asthma control programs to build capacity and implement sustainable programs and policies at the federal, state, and local levels. The NACP 's success is based on a foundation of robust surveillance data; targeted, evidence-based interventions; partnerships that conserve resources and enhance impact; and evaluation to gauge program effectiveness and make improvements. But this work has just begun.

Reducing morbidity associated with asthma remains a major public health challenge, even more so for populations disproportionately affected by asthma. The rate at which Americans are diagnosed with asthma has slowed since the 1990s, but it is still growing.

To lose momentum now, when the trends are beginning to indicate long-term progress in reducing the burden of asthma, could come at a high cost to those living with asthma and to the nation's economy.

With continued and increased funding, CDC hopes to expand the NACP to all U.S. states and territories and to build upon its many successes. Reducing asthma's burdens of mortality, morbidity, and societal costs serves the entire nation, and much work remains to be done.

Part Four

Living with Asthma

Chapter 21

Working with Your Doctor

Tips for Creating Good, Clear Communication with Your Doctor or Other Health Care Professional

Speak Up. Tell your doctor or other health care professional about what you want to achieve by improving control of your asthma. Ask for his or her help in achieving those treatment goals.

Be Open. When your doctor or other health care professional asks you questions, answer as honestly and completely as you can. Briefly describe your symptoms. Include when you started having each symptom, how often you have it, and whether it has been getting worse.

Keep It Simple. If you don't understand something your doctor or other health care professional says, ask for a simple explanation. Be especially sure that you understand how to take any medicines you are given. If you are worried about understanding what the doctor or other health care professional says, or if you have trouble hearing, bring a friend or relative with you to your appointment. You may want to ask that person to write down instructions for you.

Text in this chapter is excerpted from "So You Have Asthma," National Heart, Lung, and Blood Institute (NHLBI), March 2013; text from "Health Care Professionals," National Heart, Lung, and Blood Institute (NHLBI), April 28, 2014; and text from "When You Should See an Allergist," © 2015 Omnigraphics, Inc. Reviewed November 2015.

The gap between what the scientific literature shows us works and what we do is evident in the fact that less than a third of people with persistent asthma take inhaled corticosteroids to control asthma.

- Work closely with your doctor and other health care professionals (such as a nurse practitioner, physician assistant, nurse, respiratory therapist or asthma educator) to learn how to manage your asthma and keep it under control. Regular "asthma check-ups" with your doctor will help.

- Learn which medicines to take, when to take them, and how to use them correctly. For your quick-relief inhaler, ask your doctor if you can add a spacer to make it easier to take the medicine. Then take all of your medicines just as your doctor recommends.

- Identify the things that bring on your asthma symptoms, also called your asthma triggers. Then avoid them, or at least reduce your contact with them.

- Watch for changes in your asthma. You need to know when an asthma attack is coming and what to do. If you act quickly and follow the doctor's instructions, you can help keep your asthma symptoms from getting worse.

How often you get symptoms will let you and your doctor know if you need to do more to control your asthma. Call your doctor if—

- You have asthma symptoms more than 2 days a week.

- Your asthma wakes you up 2 or more times a month.

- You are using your quick-relief inhaler more than 2 days a week.

- Your asthma is getting in the way of your usual activities.

These are signs that your asthma is not well controlled and may be getting worse.

What to Ask the Doctor

Sample List of Questions to Ask Your Doctor or Other Health Care Professional

- Are you sure it's asthma?

- Do I need other tests to confirm the diagnosis?

- If I think my medicine isn't working, is it OK to take more right away?

- What should I do if I miss a dose?

- Will my medicine cause me any problems, like shakiness, sore throat, or upset stomach?

- What if I have problems taking my medicines or following my treatment plan?

- Is this the right way to use my inhaler? How do I use my inhaler with a spacer?

- Is this the right way to use my peak flow meter?

- How can I tell if I'm having an asthma attack? What medicines should I take and how much of each should I take? When should I call you? When should I go to the emergency room?

- Once my asthma is under control, will I be able to reduce the amount of medicine I'm taking?

- When should I see you again?

When You Should See an Allergist

Allergy/immunology is the field of medicine that deals with the human body's immune system. The immune system is a network of cells, tissues, and organs that defends the body against potentially harmful foreign organisms and particles. A physician specializing in this field of medicine is called an allergist/immunologist.

The human body is well equipped to defend itself against disease-causing organisms such as bacteria, viruses, or fungi. It also defends itself from foreign particles such as dust or mold. When the body encounters substances that it recognizes as potentially harmful, the immune system produces antibodies to eliminate them.

Under normal circumstances, this defense mechanism does a good job of protecting the body and keeping it healthy. Sometimes, though, the immune system overreacts to harmless substances—like a certain food or pollen—by releasing chemicals and triggering changes in the body to destroy the invaders. This process is called an allergic reaction. When the reaction is severe enough to require medical care, an allergist/immunologist is usually involved in diagnosing and treating the patient's condition.

Types of Allergic Reactions

Allergic reactions tend to happen in locations where the immune system has concentrated its defenses to protect against foreign substances entering the body. They frequently affect the skin, the eyes, the respiratory system (nose, sinuses, throat, lungs), and the digestive system (stomach, intestines). Some common types of allergic reactions include contact dermatitis or skin allergies, allergic rhinitis (inflammation of the lining of the nose and sinuses), and asthma. Anaphylaxis is a sudden, severe, whole-body allergic reaction that can be life-threatening without immediate medical attention.

People can develop allergies to a variety of ordinary substances that they are exposed to daily. Common types of allergens include: foods such as milk, wheat, nuts, fish, soy, and eggs; airborne particles such as dust, pollen, mold, and animal dander; insect bites and stings; certain chemicals and medications; and substances like latex. Certain plants, like poison ivy, can also trigger severe allergic reactions.

Seeing an Allergist/Immunologist

The symptoms of allergic reactions can range from a mild runny nose or skin rash to diarrhea and vomiting or anaphylaxis. Sometimes the symptoms can be controlled with occasional doses of over-the-counter allergy medications, and sometimes they get worse over time and detract from the person's quality of life. Generally speaking, patients should consider seeing an allergist/immunologist under the following circumstances:

- an abnormal reaction to inhaling, ingesting, or coming into contact with something;

- symptoms of asthma such as wheezing, difficulty breathing, or chest pressure;

- more than three infections of the ear, nose, throat, or lungs per year;

- skin conditions like rashes or hives that appear frequently or without a known cause;

- a severe reaction to a bee sting or an insect bite;

- allergic reactions that interfere with performing activities of daily living;

- symptoms that do not improve with the use of over-the-counter medications.

An allergist/immunologist has to undergo a minimum of nine years of medical education and training, including four years of medical school, three years of residency training as an internist or pediatrician, and two years of specialized study in the field of allergy/immunology. The physician then has to pass a certification examination conducted by the American Board of Allergy and Immunology.

An allergist will conduct a medical history and physical examination and perform certain tests to identify the allergen responsible for the patient's reaction. One of the most common tests is the skin-prick test, in which the allergist uses a small needle to prick the patient's skin and insert tiny quantities of allergy-causing substances. If the patient is allergic to a specific substance, they will develop a bump on the skin similar to a mosquito bite. Another test that is often performed by allergists is a challenge test, in which the patient inhales or ingests a very small quantity of allergen under medical supervision to see if they have a reaction. Finally, an allergist may conduct blood tests to check for immunoglobulin E (IgE) antibodies, which are indicators of an allergic reaction.

To prepare for a visit to an allergist, it may be helpful to keep a diary of allergic reactions, recording details about symptoms, exposure to potential allergens, and timing. This information makes it easier for the allergist to diagnose and treat the condition. Prompt diagnosis and identification of allergens will help the patient avoid exposure to these substances or control their reactions if they are exposed to them. Patients with severe allergies may be required to carry emergency medication, like an epinephrine auto-injector or an inhaler, with them at all times.

Chapter 22

How to Monitor Your Asthma

Chapter Contents

Section 22.1

Monitoring Your Symptoms

This section includes excerpts from "So You Have Asthma," National Heart, Lung, and Blood Institute (NHLBI), March 2013; and text from "Explore Asthma," National Heart, Lung, and Blood Institute (NHLBI), August 4, 2014.

What Are the Signs and Symptoms of Asthma?

Common signs and symptoms of asthma include:

- Coughing. Coughing from asthma often is worse at night or early in the morning, making it hard to sleep.

- Wheezing. Wheezing is a whistling or squeaky sound that occurs when you breathe.

- Chest tightness. This may feel like something is squeezing or sitting on your chest.

- Shortness of breath. Some people who have asthma say they can't catch their breath or they feel out of breath. You may feel like you can't get air out of your lungs.

Not all people who have asthma have these symptoms. Likewise, having these symptoms doesn't always mean that you have asthma. The best way to diagnose asthma for certain is to use a lung function test, a medical history (including type and frequency of symptoms), and a physical exam.

The types of asthma symptoms you have, how often they occur, and how severe they are may vary over time. Sometimes your symptoms may just annoy you. Other times, they may be troublesome enough to limit your daily routine.

Severe symptoms can be fatal. It's important to treat symptoms when you first notice them so they don't become severe.

With proper treatment, most people who have asthma can expect to have few, if any, symptoms either during the day or at night.

What Causes Asthma Symptoms to Occur?

Many things can trigger or worsen asthma symptoms. Your doctor will help you find out which things (sometimes called triggers) may cause your asthma to flare up if you come in contact with them. Triggers may include:

- Allergens from dust, animal fur, cockroaches, mold, and pollens from trees, grasses, and flowers

- Irritants such as cigarette smoke, air pollution, chemicals or dust in the workplace, compounds in home décor products, and sprays (such as hairspray)

- Medicines such as aspirin or other nonsteroidal anti-inflammatory drugs and nonselective beta-blockers

- Sulfites in foods and drinks

- Viral upper respiratory infections, such as colds

- Physical activity, including exercise

Other health conditions can make asthma harder to manage. Examples of these conditions include a runny nose, sinus infections, reflux disease, psychological stress, and sleep apnea. These conditions need treatment as part of an overall asthma care plan.

Asthma is different for each person. Some of the triggers listed above may not affect you. Other triggers that do affect you may not be on the list. Talk with your doctor about the things that seem to make your asthma worse.

Monitoring Your Asthma

Monitoring your asthma on a regular basis is important to keeping your asthma under control.

Keeping track of your symptoms whenever you have them is a good idea. This will help you and your doctor adjust your treatment over time.

Another way to monitor your asthma is with a peak flow meter. This is a hand-held device that shows how well air moves out of your lungs. Measuring your peak flow can help you tell how well your asthma is controlled. It can also alert you to an oncoming asthma attack hours or even days before you feel symptoms. And during an attack,it can help tell you how bad the attack is and if your medicine is working.

The peak flow meter also can be used to help you and your doctor:

- Learn what makes your asthma worse
- Decide if your treatment plan is working well
- Decide when to add or stop medicine
- Decide when to seek emergency care

Section 22.2

Peak Flow Monitoring

Text in this section is excerpted from "Management of Asthma," Federal Bureau of Prisons (BOP), May 2013.

Management of Asthma

Peak flow use during exacerbations will help determine the severity of the exacerbations and guide therapeutic decisions. Consider peak flow monitoring during exacerbations of asthma for patients who have:

- A history of severe exacerbations
- Moderate or severe persistent asthma
- Difficulty perceiving signs of worsening asthma

The frequency of peak expiratory flow (PEF) monitoring depends on the needs of the individual patient. A patient who is a poor perceiver of asthma symptoms may need to measure PEF every morning and evening, both before and after using inhaled medications, and when symptoms of asthma are noted. Another patient with more stable asthma may need to measure PEF only when experiencing symptoms or when they are at risk for an asthma flare,such as during an upper respiratory infection.

- Once baseline values are established, each patient's personal best value must be re-evaluated annually to account for disease progression.

- In addition, the PEF measurements should be compared with office spirometry at least once per year, since the PEF in some cases has been less accurate than measurement of FEV1 in detecting airflow obstruction.

Benefits

The use of peak flow monitoring can be a useful tool to monitor asthma control. Peak flow monitoring can measure the day-to-day changes in breathing patterns to help the patient to:

- Track the control of asthma over time.
- Show how well treatment is working.
- Recognize signs of flare-up before symptoms appear.
- Decide when to seek medical attention

Frequency

The frequency of monitoring asthma control with the use of peak flow monitoring is a matter of clinical judgment. The health care provider should consider the following measurement time frames:

- Consider peak flow monitoring at 2-to-6 week intervals for patients who are just starting therapy or who require a step up in therapy to achieve or regain asthma control.
- Consider peak flow monitoring for patients who have well controlled asthma during scheduled Chronic Care Clinic visits and when the patient senses the asthma is getting worse.
- Consider peak flow monitoring at 3-month intervals if a step down in therapy is anticipated.
- Consider daily peak flow monitoring for patients who have moderate or severe persistent asthma, those who have a history of severe exacerbations, and those who poorly perceive airway obstruction or worsening asthma. This could be accomplished by issuing a self-carry peak flow meter and education on its use to those patients with unstable asthma to better monitor the patient's asthma control.

Spirometry Testing Time Frames

The health care provider should consider the following spirometry testing time frames:

- At the initial assessment for patients whom the diagnosis of asthma is suspected.

- After asthma treatment is initiated and symptoms and Peak Expiratory Flow have stabilized.

- During periods of progressive or prolonged loss of asthma control.

- At least every 1–2 years; more frequently, depending on response to therapy.

Chapter 23

Asthma Action Plan

Asthma Action Plans: Help Patients Take Control

All people with asthma should receive a written asthma action plan to guide their self-management efforts.

Provide a written asthma action plan to guide daily and emergency care

Many patients have difficulty recalling instructions for care that are given by their health care provider. A written asthma action plan (AAP) provides instruction and information on how to self-manage one's asthma daily, including taking medications appropriately, and identifying and avoiding exposure to allergens and irritants that can bring about asthma symptoms. In addition, the AAP provides information on how to recognize and handle worsening asthma, and when, how, and who to contact in an emergency.

AAPs should be easy for patients and their families to understand and presented in a format that encourages self-management. In addition, AAPs serve as the vehicle of coordination across multiple caregivers and as a linking mechanism between community and clinical sites. For children, these plans should be made simple and easy for

Text in this chapter is excerpted from "Asthma Action Plan," National Heart, Lung, and Blood Institute (NHLBI), January 2013; and text from "So You Have Asthma," National Heart, Lung, and Blood Institute (NHLBI), March 2013.

schools, school nurses, and school-based health centers to use. Communicating the policies that guide use of AAPs at various points of care will reinforce their use.

Encourage patients' adherence to the written asthma action plan

- Choose treatment that achieves outcomes and addresses preferences that are important to the patient, and remind patients that adherence will help them achieve the outcomes they want.

- Review with the patient at each visit the success of the treatment plan in achieving asthma control and make adjustments as needed.

- Review patients' concerns about their asthma or treatment at every visit. Inquire about any difficulties encountered in adhering to the written asthma action plan.

- Assess the patient's and family's level of social support, and encourage family involvement.

- Tailor the self-management approach to the needs and literacy levels of the patient, and maintain sensitivity to cultural beliefs and ethnocultural practices.

- Observe skills for self-management, for example, inhaler technique, use of a valved holding chamber or spacer, and self-monitoring.

Your Asthma Management Partnership

Think of your doctor and other health care team members (such as nurse practitioner, physician assistant, nurse, respiratory therapist, pharmacist, or asthma educator) as your partners in asthma management. While you know best how your body is feeling on a day-today basis, they know best how to help you get and keep your asthma under control.

Don't hesitate to:

- Discuss your treatment goals with your doctor

- Ask questions and express concernsAsk the doctor to explain something again in a different way if you don't understand

- Get involved in decisions about your treatment so it meets your needs and is something that you know you can do

- Let your doctor know right away about any changes in your asthma condition and make time to see him or her on a regular, agreed-upon schedule

Chapter 24

Minimizing Indoor Asthma Triggers

Chapter Contents

Section 24.1

Indoor Asthma Triggers: Secondhand Smoke

Text in this section is excerpted from "Asthma Triggers: Gain Control," U.S. Environmental Protection Agency (EPA), October 26, 2015; and text from "Asthma and Secondhand Smoke," Centers for Disease Control and Prevention (CDC), September 1, 2015; and text from "Harms of Cigarette Smoking and Health Benefits of Quitting," National Cancer Institute (NCI), December 3, 2014.

About Secondhand Smoke and Asthma

Secondhand smoke is the smoke from a cigarette, cigar or pipe, and the smoke exhaled by a smoker. Secondhand smoke contains more than 4,000 substances, including several compounds that cause cancer.

Secondhand smoke can trigger asthma episodes and increase the severity of attacks. Secondhand smoke is also a risk factor for new cases of asthma in preschool-aged children. Children's developing bodies make them more susceptible to the effects of secondhand smoke and, due to their small size, they breathe more rapidly than adults, thereby taking in more secondhand smoke. Children receiving high doses of secondhand smoke, such as those with smoking parents, run the greatest relative risk of experiencing damaging health effects.

How Is Smoking Related to Asthma?

If you have asthma, an asthma attack can occur when something irritates your airways and "triggers" an attack. Your triggers might be different from other people's triggers.

Tobacco smoke is one of the most common asthma triggers. Tobacco smoke—including secondhand smoke—is unhealthy for everyone, especially people with asthma. Secondhand smoke is a mixture of gases and fine particles that includes:

- Smoke from a burning cigarette, cigar, or pipe tip

- Smoke that has been exhaled (breathed out) by someone who smokes

Secondhand smoke contains more than 7,000 chemicals, including hundreds that are toxic and about 70 that can cause cancer.

If you have asthma, it's important that you avoid exposure to secondhand smoke.

If you are among the 21% of U.S. adults who have asthma and smoke, quit smoking.

How Can Asthma Attacks Be Prevented?

If you or a family member has asthma, you can manage it with the help of your health care provider (for example, by taking your medicines exactly as your doctor tells you) and by avoiding triggers. Staying far away from tobacco smoke is one important way to avoid asthma attacks. Some other helpful tips are:

- Do not smoke or allow others to smoke in your home or car. Opening a window does not protect you from smoke.

- If your state still allows smoking in public areas, look for restaurants and other places that do not allow smoking. "No-smoking sections" in the same restaurant with "smoking sections" do not protect adequately from secondhand smoke—even if there is a filter or ventilation system.

- Make sure your children's day care centers and schools are tobacco-free. For schools, a tobacco-free campus policy means no tobacco use or advertising on school property is allowed by anyone at any time. This includes off-campus school events.

- Teach children to stay away from secondhand smoke. Be a good role model by not smoking.

Actions You Can Take

- Don't let anyone smoke near your child.

- If you smoke—until you can quit, don't smoke in your home or car.

What are the immediate benefits of quitting smoking?

The immediate health benefits of quitting smoking are substantial:

- Heart rate and blood pressure, which are abnormally high while smoking, begin to return to normal.

- Within a few hours, the level of carbon monoxide in the blood begins to decline. (Carbon monoxide reduces the blood's ability to carry oxygen.)

- Within a few weeks, people who quit smoking have improved circulation, produce less phlegm, and don't cough or wheeze as often.

- Within several months of quitting, people can expect substantial improvements in lung function.

- Within a few years of quitting, people will have lower risks of cancer, heart disease, and other chronic diseases than if they had continued to smoke.

- In addition, people who quit smoking will have an improved sense of smell, and food will taste better.

What are the long-term benefits of quitting smoking?

Quitting smoking reduces the risk of cancer and many other diseases, such as heart disease and COPD, caused by smoking.

Data from the U.S. National Health Interview Survey show that people who quit smoking, regardless of their age, are less likely to die from smoking-related illness than those who continue to smoke. Smokers who quit before age 40 reduced their chance of dying prematurely from smoking-related diseases by about 90 percent, and those who quit by age 45-54 reduced their chance of dying prematurely by about two-thirds.

People who quit smoking, regardless of their age, have substantial gains in life expectancy compared with those who continue to smoke. Those who quit between the ages of 25 and 34 years lived about 10 years longer; those who quit between ages 35 and 44 lived about 9 years longer; those who quit between ages 45 and 54 lived about 6 years longer; and those who quit between ages 55 and 64 lived about 4 years longer.

Section 24.2

Dealing with Cockroaches and Other Pests

Text in this section is excerpted from "Asthma Triggers: Gain Control," U.S. Environmental Protection Agency (EPA), October 26, 2015; and text from "Cockroaches," U.S. Department of Health and Human Services (HHS), May 22, 2014.

About Cockroaches and Other Pests

Cockroaches are one of the most common and allergenic of indoor pests. Recent studies have found a strong association between the presence of cockroaches and increases in the severity of asthma symptoms in individuals who are sensitive to cockroach allergens.

These pests are common even in the cleanest of crowded urban areas and older dwellings. They are found in all types of neighborhoods.

The proteins found in cockroach saliva are particularly allergenic but the body and droppings of cockroaches also contain allergenic proteins.

Droppings or body parts of cockroaches and other pests can trigger asthma. Certain proteins are found in cockroach feces and saliva and can cause allergic reactions or trigger asthma symptoms in some individuals.

Cockroaches are commonly found in crowded cities and the southern regions of the United States. Cockroach allergens likely play a significant role in asthma in many urban areas.

Actions You Can Take

- Insecticides and pesticides are not only toxic to pests—they can harm people too. Try to use pest management methods that pose less of a risk. Keep counters, sinks, tables and floors clean and free of clutter.

- Clean dishes, crumbs and spills right away.

- Store food in airtight containers.

- Seal cracks or openings around or inside cabinets.

Preventive Strategies

- Keep food and garbage in closed, tight-lidded containers. Never leave food out in the kitchen.

- Do not leave out pet food or dirty food bowls.

- Eliminate water sources that attract these pests, such as leaky faucets and drain pipes.

- Mop the kitchen floor and wash countertops at least once a week.

- Plug up crevices around the house through which cockroaches can enter.

- Limit the spread of food around the house and especially keep food out of bedrooms.

- Use bait stations and other environmentally safe pesticides to reduce cockroach infestation.

Section 24.3

Minimizing Dust Mites

Text in this section is excerpted from "Minimizing Dust Mites," National Institute of Environmental Health Sciences (NIEHS), May 22, 2014.

Dust Mites

Dust mites are tiny microscopic relatives of the spider and live on mattresses, bedding, upholstered furniture, carpets and curtains.

These tiny creatures feed on the flakes of skin that people and pets shed daily and they thrive in warm and humid environments.

No matter how clean a home is, dust mites cannot be totally eliminated. However, the number of mites can be reduced by following the suggestions below.

Preventive Strategies

- Use a dehumidifier or air conditioner to maintain relative humidity at about 50% or below.

- Encase your mattress and pillows in dust-proof or allergen impermeable covers (available from specialty supply mail order companies, bedding and some department stores).

- Wash all bedding and blankets once a week in hot water (at least 130–140°F) to kill dust mites. Non-washable bedding can be frozen overnight to kill dust mites.

- Replace wool or feathered bedding with synthetic materials and traditional stuffed animals with washable ones.

- If possible, replace wall-to-wall carpets in bedrooms with bare floors (linoleum, tile or wood) and remove fabric curtains and upholstered furniture.

- Use a damp mop or rag to remove dust. Never use a dry cloth since this just stirs up mite allergens.

- Use a vacuum cleaner with either a double-layered microfilter bag or a HEPA filter to trap allergens that pass through a vacuum's exhaust.

- Wear a mask while vacuuming to avoid inhaling allergens, and stay out of the vacuumed area for 20 minutes to allow any dust and allergens to settle after vacuuming.

Section 24.4

Preventing and Eradicating Mold

Text in this section is excerpted from "You Can
Control Mold," Centers for Disease Control and
Preventation (CDC), February 10, 2015.

You Can Control Mold!

Mold can cause many health effects. For some people, mold can
cause a stuffy nose, sore throat, coughing or wheezing, burning eyes,
or skin rash. People with asthma or who are allergic to mold may have
severe reactions. Immune-compromised people and people with chronic
lung disease may get infections in their lungs from mold.

There is always some mold around. Molds have been on the Earth for
millions of years. Mold can get in your home through open doors, windows, vents, and heating and air conditioning systems. Mold in the air
outside can be brought indoors on clothing, shoes, bags, and even pets.

Mold will grow where there is moisture, such as around leaks in
roofs, windows, or pipes, or where there has been a flood. Mold grows
on paper, cardboard, ceiling tiles, and wood. Mold can also grow in dust,
paints, wallpaper, insulation, drywall, carpet, fabric, and upholstery.

If You Have Mold in Your Home

Mold can look like spots. It can be many different colors, and it can
smell musty. If you see or smell mold, you should remove it. You do
not need to know the type of mold.

If mold is growing in your home, you need to clean up the mold and
fix the moisture problem. Mold can be removed from hard surfaces with
household products, soap and water, or a bleach solution of no more
than 1 cup of household laundry bleach in 1 gallon of water.

If You Use Bleach to Clean Up Mold

- Never mix bleach with ammonia or other household cleaners.
  Mixing bleach with ammonia or other cleaning products will

produce a poisonous gas. Always follow the manufacturer's instructions when you use bleach or any other cleaning product.

- Open windows and doors to provide fresh air.

- Wear waterproof gloves and eye protection.

To Prevent Mold Growth in Your Home

- Keep humidity levels in your home as low as you can—no higher than 50%—all day long. An air conditioner or dehumidifier will help you keep the level low. You can buy a meter to check your home's humidity at a home improvement store. Humidity levels change over the course of a day so you will need to check the humidity levels more than once a day.

- Be sure the air in your home flows freely. Use exhaust fans that vent outside your home in the kitchen and bathroom. Make sure your clothes dryer vents outside your home.

- Fix any leaks in your home's roof, walls, or plumbing so mold does not have moisture to grow.

- Clean up and dry out your home fully and quickly (within 24–48 hours) after a flood.

- Add mold inhibitors to paints before painting. You can buy mold inhibitors at paint and home improvement stores.

- Clean bathrooms with mold-killing products.

- Remove or replace carpets and upholstery that have been soaked and cannot be dried right away. Think about not using carpet in places like bathrooms or basements that may have a lot of moisture.

Section 24.5

Nitrogen Dioxide and Asthma Trigger

Text in this section is excerpted from "Asthma
Triggers: Gain Control," U.S. Environmental Protection
Agency (EPA), October 26, 2015.

Dealing with Nitrogen Dioxide

Nitrogen dioxide (NO_2) is an odorless gas that can irritate your eyes, nose and throat and cause shortness of breath. NO_2 can come from appliances inside your home that burn fuels such as gas, kerosene and wood. NO_2 forms quickly from emissions from cars, trucks and buses, power plants and off-road equipment. Smoke from your stove or fireplace can trigger asthma.In people with asthma, exposure to low levels of NO_2 may cause increased bronchial reactivity and make young children more susceptible to respiratory infections. Long-term exposure to high levels of NO_2 can lead to chronic bronchitis. Studies show a connection between breathing elevated short-term NO_2 concentrations, and increased visits to emergency departments and hospital admissions for respiratory issues, especially asthma.

Actions You Can Take

If possible, use fuel-burning appliances that are vented to the outside. Always follow the manufacturer's instructions on how to use these appliances.

- Gas cooking stoves: If you have an exhaust fan in the kitchen, use it when you cook. Never use the stove to keep you warm or heat your house.

- Unvented kerosene or gas space heaters: Use the proper fuel and keep the heater adjusted the right way. Open a window slightly or use an exhaust fan when you are using the heater.

Section 24.6

Managing Pets When You Have Asthma

Text in this section is excerpted from "Asthma
Triggers: Gain Control," U.S. Environmental Protection
Agency (EPA), October 26, 2015.

About Pets and Asthma

Proteins in your pet's skin flakes, urine, feces, saliva and hair can trigger asthma. Dogs, cats, rodents (including hamsters and guinea pigs) and other warm-blooded mammals can trigger asthma in individuals with an allergy to animal dander.

The most effective method to control animal allergens in the home is to not allow animals in the home. If you remove an animal from the home, it is important to thoroughly clean the floors, walls, carpets and upholstered furniture.

Some individuals may find isolation measures to be sufficiently effective. Isolation measures that have been suggested include keeping pets out of the sleeping areas, keeping pets away from upholstered furniture, carpets and stuffed toys, keeping the pet outdoors as much as possible and isolating sensitive individuals from the pet as much as possible.

Actions You Can Take

- Find another home for your cat or dog.

- Keep pets outside if possible.

- If you have to have a pet inside, keep it out of the bedroom of the person with asthma.

- Keep pets off of your furniture.

- Vacuum carpets and furniture when the person with asthma is not around.

Section 24.7

Dealing with Wood Smoke

Text in this section is excerpted from "Asthma Triggers:
Gain Control," U.S. Environmental Protection Agency (EPA),
October 26, 2015; and text from "Wood Smoke and Your Health,"
U.S. Environmental Protection Agency (EPA), October 19, 2015.

What is Wood Smoke?

Smoke forms when wood or other organic matter burns. The smoke from wood burning is made up of a complex mixture of gases and fine particles (also called particle pollution, particulate matter, or PM). These microscopic particles can get into your eyes and respiratory system, where they can cause health problems such as burning eyes, runny nose, and illnesses such as bronchitis. In addition to particle pollution, wood smoke contains several toxic harmful air pollutants including: benzene, formaldhyde, acrolein and polycyclic aromatic hydrocarbons (PAHs).

About Wood Smoke and Asthma

Smoke from wood-burning stoves and fireplaces contain a mixture of harmful gases and small particles. Breathing these small particles can cause asthma attacks and severe bronchitis, aggravate heart and lung disease and may increase the likelihood of respiratory illnesses. If you're using a wood stove or fireplace and smell smoke in your home, it probably isn't working as it should.

Health Effects of Wood Smoke

Smoke may smell good, but it's not good for you. Both short- and long-term exposures to particle pollution from wood smoke have been linked to a variety of health effects.

Short-term exposures to particles (hours or days) can aggravate lung disease, causing asthma attacks and acute bronchitis, and may also increase susceptibility to respiratory infections. Long-term exposures (months or years) have been associated with problems such as reduced lung function and the development of chronic bronchitis—and even premature death. Some studies also suggest that long-term PM 2.5 exposures may be linked to cancer and to harmful developmental and reproductive effects, such as infant mortality and low birth weight.

Who Is at Risk from Wood Smoke?

Wood smoke can affect everyone, but children, teenagers, older adults, people with lung disease, including asthma and COPD or people with heart diseases are the most vulnerable. Research indicates that obesity or diabetes may also increase risk. New or expectant mothers may also want to take precautions to protect the health of their babies, because some studies indicate they may be at increased risk.

It's important to limit your exposure to smoke—especially if you are more susceptible than others:

- If you have heart or lung disease, such as congestive heart failure, angina, chronic obstructive pulmonary disease, emphysema or asthma, you may experience health effects earlier and at lower smoke levels than healthy people.

- Older adults are more likely to be affected by smoke, possibly because they are more likely to have chronic heart or lung diseases than younger people.

- Children also are more susceptible to smoke for several reasons: their respiratory systems are still developing; they breathe more air (and air pollution) per pound of body weight than adults; and they're more likely to be active outdoors.

Environmental Effects of Wood Smoke

The particles in wood smoke can reduce visibility (haze) and create environmental and aesthetic damage in our communities and scenic areas – like national parks.

Actions You Can Take

- To help reduce smoke, make sure to burn dry wood that has been split, stacked, covered and stored for at least 6 months.

- Have your stove and chimney inspected every year by a certified professional to make sure there are no gaps, cracks, unwanted drafts or to remove dangerous creosote build-up.

- If possible, replace your old wood stove with a new, cleaner heating appliance. Newer wood stoves are at least 50% more efficient and pollute 70% less than older models.

- This can help make your home healthier and safer and help cut fuel costs.

Section 24.8

What You Need to Know about Air Filters

Text in this section is excerpted from "Indoor Air Quality (IAQ),"
U.S. Environmental Protection Agency (EPA), October 15, 2015.

Air Filters—Available Evidence of Their Usefulness

Whether installed in the ducts of HVAC systems or used in portable air cleaners, most air filters have a good efficiency rating for removing larger particles when they remain airborne. These particles include dust, pollen, some molds, animal dander, and those that contain dust mite and cockroach body parts and droppings. But because these particles settle rather rapidly from the air, air filters are somewhat ineffective in removing them from indoor areas. And although human activities such as walking and vacuuming, or the high velocity air exiting supply vents, can re-suspend particles, most of the larger particles will resettle before they enter the HVAC system or portable air cleaner and are removed by a particle air filter.

Large particles settle from the air rapidly; therefore, air filters are somewhat ineffective in their removal.

The appropriate type of particle removal air filter can be chosen by looking at its MERV rating in removing airborne particles from the airstream that passes through it. MERV ratings can also be used to compare air filters made by different manufacturers.

Flat or panel air filters with a MERV of 1 to 4 have low efficiency on smaller airborne particles, but reasonable efficiency on large particles when they remain airborne. These filters have low airflow resistance and are relatively inexpensive. Typically < to 1 inch thick, they are commonly used in residential furnaces and air-conditioning systems, and they are often used as pre-filters for higher efficiency filters. For the most part, such filters are used to protect the HVAC equipment from the buildup of unwanted materials on fan motors, heat exchangers, and other surfaces.

Pleated or extended surface filters with a MERV of 5 to 13 have higher efficiency ratings than panel filters. These medium-efficiency filters are reasonably efficient at removing small-to-large airborne particles. The airflow resistance of these filters does not necessarily increase as the MERV increases. Higher efficiency filters with a MERV of 14 to 16 have a higher average resistance to airflow than medium-efficiency filters. Higher efficiency pleated filters, sometimes inaccurately called "high efficiency," "HEPA," or "HEPA-type" filters, are similar in appearance to true HEPA filters, which have MERV values of 17 to 20, but use less efficient filter media.

The depth of these pleated or extended surface filters may vary from approximately 1 to 6 inches for medium-efficiency models and 6 to 12 inches for higher efficiency filters. As the depth and pleating increases, so does the area of the filtration medium, helping to offset the increase in resistance to airflow across the filter. Because of their increased surface area, these filters often have an extended life. The operating resistance of a fully dust-loaded filter must be considered in the design, because it is the maximum resistance against which the fan operates. Generally, dust loading results in increased filtration efficiency along with an increase in pressure drop. Pressure drop in media-type filters is greater than that in electronic-type cleaners and slowly increases over the filters' useful life. Some residential HVAC systems may not have enough fan or motor capacity to accommodate higher efficiency filters. Therefore, the HVAC manufacturer's information should be checked prior to upgrading filters to determine whether it is feasible to use more efficient filters.

Filters that have a MERV between 7 and 13 are likely to be nearly as effective as true HEPA filters.

True HEPA filters with a MERV between 17 and 19 are defined by the IEST test method as having a minimum efficiency between 99.97 percent and 99.999 percent in removing 0.3 μm particles. A MERV of 20 is rated for 0.1 to 0.2 μm particles. HEPA filters have higher efficiencies for removing both larger and smaller airborne particles. True HEPA filters normally are not installed in residential HVAC systems; installing a HEPA filter in an existing HVAC system would probably require professional modification of the system. A typical residential air-handling unit and the associated ductwork would not be able to accommodate such filters because of their size and increased airflow resistance. Specially built high performance homes may occasionally be equipped with true HEPA filters installed in a properly designed HVAC system.

Some air filters may be effective at reducing tobacco smoke particles, but they will not remove gaseous pollutants from tobacco smoke. While some gas-phase filters may remove specific gaseous pollutants from the complex mixture of chemical compounds in tobacco smoke, none is expected to remove all unwanted gaseous combustion products. Odorous and toxic organic gases may also evaporate from liquid tobacco smoke particles trapped by the air filter12.

Manufacturers market HEPA filters to allergy and asthma patients. Experimental data and theoretical predictions indicate that medium-efficiency air filters, MERV between 7 and 13, are likely to be almost as effective as true HEPA filters in reducing the concentrations of most indoor particles linked to health effects.17Available data indicate that even for very small particles, HEPA filters are not necessarily the preferred option. For these small particles, relatively large decreases in indoor concentrations (around 80 percent) are attainable with medium filter efficiency (such as a MERV of 13).

Increasing filter efficiency above a MERV of 13 results in only modest predicted decreases in indoor concentrations of these particles. Predicted reductions in indoor concentrations of cat and dust mite allergens carried on small particles vary from 20 percent with a MERV 7 filter to 60 percent using a HEPA filter. Increasing filter efficiency above a MERV of 11 does not significantly reduce predicted indoor concentrations of animal dander. Medium-efficiency air filters are generally less expensive than HEPA filters and allow quieter HVAC fan operation and higher airflow rates than HEPA filters because they have less airflow resistance. Pleated filters 1 to 2 inches thick that have a MERV of 12 are available for use in homes and may often be installed without modifying residential HVAC systems; however, manufacturer's information should be checked prior to installation.

Electrostatic precipitators remove and collect small airborne particles and have an initial ASHRAE dust spot efficiency of up to 98 percent at low airflow velocity. This efficiency will be highest for clean electronic air cleaners. Electronic air cleaners exhibit high initial efficiencies in cleaning air, largely because of their ability to remove fine particles. Their efficiency decreases as the collecting plates become loaded with particles, or as airflow velocity increases or becomes less uniform.

Chapter 25

Managing Outdoor Asthma Triggers

Chapter Contents

Section 25.1

What Are the Health Effects of Outdoor Air Pollution?

Text in this section is excerpted from "Our Nation's Air," U.S.
Environmental Protection Agency (EPA), February 2012.
Reviewed December 2015.

Health and Environmental Impacts

Air pollution can affect our health in many ways. Numerous scientific studies have linked air pollution to a variety of health problems including: (1) aggravation of respiratory and cardiovascular disease; (2) decreased lung function; (3) increased frequency and severity of respiratory symptoms such as difficulty in breathing and coughing; (4) increased susceptibility to respiratory infections; (5) effects on the nervous system, including the brain, such as IQ loss and impacts on learning, memory, and behavior; (6) cancer; and (7) premature death. Some sensitive individuals appear to be at greater risk for air pollution-related health effects, for example, those with pre-existing heart and lung diseases (e.g., heart failure/ischemic heart disease, asthma, emphysema, and chronic bronchitis), diabetics, older adults, and children.

Air pollution also damages our environment. For example, ozone can damage vegetation, adversely impacting the growth of plants and trees. These impacts can reduce the ability of plants to uptake carbon dioxide (CO_2) from the atmosphere and indirectly affect entire ecosystems.

Table 25.1. Sources and Health Effects of Air Pollution

Pollutant	Sources	Health Effects
Ozone (O_3)	Secondary pollutant typically formed by chemical reaction of volatile organic compounds (VOCs) and NOx in the presence of sunlight.	Decreases lung function (FEV1) and causes respiratory symptoms, such as coughing and shortness of breath; aggravates asthma and other lung diseases leading to increased medication use, hospital admissions, emergency department (ED) visits, and premature mortality.
Particulate Matter (PM)	Emitted or formed through chemical reactions; fuel combustion (e.g., burning coal, wood, diesel); industrial processes; agriculture (plowing, field burning); unpaved roads, spores and pollen.	Short-term exposures can aggravate heart or lung diseases leading to respiratory symptoms, increased medication use, hospital admissions, ED visits, and premature mortality; long-term exposures can lead to the development of heart or lung disease and premature mortality.
Lead	Smelters (metal refineries) and other metal industries; combustion of leaded gasoline in piston engine aircraft; waste incinerators; and battery manufacturing.	Damages the developing nervous system, resulting in IQ loss and impacts on learning, memory, and behavior in children. Cardiovascular and renal effects in adults and early effects related to anemia.

Table 25.1. Sources and Health Effects of Air Pollution

Pollutant	Sources	Health Effects
Oxides of Nitrogen (NOx)	Fuel combustion (e.g., electric utilities, industrial boilers, and vehicles), wood burning, and gas stove.	Aggravate lung diseases leading to respiratory symptoms, hospital admissions, and ED visits; increased susceptibility to respiratory infection.
CarbonMonoxide(CO)	Fuel combustion (e.g., electric utilities, industrial boilers, and vehicles), wood burning, and coal burning.	Aggravate lung diseases leading to respiratory symptoms, hospital admissions, and ED visits; increased susceptibility to respiratory infection.
SulfurDioxide(SO_2)	Fuel combustion (especially high-sulfur coal); electric utilities and industrial processes; and natural sources such as volcanoes.	Aggravates asthma and increased respiratory symptoms. Contributes to particle formation with associated health effects.

Section 25.2

Dealing with Air Pollution

Text in this section is excerpted from "Dealing with Air Pollution,"
U.S. Environmental Protection Agency (EPA), August 2014.

You can take steps to help protect your health from air pollution

- Get to know how sensitive you are to air pollution.

- Notice your asthma symptoms when you are physically active. Do they happen more often when the air is more polluted? If so, you may be sensitive to air pollution.

- Also notice any asthma symptoms that begin up to a day after you have been outdoors in polluted air. Air pollution can make you more sensitive to asthma triggers, like mold and dust mites. If you are more sensitive than usual to indoor asthma triggers, it could be due to air pollution outdoors.

Know when and where air pollution may be bad.

- Ozone is often worst on hot summer days, especially in the afternoons and early evenings.

- Particle pollution can be bad any time of year, even in winter. It can be especially bad when the weather is calm, allowing air pollution to build up. Particle levels can also be high:

  - Near busy roads, during rush hour, and around factories.

  - When there is smoke in the air from wood stoves, fireplaces, or burning vegetation.

Plan activities when and where pollution levels are lower. Regular exercise is important for staying healthy, especially for people with asthma. By adjusting when and where you exercise, you can lead a healthy lifestyle and help reduce your asthma symptoms when the air is polluted. In summer, plan your most vigorous activities for the morning. Try to exercise away from busy roads or industrial areas. On hot, smoggy days when ozone levels are high, think about exercising indoors.

Change your activity level. When the air is polluted, try to take it easier if you are active outdoors. This will reduce how much pollution you breathe. Even if you can't change your schedule, you might be able to change your activity so it is less intense. For example, go for a walk instead of a jog. Or, spend less time on the activity. For example, jog for 20 minutes instead of 30.

Listen to your body. If you get asthma symptoms when the air is polluted, stop your activity. Find another, less intense activity

Keep your quick-relief medicine on hand when you're active outdoors. That way, if you do have symptoms, you'll be prepared. This is especially important if you're starting a new activity that is more intense than you are used to.

Consult your health care provider. If you have asthma symptoms when the air is polluted, talk with your health care provider.

- If you will be exercising more than usual, discuss this with your health care provider. Ask whether you should use medicine before you start outdoor activities.

- If you have symptoms during a certain type of activity, ask your health care provider if you should follow an asthma action plan.

Get up-to-date information about your local air quality:

Sometimes you can tell that the air is polluted—for example, on a smoggy or hazy day. But often you can't. In many areas, you can find air quality forecasts and reports on local TV or radio. These reports use the Air Quality Index, or AQI, a simple color scale, to tell you how clean or polluted the air is. You can also find these reports on the Internet at: www.epa.gov/airnow. You can use the AQI to plan your activities each day to help reduce your asthma symptoms.

Section 25.3

Pollen and Asthma

Text in this section is excerpted from "Pollen and Asthma," National Institute of Allergy and Infectious Diseases (NIAID), April 22, 2015.

Pollen

Each spring, summer, and fall, plants release tiny pollen grains to fertilize other plants of the same species.

People with allergic rhinitis or asthma aggravated by pollen have symptoms only for the period or season when the pollen grains to which they are allergic are in the air. For example, in most parts of the United States, grass pollen is present during the spring. Allergic rhinitis caused by pollen, also called "seasonal allergic rhinitis," affects approximately 7 percent of adults and 9 percent of children in the United States. However, not all seasonal symptoms are due to pollen.

Rhinovirus, the cause of the common cold, causes runny noses and triggers asthma attacks in the fall and spring. It is not always easy to figure out whether allergy or a common cold is the cause of these symptoms, although some clues can help tell the two apart. For example, a fever suggests a cold rather than an allergy, and symptoms lasting more than two weeks suggest allergies rather than a cold.

Most of the pollens that generate allergic reactions come from trees, weeds, and grasses. These plants make small, light, and dry pollen grains that are carried by wind. Among North American plants, grasses are the most common cause of allergy. Ragweed is a main culprit among the weeds, but other major sources of weed pollen include sagebrush, pigweed, lamb's quarters, and tumbleweed. Certain species of trees, including birch, cedar, and oak, also produce highly allergenic pollen. Plants that are pollinated with the help of insects, such as roses and ornamental flowering trees like cherry and pear trees, usually do not cause allergic rhinitis or asthma.

A pollen count, often reported by local weather broadcasts or allergy websites, is a measure of how much pollen is in the air. Pollen counts tend to be highest early in the morning on warm, dry, breezy days and lowest during chilly, wet periods. Although pollen counts reflect the past 24 hours, they are useful as a general guide for when it may be wise to stay indoors with windows closed to avoid contact with a certain pollen.

Section 25.4

Pollens and Preventive Strategies

Text in this section is excerpted from "Avoidance Strategies for
Common Pollens (Pollens and Preventive Strategies)," National
Institute of Environmental Health Sciences (NIEHS), April 24, 2015.

Ragweed Pollen

Ragweed and other weeds such as curly dock, lambs quarters, pigweed, plantain, sheep sorrel and sagebrush are some of the most pro-
lific producers of pollen allergens.

Although the ragweed pollen season runs from August to November,
ragweed pollen levels usually peak in mid-September in many areas
in the country.

In addition, pollen counts are highest between 5:00 – 10:00 A.M.
and on dry, hot and windy days.

Preventive Strategies

- Avoid the outdoors between 5:00 – 10:00 A.M. Save outside
  activities for late afternoon or after a heavy rain, when pollen
  levels are lower.

- Keep windows in your home and car closed to lower exposure to
  pollen. To keep cool, use air conditioners and avoid using window and attic fans.

- Be aware that pollen can also be transported indoors on people
  and pets.

- Dry your clothes in an automatic dryer rather than hanging
  them outside. Otherwise pollen can collect on clothing and be
  carried indoors.

Grass Pollen

As with tree pollen, grass pollen is regional as well as seasonal. In
addition, grass pollen levels can be affected by temperature, time of
day and rain.

Of the 1,200 species of grass that grow in North America, only a small percentage of these cause allergies. The most common grasses that can cause allergies are:

- Bermuda grass
- Johnson grass
- Kentucky bluegrass
- Orchard grass
- Sweet vernal grass
- Timothy grass

Preventive Strategies

- If you have a grass lawn, have someone else do the mowing. If you must mow the lawn yourself, wear a mask.
- Keep grass cut short.
- Choose ground covers that don't produce much pollen, such as Irish moss, bunch, and dichondra.
- Avoid the outdoors between 5:00–10:00 A.M. Save outside activities for late afternoon or after a heavy rain, when pollen levels are lower.
- Keep windows in your home and car closed to lower exposure to pollen. To keep cool, use air conditioners and avoid using window and attic fans.
- Be aware that pollen can also be transported indoors on people and pets.
- Dry your clothes in an automatic dryer rather than hanging them outside. Otherwise pollen can collect on clothing and be carried indoors.

Tree Pollen

Trees can aggravate your allergy whether or not they are on your property, since trees release large amounts of pollen that can be distributed miles away from the original source.

Trees are the earliest pollen producers, releasing their pollen as early as January in the Southern states and as late as May or June in the Northern states.

Most allergies are specific to one type of tree such as:

- catalpa
- elm
- hickory
- olive
- pecan
- sycamore
- walnut

or to the male cultivar of certain trees. The female of these species are totally pollen-free:

- ash
- box elder
- cottonwood
- date palm
- maple (red)
- maple (silver)
- Phoenix palm
- poplar
- willow

Some people, though, do show cross-reactivity among trees in the alder, beech, birch and oak family, and the juniper and cedar family.

Preventive Strategies

- If you buy trees for your yard, look for species that do not aggravate allergies such as crape myrtle, dogwood, fig, fir, palm, pear, plum, redbud and redwood trees or the female cultivars of ash, box elder, cottonwood, maple, palm, poplar or willow trees.

- Avoid the outdoors between 5:00–10:00 A.M. Save outside activities for late afternoon or after a heavy rain, when pollen levels are lower.

- Keep windows in your home and car closed to lower exposure to pollen. To keep cool, use air conditioners and avoid using window and attic fans.

- Be aware that pollen can also be transported indoors on people and pets.

- Dry your clothes in an automatic dryer rather than hanging them outside. Otherwise pollen can collect on clothing and be carried indoors.

Chapter 26

Managing Other Types of Asthma Triggers

Chapter Contents

Section 26.1

Stress

"Managing Asthma Triggers—Stress," © 2016 Omnigraphics, Inc.
Reviewed January 2016.

Managing Asthma Triggers—Stress

Many people find that their asthma symptoms worsen when they are under stress. Countless everyday situations can contribute to stress, from work deadlines and money problems to school exams and peer pressure. Major life changes like getting married, starting a family, changing jobs, moving, or experiencing a death in the family can be tremendously stressful.

For people with asthma, stress can trigger symptoms such as wheezing, coughing, and shortness of breath. As these symptoms grow worse, they can make people feel worried, anxious, frightened, and even panicked—thus increasing their stress levels further. This cyclical relationship makes it especially important for people with asthma to learn how to manage stress.

Stress and Asthma

Stress impacts the body in many ways, and some of these physical changes can trigger asthma. One common reaction to stressful situations is the "fight or flight" response. The body releases a surge of hormones that cause an increase in heart rate, muscle tension, and breathing rate. Although these changes prepare the body to face danger, they also increase the risk of asthma symptoms.

Some people react to stress in unhealthy ways, by drinking alcohol, smoking cigarettes, or overeating. Similarly, stress and anxiety can cause people to lose sleep, forego exercise, and stop taking their medication as directed. All of these behaviors can trigger asthma symptoms. Even some asthma treatments—such as oral steroids (like prednisone) —can affect mood and increase stress and anxiety.

Managing Stress

While it is impossible to avoid stress entirely, there are a number of proven methods that can help people manage it.

- Recognize and Avoid Sources of Stress: Identifying major sources of stress—such as relationship issues, money problems, or work situations—is the first step in managing stress-related asthma. When people recognize the stressors that have the greatest impact on their lives, they can often be proactive, plan ahead, and cope with problems in a calmer manner. If the underlying causes of stress are hard to pinpoint, or if a certain situation seems overwhelming, it may be helpful to consult with a mental health professional.

- Make a Plan and Get Organized: A large part of stress comes from feeling unprepared and worrying about what might happen. To regain a feeling of control over stressful situations, many people apply organization and time-management skills. It may be helpful to make a list of tasks that must be accomplished and prioritize them, so that the most important things can be done first. Checking tasks off the list can help alleviate stress.

- Learn to Delegate: Many people feel stress because they try to handle too many responsibilities on their own. Delegating some tasks to other qualified people can help free up time and reduce stress. It is important to provide clear instructions and deadlines, yet also give others room to perform tasks in their own way, rather than looking over their shoulder and micromanaging.

- Seek Support When Needed: Acknowledging feelings of stress and seeking social support from family and friends is a valuable tool in managing tough situations. In addition to offering encouragement and emotional support, a trusted friend or relative can often provide a new perspective on a problem. Many people find that talking things over helps them feel better.

- Maintain Healthy Habits: To counteract the physical effects of stress, it is important to maintain healthy habits. Eating a healthy, well-balanced diet becomes even more vital during stressful times. It is particularly helpful to avoid eating processed foods that can cause extreme fluctuations in blood sugar levels, as well as to avoid drinking alcohol or smoking in response to stress. Daily exercise offers proven benefits in reducing stress, improving mood, and increasing overall health. Finally, getting plenty of sleep can help renew the physical energy and mental resources needed for coping with stress.

- Make Time to Relax and Have Fun: A wide variety of relaxation techniques are available to help people deal with stress, including yoga, meditation, deep breathing exercises, progressive muscle relaxation, and guided imagery. It is also important to step back from the stresses of daily life periodically and reconnect with things that provide enjoyment and fulfillment. Taking a break and doing a fun activity or hobby can restore the positive energy needed to deal with stress.

References

1. "Stress and Anxiety." Asthma UK, March 2015.

2. "Stress and Asthma." WebMD Asthma Health Center, 2014.

Section 26.2

Weather

"Managing Asthma Triggers—Weather," © 2016 Omnigraphics, Inc.
Reviewed January 2016.

Managing Asthma Triggers—Weather

Numerous studies have indicated that the weather can trigger asthma. Although the connection is not fully understood, it is clear that many people experience a worsening of asthma symptoms in certain types of weather conditions or at certain times of year. Some of the factors that may influence asthma symptoms include temperature, humidity, barometric pressure, wind, seasonal allergens, air pollution, and viruses. Understanding seasonal and weather-related trends enables people to take steps to limit their exposure to asthma triggers and reduce their risk of asthma attacks.

Seasonal Impacts on Asthma

Fall

Autumn is historically a peak season for asthma episodes. In fact, some studies have found that more than twice as many asthma-related hospitalizations occur in October than during the summer months. Allergens like ragweed can cause problems for people with asthma in the late summer and fall. Cooler weather may also be a factor in the increase of asthma-related emergency-room visits, although the same seasonal pattern can be found in tropical locations.

Based on this evidence, researchers believe that the main culprit in the increase in asthma attacks in the fall is that it coincides with the start of the school year. As children return to school, they come into increased contact with cold and flu viruses, which they soon spread to their families. Respiratory illnesses increase the risk of asthma symptoms by aggravating the chronic lung inflammation that is characteristic of asthma. In addition, respiratory illnesses tend to last longer and be more severe for people with asthma. Asthma also makes people more vulnerable to pneumonia and other complications from the flu.

Winter

Winter weather can be difficult for people with asthma. Breathing cold, dry air can irritate sensitive airways and cause asthma symptoms. People with asthma who exercise outdoors in the winter are particularly prone to problems because they inhale larger quantities of cold air.

Indoor conditions can also be troublesome during the winter months. With windows closed and homes sealed, indoor air pollutants and allergens can reach high levels. Using furnaces and humidifiers creates conditions that are favorable to mold, dust mites, and other common allergens that can aggravate asthma. Smoke from fireplaces and woodstoves is another lung irritant that is found mainly in the winter.

Spring

Spring is the season when trees, grasses, and flowers release pollen into the air. Many people have an allergic reaction upon inhaling these tiny particles, which can be carried by wind over hundreds of miles. In people with asthma, breathing air with a high concentration of pollen can exacerbate inflammation in the airways and cause asthma attacks. The unpredictable nature of spring weather is another potential asthma trigger. Rapid increases in temperature and humidity have been associated with an increase in asthma-related hospitalizations in some studies.

Summer

Although summer is generally considered a good season for people with asthma, hot, humid weather can trigger asthma episodes in some people. In addition, warm, wet air creates favorable conditions for the growth of mold spores. In urban areas, air quality tends to be poorer in the summer. Car exhaust and other sources of air pollution combine with heat and sunlight to create ground-level ozone, which is a powerful asthma trigger.

Some studies have found that thunderstorms are associated with a 15 percent increase in asthma-related emergency-room visits. Sudden changes in barometric pressure may trigger asthma episodes in some people. In addition, the strong winds that often accompany summertime storms stir up fungal spores, nearly doubling the amount usually found in the air. Meanwhile, rain breaks up grains of pollen into tiny pieces that spread more easily.

Avoiding Weather-Related Triggers

Keeping a diary of asthma symptoms is a good way to determine if they are triggered by weather and seasonal conditions. Any weather triggers should be included in a written asthma action plan. Sometimes asthma medication can be adjusted seasonally to correlate with increases or decreases in weather-related triggers. The following suggestions can also help people avoid these triggers and minimize the risk of asthma attacks:

- Pay attention to weather forecasts. Many sources of weather-related news provide information about pollen and mold counts, ozone levels, extreme temperatures, high humidity, thunderstorms, and other conditions that can trigger asthma. Remain indoors as much as possible on days when these conditions are unfavorable.

- Get an annual flu shot to protect against respiratory viruses.

- To limit exposure to pollen, stay indoors in the morning when levels are highest. Also avoid raking leaves or mowing the lawn.

Close windows at night to keep allergens out, and dry clothes and sheets in a dryer rather than hanging them outdoors.

- Avoid going outdoors in urban areas on very hot days when air pollution and ozone levels are highest.

- In cold weather, cover the nose and mouth with a scarf to help warm and humidify inhaled air. While exercising outdoors in winter, consider wearing a mask containing a heat exchanger. Using an inhaler containing albuterol before going outdoors can also help minimize the effects of cold air on the lungs.

- Limit exposure to fireplaces and wood-burning stoves, and keep flues and ducts clean and well ventilated.

- Always keep a fast-acting rescue inhaler on hand in case unexpected weather-related triggers occur.

References

1. Hainer, Ray. "Why Asthma Symptoms Can Vary with the Weather." Health, October 29, 2009.

2. "Weather and Asthma." KidsHealth, 2014.

Chapter 27

Prevention Strategies for Asthma

Primary Prevention Strategies in Children

Avoid smoking and environmental tobacco smoke (ETS)

For children, studies indicate that in utero exposure to tobacco smoke products is an important predictor of wheezing within the first year of life. Exposure to ETS places children at increased risk for the development and exacerbation of asthma as well as

- Sinusitis,
- Otitis media,
- Bronchiolitis, and
- Diminished pulmonary function.

Both in utero and passive (environmental) tobacco smoke exposure adversely affect pulmonary function, and predispose to asthma symptoms and possibly bronchial hyper responsiveness in childhood. Exposure to tobacco smoke products in utero is a risk factor for wheezing

---

Text in this chapter is excerpted from "ATSDR Case Studies in Environmental Triggers of Asthma," Agency for Toxic Substances and Disease Registry (ATSDR), November 28, 2014.

in the first year of life. Children who have asthma and whose parents smoke have more frequent asthma attacks and more severe symptoms.

Avoid exposure to insect allergens.

House dust mite and cockroach allergens have a very close association between exposure and the sensitization of an individual.

Avoid exposure to molds.

Exposure to mold in homes as much as doubles the risk of asthma development in children.

Breast-feed infants.

A study demonstrated that exclusively breastfeeding for the first 4 months is associated with a statistically significant decrease in the risk of asthma and wheezing in children until the age of 6 years.

Primary Prevention in Adults

In adult-onset asthma, primary prevention relies mainly on smoking cessation and control of workplace exposures. Studies of factory workforces in the past decade have provided consistent evidence of exposure-response relationships for both sensitization (IgE production) and asthma. New-onset occupational asthma may be immunological or nonimmunological in origin. The immunologic variants are usually caused by high molecular-weight allergens such as grain dust and animal or fish protein. Symptoms may take months or years to develop.

A brief, high-level exposure to a strong irritant can precipitate nonimmunologic occupational asthma. Symptoms occur immediately or within a few hours of the exposure. Multiple lower level exposures to an irritant can also cause asthma. The worker should be removed from further exposure once the diagnosis of occupational asthma is established, whether immunologic or nonimmunologic in origin. Continued exposure to sensitizers or irritants following sensitization may cause persistent problems that can lead to permanent impairment. In addition, once sensitized, individuals may have a substantial response to extremely low levels of sensitizers or irritants. If the diagnosis is made in a timely fashion and steps are taken to stop exposure, most workers experience improvement. Prevention is the best therapeutic intervention.

Avoidance of exposure to occupational irritants and allergens is the mainstay of primary prevention. Especially notorious for producing occupational asthma are jobs that use

- Isocyanates,

- Enzymes, or

- Latex.

Prospective surveillance can detect the development of specific IgE antibody before the onset of allergic symptoms. This allows continuing interventions to reduce exposures and minimize or eliminate those associated with symptoms. Workers with IgE to specific allergens can continue to work in the industry symptom-free for their entire careers. This indicates that exposures needed to induce sensitization are different and probably lower than exposures needed to elicit allergic symptoms.

Secondary Prevention in Children and Adults

Patients can take a number of steps to reduce or avoid exposure to:

- Pollutants,

- Irritants, and

- Allergens.

that may trigger or exacerbate asthma episodes. The National Environmental Education and Training Foundation outlined possible preventive measures in Environmental Management of Pediatric Asthma: *Guidelines for Health Care Providers*. Summarized below are those environmental intervention guidelines. It is important to note that no single intervention will likely achieve sufficient benefits to be cost effective and that a comprehensive environmental intervention may be needed to improve asthmaassociated morbidity.

Dust Mites

No matter how clean the home is, dust mites cannot be eliminated. However, household interventions can decrease exposure to dust mites and possibly reduce asthma exacerbations. Cleaning with a high-efficiency particulate air (HEPA) filter vacuum is particularly effective in removing allergens and thus decreasing asthma symptoms.

Listed below are recommended steps to reduce dust mites in the home.

- Remove carpet from bedrooms.
- Use an air conditioner or dehumidifier to reduce household humidity.
- Remove upholstered furniture.
- Replace draperies with blinds or other wipeable window coverings.
- Encase pillow and mattress in allergen impermeable cover.
- Remove humidifiers.
- Replace wool or feathered bedding with synthetic materials that will withstand repeated hot water washing.
- Use a damp mop or rag to remove dust (a dry cloth just stirs up mite allergens).
- Vacuum regularly using a cleaner with a HEPA filter or a double-layered microfilter bag (try not to vacuum when the asthmatic is in the room).
- Wash and thoroughly dry stuffed toys weekly in hot water, or freeze them weekly.
- Wash bedding in hot water (at least 130°F) weekly.

Animal Allergens

Modifications to the home environment can significantly reduce animal allergens and the frequency of asthma episodes. The following steps can reduce exposure to animal allergens.

- Find a new home for indoor cats, dogs, and pet rodents that have caused allergy symptoms.
- Keep pets outside.
- Select low-dander pets in place of those with fur or feathers.

If those options are not possible, the following steps may help reduce exposure.

- Keep pets out of the bedroom.
- Enclose mattresses and pillows in zippered plastic cases.

- Remove carpets.

- Vacuum regularly using a cleaner with a HEPA filter or a double-layered microfilter bag (try not to vacuum when the asthmatic is in the room).

- Use a portable air cleaner with HEPA filter for the child's bedroom.

- Keep pets off furniture.

Cockroach Allergen

The first step in limiting cockroach allergens is to keep the house clean and in good shape. In general, use the least hazardous methods of roach control first.

Food

- Clean up all food items and crumbs.

- Limit spread of food around house, especially bedrooms.

- Restrict food consumption to the kitchen and dining room.

- Store food (including pet food) in closed containers.

Hygiene and maintenance

- Fix water leaks under sinks

- Mop the kitchen floor and clean countertops at least once a week.

- Check for and plug crevices outside your house that cockroaches may enter.

- Caulk or patch holes in walls, cupboards, and cabinets.

Pest management

- Use the integrated pest management (IPM) approach for least toxic extermination methods first.

- Use boric acid powder under stoves and other appliances.

- Use bait stations and gels.

- Use outdoor treatments as much as possible to prevent insects from entering your house.

- If those steps are unsuccessful, seek help from a professional, licensed exterminator rather than spraying chemicals yourself.

- Stay away from the house for several hours after pesticides are applied.

- Avoid using liquid sprays inside the house, especially near places children crawl, play, or sleep.

Mold and Mildew

Mold spores are allergens found indoors and outdoors. Outdoor molds are present year-round throughout the West (lower altitudes) and South, and in the North during the fall. Outdoor molds in the North generally peak in late summer. There is no definite seasonal pattern to molds that grow indoors. Moisture control is the key step in limiting indoor mold growth.

Tips to help keep exposure to mold spores as low as possible.

- Use air-conditioning to cool the house; evaporative coolers are not recommended.

- When first turning on home or car air-conditioners, leave the room or drive with the windows open for several minutes to allow mold spores to disperse.

- Use a dehumidifier or air-conditioner (nonevaporative or water-filled type) to maintain relative humidity below 50%.

- Do not use a humidifier.

- Check faucets, pipes, and ductwork and repair any that are leaking.

- Clean mold with chlorine solution diluted 1:10 with water.

- Do not install carpet and wallpaper in rooms prone to dampness.

- Leave a light on inside a closet that has mold in it to dry the air.

- Install and use exhaust fans in the kitchen, bathrooms, and damp areas.

- Vent bathrooms and clothes dryers to the outside.

- Remove decaying debris from the yard, roof, and gutters.

- Avoid raking leaves, mowing lawns, or working with peat, mulch, hay, or dead wood if you are allergic to mold spores.

Environmental Tobacco Smoke

Cigarette smoke contains many toxic chemicals and irritants. Approximately 42% of children 2 months to 11 years of age live in a home with at least one smoker. Children exposed to tobacco smoke have increased asthma exacerbations. Studies suggest that asthma symptoms may be less severe for asthmatic children if parents expose them to less cigarette smoke. Complete cessation of indoor smoking in the homes of children with asthma may be needed to achieve significant health improvement. The following are the most important preventive strategies to reduce exposure to environmental tobacco smoke.

- Keep your home and car smoke-free.

- If you smoke, do not smoke near children or other nonsmokers.

- Seek support to quit smoking; consider aids such as nicotine gum, patch, and medication from your doctor to help you in quitting.

- Change clothes after smoking while you are in the process of cutting down on the number of cigarettes.

- Choose smoke-free childcare and social settings.

- Seek smoke-free environments in restaurants, theaters, and hotel rooms.

Chapter 28

Preventing Asthma in Animal Handlers

Animal handlers should take steps to protect themselves from exposure to animals and animal products:

- Perform animal manipulations within ventilated hoods or safety cabinets when possible.

- Avoid wearing street clothes while working with animals.

- Leave work clothes at the workplace to avoid potential exposure problems for family members.

- Keep cages and animal areas clean.

- Reduce skin contact with animal products such as dander, serum, and urine by using gloves, lab coats, and approved particulate respirators with faceshields.

Employers of animal handlers should take steps to protect workers from exposure to animals and animal products:

- Modify ventilation and filtration systems:

- Increase the ventilation rate and humidity in the animal-housing areas.

- Ventilate animal-housing and -handling areas separately from the rest of the facility.

Text in this chapter is excerpted from "Preventing Asthma in Animal Handlers," Centers for Disease Control and Prevention (CDC), June 6, 2014.

- Direct airflow away from workers and toward the backs of the animal cages.

- Install ventilated animal cage racks or filter-top animal cages.

- Decrease animal density (number of animals per cubic meter of room volume).

- Keep cages and animal areas clean.

- Use absorbent pads for bedding. If these are not available, use corncob bedding instead of sawdust bedding.

- Use an animal species or sex that is known to be less allergenic than others.

- Provide protective equipment for animal handlersgloves, lab coats, and approved particulate respirators with faceshields.

- Provide training to educate workers about animal allergies and steps for risk reduction.

- Provide health monitoring and appropriate counseling and medical followup for workers who have become sensitized or have developed allergy symptoms.

Chapter 29

Dealing with Co-Existing Respiratory Conditions

Chapter Contents

Section 29.1

Chronic Obstructive Pulmonary Disease (COPD)

Text in this section is excerpted from "Chronic Obstructive
Pulmonary Disease (COPD)," U.S. Environmental Protection
Agency (EPA), October 26, 2015.

What Is COPD?

Chronic obstructive pulmonary disease, or COPD, is a progressive
lung disease in which the airways of the lungs become damaged, making it hard to breathe. You may also have heard COPD called other
names, like emphysema or chronic bronchitis.

In people who have COPD, the airways that carry air in and out of
the lungs are partially blocked, making it difficult to get air in and out.
COPD is a major cause of death and illness throughout the world. It
kills more than 120,000 Americans each year. That's one death every
4 minutes.

How COPD Affects Airways

The "airways" are the tubes that carry air in and out of the lungs
through the nose and mouth. The airways of the lungs branch out
like an upside-down tree. At the end of each branch are many small,
balloon-like air sacs. In healthy people, the airways and air sacs are
elastic (stretchy). When you breathe in, each air sac fills up with air,
like a small balloon, and when you breathe out, the balloon deflates
and the air goes out.

In people with COPD, the airways and air sacs lose their shape and
become floppy. Less air gets in and less air goes out of the airways
because

- The airways and air sacs lose their elasticity like an old rubber
  band.

- The walls between many of the air sacs are destroyed.

- The walls of the airways become thick and inflamed or swollen.

- Cells in the airways make more mucus or sputum than usual, which tends to clog the airways.

COPD Develops Slowly, Has No Cure

When COPD is severe, shortness of breath and other symptoms of COPD can get in the way of even the most basic tasks, such as doing light housework, taking a walk, even washing and dressing.

COPD develops slowly, and it may be many years before you notice symptoms like feeling short of breath. Most of the time, COPD is diagnosed in middle-aged or older people.

There is no cure for COPD. The damage to your airways and lungs cannot be reversed, but there are things you can do to control the disabling effects of the disease.

COPD is not contagious. You cannot catch it from someone else.

Causes

Smoking

Most cases of COPD develop over time, from breathing in fumes and other things that irritate the lungs. Some of the things that put you at risk for COPD include smoking, environmental exposure, and genetic factors.

Cigarette smoking is the most common cause of COPD in the United States (either current or former smokers). Pipe, cigar, and other types of tobacco smoking can also cause COPD, especially if the smoke is inhaled.

Environmental Exposure

COPD can also occur in people who have had long-term exposure to things that can irritate your lungs, like chemical fumes, or dust from the environment or workplace. Heavy or long-term exposure to secondhand smoke or other air pollutants may also contribute to COPD even if you have never smoked or had long-term exposure to harmful pollutants. Secondhand smoke is smoke in the air from other people smoking.

Genetic Factors

In a small number of people, COPD is caused by a genetic condition known as alpha-1 antitrypsin, or AAT, deficiency. People who have this condition have low levels of alpha-1 antitrypsin (AAT)—a protein made in the liver. Having a low level of the AAT protein can lead to lung damage and COPD if you're exposed to smoke or other lung irritants. If you have this condition and smoke, COPD can worsen very quickly. While very few people know if they have AAT deficiency, it is estimated that about 1 in every 1,600 people to about 1 in every 5,000 people have it. People with AAT deficiency can get COPD even if they have never smoked or had long-term exposure to harmful pollutants.

Asthma

Although uncommon, some people who have asthma can develop COPD. Asthma is a chronic (long-term) lung disease that inflames and narrows the airways. Treatment usually can reverse the inflammation and narrowing. However, if not, COPD can develop.

Section 29.2

Influenza

Text in this section is excerpted from "People with Asthma Are at High Risk of Severe Disease and Complications from Flu," Centers for Disease Control and Preventions (CDC), August 14, 2015.

Complications from Flu

Though people with asthma are not more likely to get the flu, influenza (flu) can be more serious for people with asthma, even if their asthma is mild or their symptoms are well-controlled by medication. This is because people with asthma have swollen and sensitive airways, and influenza can cause further inflammation of the airways and lungs. Influenza infection in the lungs can trigger asthma attacks and a worsening of asthma symptoms. It also can lead to pneumonia and other acute respiratory diseases. In fact, adults and children with asthma are more likely to develop pneumonia after getting sick with the flu than people who do not have asthma. Asthma is the most common medical condition among children hospitalized with the flu and one of the more common medical conditions among hospitalized adults. For information about underlying health conditions in reported flu hospitalizations, see the FluView Interactive application.

If You Have Asthma, You Need to Take Steps to Fight the Flu

Everyone with asthma who is six months and older should get a flu vaccine to protect against getting the flu.
Vaccination is the first and most important step in protecting against influenza. Even if you don't have a regular doctor or nurse, you can get a flu vaccine.

Flu vaccines are offered in many locations including doctors' offices, clinics, health departments, pharmacies, college health centers and increasingly by a number of employers and public schools.

Which flu vaccine should people with asthma get?

- Flu shots (made with inactivated (killed) flu virus) are approved for use in people 6 months and older regardless of whether or not they have asthma or other health conditions.

- The flu shot has a long established safety record in people with asthma.

- Nasal spray vaccine: The nasal spray vaccine is approved for use in people 2 through 49 years of age.

- Children 2 years through 4 years who have asthma or who have had a history of wheezing in the past 12 months should not get the nasal spray vaccine.

- People of any age with asthma might be at increased risk for wheezing after getting the nasal spray flu vaccine. This should be considered a precaution for the use of LAIV.

- Also, the safety of the nasal spray flu vaccine in people with lung disease and some other high risk conditions has not been established.

Pneumococcal infections are a serious complication of influenza infections and can cause death. Pneumococcal vaccines may be given at the same time as influenza vaccine.

Take everyday preventive actions to stop the spread of flu:

Stay home when you are sick, except to get medical care. Stay away from other people who are sick.

Cover your nose and mouth with a tissue when coughing or sneezing and throw the tissue away. If you do not have a tissue, cough or sneeze into your elbow or shoulder not your bare hands;

Wash your hands often with soap and water, especially after coughing or sneezing;

Avoid touching your eyes, nose, or mouth (germs are spread that way); and

Clean and disinfect frequently touched surfaces at home, work or school, especially when someone is ill.

Follow an updated, written Asthma Action Plan developed with your doctor.

Follow this plan for daily treatment to control asthma long-term and to handle worsening asthma, or attacks.

If your child has asthma, make sure that his or her up-to-date written Asthma Action Plan is on file at school or at the daycare center. Be sure that the plan and medication(s) are easy to get to when needed.

If you do get sick with flu symptoms, call your doctor and take flu antiviral drugs if your doctor recommends them.

Treatment should begin as soon as possible because antiviral drug treatment works best when started early (within 48 hours after symptoms start).

Antiviral drugs can make your flu illness milder and make you feel better faster. They may also prevent serious health problems that can result from flu illness.

Oseltamivir (Tamiflu®) is an antiviral drug that can be used to treat flu. To get oseltamivir (Tamiflu®), a doctor needs to write a prescription. This medicine fights against the flu by keeping flu viruses from making more viruses in your body.

People with asthma should not use zanamivir (Relenza®), a different antiviral drug, because there is a risk it may cause wheezing in people that already have asthma or other lung problems.

Section 29.3

Rhinitis

Text in this section is excerpted from "Pollen Allergy," National Institute of Allergy and Infectious Diseases (NIAID), July 2015.

Pollen is one of the most common triggers of seasonal allergies. Many people know pollen allergy as "hay fever," but health experts usually refer to it as "seasonal allergic rhinitis." Pollen allergy affects approximately 7 percent of adults and 9 percent of children in the United States. An allergic reaction is a specific response of the body's immune system to a normally harmless substance called an allergen. People who have allergies often are sensitive to more than one allergen. In addition to pollen, other airborne allergens that can cause allergic reactions include materials from house dust mites, animal dander, and cockroaches.

Pollen Overview

Each spring, summer, and fall, plants release tiny pollen grains to fertilize other plants of the same species. Most of the pollens that cause allergic reactions come from trees, weeds, and grasses. These plants make small, light, and dry pollen grains that are carried by the wind. Among North American plants, grasses are the most common cause of allergy. Ragweed is a main culprit among the weeds, but other major sources of weed pollen include sagebrush, pigweed, lamb's quarters, and tumbleweed.

Certain species of trees, including birch, cedar, and oak, also produce highly allergenic pollen. Plants that are pollinated with the help of insects, such as roses and ornamental flowering trees like cherry and pear trees, usually do not cause allergic rhinitis. People with pollen allergy only have symptoms for the period or season when the pollen grains to which they are allergic are in the air. For example, in most parts of the United States, grass pollen is present during the spring.

Medications

Certain over-the-counter and prescription medications may help reduce the severity of pollen allergy symptoms.

Antihistamines

Antihistamines, which are taken by mouth or as a nasal spray, can relieve sneezing and itching in the nose and eyes. They also reduce runny nose and, to a lesser extent, nasal stuffiness. Some older antihistamines can cause side effects such as drowsiness and loss of alertness and coordination. Effective, newer antihistamines cause fewer or no side effects.

Nasal Corticosteroids

Nasal corticosteroid sprays are anti-inflammatory medicines that help block allergic reactions. They are widely considered to be the most effective medication type for allergic rhinitis and can reduce all symptoms, including nasal congestion. Unlike corticosteroids taken by mouth or as an injection, nasal corticosteroids have few side effects. Combining a nasal antihistamine with a nasal corticosteroid appears to be more effective than using either of the sprays alone. However, it is not clear if taking an oral antihistamine with a nasal corticosteroid is helpful.

Decongestants

Oral and nasal decongestants help shrink the lining of the nasal passages, relieving nasal stuffiness. Decongestant nose drops and sprays are intended for short-term use. When used for more than a few days, these medicines may lead to even more congestion and swelling inside the nose. Doctors may recommend using decongestants along with an antihistamine because antihistamines do not have a strong decongestant effect.

Leukotriene Receptor

Antagonists Leukotriene receptor antagonists, such as the prescription drug montelukast, block the action of important chemical messengers other than histamine that are involved in allergic reactions.

Cromolyn Sodium

Cromolyn sodium is a nasal spray that blocks the release of chemicals that cause allergy symptoms, including histamine and leukotrienes. The drug causes few side effects but must be taken four times a day.

Many people with pollen allergy do not get complete relief from medications and may be candidates for immunotherapy. Immunotherapy is a long-term treatment that can help prevent or reduce the severity of allergic reactions and change the course of allergic disease by modifying the body's immune response to allergens.

Allergy Shots (Subcutaneous Immunotherapy)

Allergy shots, also known as subcutaneous immunotherapy (SCIT), have been used for more than 100 years and can provide long-lasting symptom relief. SCIT involves a series of shots containing small amounts of allergen into the fat under the skin. SCIT includes two phases: a buildup phase and a maintenance phase. During the buildup phase, doctors administer injections containing gradually increasing amounts of allergen once or twice per week. This phase generally lasts from 3 to 6 months, depending on how often the shots are given and the body's response. The aim is to reach a target dose that has been shown to be effective. Once the target dose is reached, the maintenance phase begins. Shots are given less frequently during the maintenance phase, typically every 2 to 4 weeks.

Some people begin experiencing a decrease in symptoms during the buildup phase, but others may not notice an improvement until the maintenance phase. Maintenance therapy generally lasts 3 to 5 years. The decision about how long to continue SCIT is based on how well it is working and how well a person tolerates the shots. Many people continue to experience benefits for several years after the shots are stopped. Side effects from SCIT are usually minor and may include swelling or redness at the injection site.However, there is a small risk of serious allergic reactions such as anaphylaxis, a potentially life-threatening reaction that can develop very rapidly. Because most severe reactions occur shortly after injection, it is recommended that patients remain under medical supervision for at least 30 minutes after receiving a shot.

Sublingual Immunotherapy

In 2014, the U.S. Food and Drug Administration (FDA) approved three types of under-the-tongue tablets to treat allergies to grass and ragweed. The treatments, called sublingual immunotherapy (SLIT), offer people with these allergies a potential alternative to allergy shots. People taking SLIT place a tablet containing allergen under the tongue for 1 to 2 minutes and then swallow it. SLIT tablets are taken daily before and during grass or ragweed season.

Studies show that there are fewer allergic reactions to SLIT compared with SCIT. After the first SLIT dose is given at the doctor's office, patients can take subsequent doses at home. Side effects of SLIT are usually minor and may include itching of the mouth, lips, or throat. Although severe allergic reactions to SLIT are extremely rare, because SLIT treatment takes place at home, doctors usually prescribe an epinephrine auto-injector (EpiPen) for use in the event of a serious reaction.

Section 29.4

Sinusitis

Text in this section is excerpted from "Sinusitis," National Institute of Allergy and Infectious Diseases (NIAID), June 2015.

What Is Sinisitis (Sinus Infections)?

Sinusitis is an inflammation of the membranes lining the paranasal sinuses—small air-filled spaces located within the skull or bones of the head surrounding the nose. Sinusitis can be caused by an infection or other health problem. Symptoms include facial pain and nasal discharge, or "runny nose." Nearly 30 million adults in the United States are diagnosed with sinusitis each year, according to the Centers for Disease Control and Prevention (CDC).

The paranasal sinuses comprise four pairs of air-filled spaces:

- Frontal sinuses—over the eyes in the brow area
- Ethmoid sinuses—just behind the bridge of the nose, between the eyes
- Maxillary sinuses—inside each cheekbone
- Sphenoid sinuses—behind the ethmoids in the upper region of the nose and behind the eyes

There are two basic types of sinusitis:

- Acute, which lasts up to 4 weeks
- Chronic, which lasts more than 12 weeks and can continue for months or years

What Are the Symptoms of Sinusitis?

Most people with sinusitis have facial pain or tenderness in several places, and their symptoms usually do not clearly indicate which sinuses are inflamed. The pain of a sinus attack arises because trapped air and mucus put pressure on the membranes of the sinuses and the bony wall behind them. Also, when a swollen membrane at the opening of a paranasal sinus prevents air from entering into the sinuses, it can create a vacuum that causes pain.

People with sinusitis also have thick nasal secretions that can be white, yellowish, greenish, or blood-tinged. Sometimes these secretions drain in the back of the throat and are difficult to clear. This is referred to as "post-nasal drip" or "post-nasal drainage." Chronic post-nasal discharge may indicate sinusitis, even in people who do not have facial pain.

However, facial pain without either nasal or post-nasal drainage is rarely caused by inflammation of the sinuses. People who experience facial pain but no nasal discharge often are diagnosed with a pain disorder—such as migraines, cluster headaches, or tension-type headaches—rather than sinusitis.

Less common symptoms of acute or chronic sinusitis include the following:

- Tiredness
- Decreased sense of smell
- Cough that may be worse at night
- Sore throat
- Bad breath
- Fever

On very rare occasions, acute sinusitis can result in brain infection and other serious complications.

What Causes Sinusitis?

Colds, bacterial infections, allergies, asthma, and other health conditions can cause sinusitis.

Acute Sinusitis

Acute sinusitis usually is caused by a viral or bacterial infection. The common cold, which is caused by a virus, may lead to swelling of the sinuses, trapping air and mucus behind the narrowed sinus openings. Both the nasal and the sinus symptoms usually go away within 2 weeks. Sometimes, viral infections are followed by bacterial infections. Many cases of acute sinusitis are caused by bacteria that frequently colonize the nose and throat, such as Streptococcus pneumoniae, Haemophilus influenzae, and Moraxella catarrhalis. These bacteria typically do not cause problems in healthy people, but in some cases they begin to multiply in the sinuses, causing acute sinusitis. NIAID supports studies to better understand the factors that put people at risk for bacterial sinusitis.

People who have allergies or other chronic nasal problems are prone to episodes of acute sinusitis. In general, people who have reduced immune function, such as those with HIV infection, are more likely to have sinusitis. Sinusitis also is common in people who have abnormal mucus secretion or mucus movement, such as people with cystic fibrosis, an inherited disease in which thick and sticky mucus clogs the lungs.

Chronic Sinusitis (Rhinosinusitis)

In chronic sinusitis, also known as chronic rhinosinusitis, the membranes of both the paranasal sinuses and the nose thicken because they are constantly inflamed. This condition can occur with or without nasal polyps, grape-like growths on the mucous membranes that protrude into the sinuses or nasal passages. The causes of chronic rhinosinusitis are largely unknown. NIAID supports basic research to help explain why people develop this chronic inflammation.People with asthma and allergies, recurrent acute sinusitis, and other health conditions are at higher risk of developing chronic rhinosinusitis.

In fact, some evidence suggests that chronic rhinosinusitis and asthma may be the same disease occurring in the upper and lower parts of the respiratory system, respectively. NIAID supports research to understand the causes of chronic airway inflammation in asthma and its link to chronic rhinosinusitis. For example, NIAID-supported researchers are investigating and developing improved treatments for aspirin-exacerbated respiratory disease (AERD). People with AERD have asthma and chronic rhinosinusitis with nasal polyps, and they experience potentially severe respiratory reactions to aspirin and other nonsteroidal anti-inflammatory drugs. NIAID-supported scientists also are examining whether viral infections cause worsening of chronic rhinosinusitis and identifying differences in genes and proteins in people with chronic rhinosinusitis and those whose sinuses are healthy.

How Is Sinusitis Diagnosed?

Often, healthcare providers can diagnose acute sinusitis by reviewing a person's symptoms and examining the nose and face. Doctors may perform a procedure called rhinoscopy, in which they use a thin, flexible tube-like instrument to examine the inside of the nose. If symptoms do not clearly indicate sinusitis or if they persist for a long time and do not get better with treatment, the doctor may order a computerized tomography (CT) scan—a form of X-ray that shows some soft tissue and other structures that cannot be seen in conventional X-rays—to confirm the diagnosis of sinusitis and to evaluate how severe it is.

Laboratory tests that a healthcare professional may use to check for possible causes of chronic rhinosinusitis include:

- Allergy testing
- Blood tests to rule out conditions that are associated with sinusitis, such as an immune deficiency disorder
- A sweat test or a blood test to rule out cystic fibrosis
- Tests on the material inside the sinuses to detect a bacterial or fungal infection
- An aspirin challenge to test for AERD. In an aspirin challenge, a person takes small but gradually increasing doses of aspirin under the careful supervision of a healthcare professional.

How Is Sinusitis Treated?

Acute Sinusitis

Medications can help ease the symptoms of acute sinusitis. Healthcare providers may recommend pain relievers or decongestants—medicines that shrink the swollen membranes in the nose and make it easier to breathe. Decongestant nose drops and sprays should be used for only a few days, as longer term use can lead to even more congestion and swelling of the nasal passages. A doctor may prescribe antibiotics if the sinusitis is caused by a bacterial infection.

Chronic Rhinosinusitis

Chronic rhinosinusitis can be difficult to treat. Medicines may offer some symptom relief. Surgery can be helpful if medication fails.

Medicine

Nasal steroid sprays are helpful for many people, but most do not get full relief of symptoms with these medicines. Saline (salt water) washes or nasal sprays can be helpful because they remove thick secretions and allow the sinuses to drain. Doctors may prescribe oral steroids, such as prednisone, for severe chronic rhinosinusitis. However, oral steroids are powerful medicines that can cause side effects such as weight gain and high blood pressure if used over the long term.

Oral steroids typically are prescribed when other medicines have failed. Desensitization to aspirin may be helpful for patients with AERD. During desensitization, which is performed under close medical supervision, a person is given gradually increasing doses of aspirin over time to induce tolerance to the drug.

Surgery

When medicine fails, surgery may be the only alternative for treating chronic rhinosinusitis. The goal of surgery is to improve sinus drainage and reduce blockage of the nasal passages. Sinus surgery usually is performed to:

- Enlarge the natural openings of the sinuses

- Remove nasal polyps

- Correct significant structural problems inside the nose and the sinuses if they contribute to sinus obstruction

Although most people have fewer symptoms and a better quality of life after surgery, problems can reoccur, sometimes even after a short period of time.

In children, problems can sometimes be eliminated by removing the adenoids. These gland-like tissues, located high in the throat behind and above the roof of the mouth, can obstruct the nasal passages.

Can Sinusitis Be Prevented?

There is little information about the prevention of acute or chronic sinusitis, but the following measures may help:

- Avoid exposure to irritants such as cigarette and cigar smoke or strong chemicals.

- To avoid infections, wash hands frequently during common cold season and try to avoid touching your face.

- If you have allergies, avoid exposure to allergy-inducing substances, or consider asking your healthcare provider for an allergy evaluation or a referral to an allergy specialist.

Section 29.5

Nasal Polyps

"Nasal Polyps," © 2016 Omnigraphics, Inc.
Reviewed November 2015.

What Is a Nasal Polyp?

Nasal polyps are small, polypoidal, noncancerous growths that can occur anywhere in the mucous membranes lining the nose or the paranasal sinuses. They may occur singly or in clusters, and they usually form where the sinuses open into the nasal cavity. While small polyps may not cause problems as they are freely movable, larger ones can block the sinuses or the nasal airway.

Nasal polyps can develop at any age, but they are most common in adults over age 40. Men are more prone to this disease, while it is uncommon in children under ten years. When young children are diagnosed with nasal polyps, in fact, doctors should conduct further tests to rule out cystic fibrosis, a genetic disorder characterized by a buildup of mucus in the lungs. Nasal polyps occur in nearly two-thirds of cystic fibrosis patients.

Causes

It is not entirely clear why some people develop nasal polyps and others do not. Although there is no definite cause of nasal polyposis, some factors may contribute to an increased risk of developing nasal polyps. One of the most common triggers is nasal congestion arising from chronic inflammation of the sinuses,which may be caused by allergies or recurring sinus infections. A certain degree of genetic predisposition has been observed in patients with nasal polyps, and it may explain why the mucosa in some people reacts differently to inflammation. Polyps are also commonly seen in patients with late onset of asthma and aspirinsensitivity, allergic rhinitis, and sinusitis.

Types of Nasal Polyps

Nasal polyps can be classified as a) Antrochoanal and b) Ethmoidal.
Antrochoanal nasal polyp is single, unilateral, and originates from maxillary sinus; it is mostly found in children. Ethmoidal polyps are bilateral and usually found in adults.

Symptoms and Diagnosis

Polyposis may be asymptomatic in some people, particularly if the polyps are small. Larger polyps are usually associated with catarrh (excessive secretion of mucus), breathing difficulties, inflammation of the paranasal cavities, and loss of smell and taste. Other symptoms of nasal polyps may include postnasal drip (drainage of mucous down the back of the throat) and a dull, achy feeling in the face because of fluid buildup.

Diagnosis of nasal polyps is generally made using a procedure called nasal endoscopy. Although a routine examination with a rhinoscope (a lighted device fitted with a lens that can be inserted into the nose) can find polyps located in the nasal cavity, an endoscope (a long, flexible tool fitted with a miniature camera on its end) is required to find polyps that are deep-seated in the sinuses. The doctor may also request a Computerized Tomography (CT) scan to diagnose polyps and additional tests such as biopsy to rule out nasal and sinus cancer, and non-malignant conditions such as nasal papilloma.

Treatment Options

Although various forms of medicine can alleviate symptoms associated with nasal polyps, they may provide only temporary relief. The first line of treatment is usually nasal drops or sprays containing steroids. Steroid treatment is often beneficial if the polyps are small, and the patient is likely to experience marked improvement in breathing as the polyps shrink and free up the airways. Tapered oral steroid medications can prevent sinus inflammation associated with allergies and effectively reduce the size of inflammatory polyps, but these drugs are used sparingly because they may increase the risk of such health concerns as diabetes, high blood pressure, and osteoporosis. Steroids, both topical and oral, are also frequently used after surgery to prevent the recurrence of polyps.

Doctors may also prescribe antibiotics to treat chronic sinusitis that may be associated with nasal polyps.

Endoscopic nasal surgery is the most commonly used treatment option for polyposis when the polyps are too large to respond to corticosteroids. This minimally invasive surgical procedure, known as a polypectomy, is performed with a nasal endoscope and can be done on an outpatient basis. The procedure, which is done in approximately 45 minutes to an hour, is carried out under general anaesthesia using a suction device or a microdebrider (a minuscule, motorized shaver) to remove the polyps. If there is no bleeding, the patient is discharged after a few hours of observation. Antibiotics are usually prescribed to prevent infection at the site of surgery.

Although surgery can provide symptomatic relief for a few years, the nasal polyps grow back in at least 15 percent of patients. In such cases, postoperative use of steroidal sprays and saline washes is usually prescribed to extend the period before the polyps recur.

References

1. Case-Lo, Christine. "Nasal Polyps." Healthline, October 5, 2015.

2. "Nasal Polyps—Treatment." NHS Choices, February 12, 2015.

Section 29.6

Aspergillosis: People with Asthma at Highest Risk

Text in this section is excerpted from "Fungal Diseases," Centers for
Disease Control and Prevention (CDC), September 8, 2014.

What Is Aspergillosis?

Aspergillosis is a disease caused by *Aspergillus*, a common mold (a
type of fungus) that lives indoors and outdoors. Most people breathe
in *Aspergillus* spores every day without getting sick. However, people
with weakened immune systems or lung diseases are at a higher risk
of developing health problems due to *Aspergillus*. There are different
types of aspergillosis. Some types are mild, but some of them are very
serious.

Types of Aspergillosis

- **Allergic bronchopulmonary aspergillosis (ABPA):** *Aspergillus* causes inflammation in the lungs and allergy symptoms
  such as coughing and wheezing, but doesn't cause an infection.

- **Allergic Aspergillus sinusitis:** *Aspergillus* causes inflammation in the sinuses and symptoms of a sinus infection (drainage,
  stuffiness, headache) but doesn't cause an infection.

- **Aspergilloma:** also called a "fungus ball." As the name suggests, it is a ball of *Aspergillus* that grows in the lungs or
  sinuses, but usually does not spread to other parts of the body.

- **Chronic pulmonary aspergillosis:** a long-term (3 months or
  more) condition in which *Aspergillus* can cause cavities in the
  lungs. One or more fungal balls (aspergillomas) may also be
  present in the lungs.

- **Invasive aspergillosis:** a serious infection that usually affects
  people who have weakened immune systems, such as people who

have had an organ transplant or a stem cell transplant. Invasive aspergillosis most commonly affects the lungs, but it can also spread to other parts of the body.

- **Cutaneous (skin) aspergillosis:** Aspergillus enters the body through a break in the skin (for example, after surgery or a burn wound) and causes infection, usually in people who have weakened immune systems. Cutaneous aspergillosis can also occur if invasive aspergillosis spreads to the skin from somewhere else in the body, such as the lungs.

Symptoms of Aspergillosis

The different types of aspergillosis can cause different symptoms. The symptoms of **allergic bronchopulmonary aspergillosis (ABPA)** are similar to asthma symptoms, including:

- Wheezing
- Shortness of breath
- Cough
- Fever (in rare cases)

Symptoms of **allergic Aspergillus** sinusitis include:

- Stuffiness
- Runny nose
- Headache

Symptoms of an **aspergilloma** ("fungus ball") include:

- Cough
- Coughing up blood
- Shortness of breath

Symptoms of **chronic pulmonary aspergillosis** include:

- Weight loss
- Cough
- Coughing up blood
- Fatigue
- Shortness of breath

Invasive aspergillosis usually occurs in people who are already sick from other medical conditions, so it can be difficult to know which symptoms are related to an *Aspergillus* infection. However, the symptoms of invasive aspergillosis in the lungs include:

- Fever

- Chest pain

- Cough

- Coughing up blood

- Shortness of breath

- Other symptoms can develop if the infection spreads from the lungs to other parts of the body.

Contact your healthcare provider if you have symptoms that you think are related to any form of aspergillosis.

People at Risk and Prevention

Who Gets Aspergillosis?

The different types of aspergillosis affect different groups of people.

- Allergic bronchopulmonary aspergillosis (ABPA) most often occurs in people who have cystic fibrosis or asthma.

- Aspergillomas usually affect people who have other lung diseases like tuberculosis.

- Chronic pulmonary aspergillosis typically occurs in people who have other lung diseases, including tuberculosis, chronic obstructive pulmonary disease (COPD), or sarcoidosis.

- Invasive aspergillosis affects people who have weakened immune systems, such as people who have had a stem cell transplant or organ transplant, are getting chemotherapy for cancer, or are taking high doses of corticosteroids.

How Does Someone Get Aspergillosis?

People can get aspergillosis by breathing in microscopic Aspergillus spores from the environment. Most people breathe in Aspergillus spores every day without getting sick. However, people with weakened immune systems or lung diseases are at a higher risk of developing health problems due to Aspergillus.

Is Aspergillosis Contagious?

No. Aspergillosis can't spread between people or between people and animals from the lungs.

How Can I Prevent Aspergillosis?

- It's difficult to avoid breathing in *Aspergillus* spores because the fungus is common in the environment. For people who have weakened immune systems, there may be some ways to lower the chances of developing a severe *Aspergillus* infection.

- Protect yourself from the environment. It's important to note that although these actions are recommended, they haven't been proven to prevent aspergillosis.

  - Try to avoid areas with a lot of dust like construction or excavation sites. If you can't avoid these areas, wear an N95 respirator (a type of face mask) while you're there.

  - Avoid activities that involve close contact to soil or dust, such as yard work or gardening. If this isn't possible,

    - Wear shoes, long pants, and a long-sleeved shirt when doing outdoor activities such as gardening, yard work, or visiting wooded areas.

    - Wear gloves when handling materials such as soil, moss, or manure.

  - To reduce the chances of developing a skin infection, clean skin injuries well with soap and water, especially if they have been exposed to soil or dust.

- Antifungal medication. If you are at high risk for developing invasive aspergillosis (for example, if you've had an organ transplant or a stem cell transplant), your healthcare provider may prescribe medication to prevent aspergillosis. Scientists are still learning about which transplant patients are at highest risk and how to best prevent fungal infections.

- Testing for early infection. Some high-risk patients may benefit from blood tests to detect invasive aspergillosis. Talk to your doctor to determine if this type of test is right for you.

Sources of Aspergillosis

Aspergillus lives in the environment

Aspergillus, the mold (a type of fungus) that causes aspergillosis, is very common both indoors and outdoors, so most people breathe in fungal spores every day. It's probably impossible to completely avoid breathing in some Aspergillus spores. For people with healthy immune systems, breathing in Aspergillus isn't harmful. However, for people who have weakened immune systems, breathing in Aspergillus spores can cause an infection in the lungs or sinuses which can spread to other parts of the body.

I'm worried that the mold in my home is Aspergillus. Should someone test the mold to find out what it is?

No. Generally, it's not necessary to identify the species of mold growing in a home, and CDC doesn't recommend routine sampling for molds.

Types of Aspergillus

There are approximately 180 species of Aspergillus, but fewer than 40 of them are known to cause infections in humans. Aspergillus fumigatus is the most common cause of human Aspergillus infections. Other common species include A. flavus, A. terreus, and A. niger.

Diagnosis and Testing for Aspergillosis

Healthcare providers consider your medical history, risk factors, symptoms, physical examinations, and lab tests when diagnosing aspergillosis. You may need imaging tests such as a chest X-ray or a CT scan of your lungs or other parts of your body depending on the location of the suspected infection. If your healthcare provider suspects that you have an *Aspergillus* infection in your lungs, he or she might collect a sample of fluid from your respiratory system to send to a laboratory. Healthcare providers may also perform a tissue biopsy, in which a small sample of affected tissue is analyzed in a laboratory for evidence of *Aspergillus* under a microscope or in a fungal culture. A blood test can help diagnose invasive aspergillosis early in people who have severely weakened immune systems.

Treatment for Aspergillosis

Allergic Forms of Aspergillosis

For allergic forms of aspergillosis such as allergic bronchopulmonary aspergillosis (ABPA) or allergic *Aspergillus* sinusitis, the recommended treatment is itraconazole, a prescription antifungal medication. Corticosteroids may also be helpful.

Invasive Aspergillosis

Invasive aspergillosis needs to be treated with prescription antifungal medication, usually voriconazole. There are other medications that can be used to treat invasive aspergillosis in patients who can't take voriconazole or whose infections don't get better after taking voriconazole. These include itraconazole, lipid amphotericin formulations, caspofungin, micafungin, and posaconazole. Whenever possible, immunosuppressive medications should be discontinued or decreased. People who have severe cases of aspergillosis may need surgery.

Chapter 30

Dealing with Other Co-Existing Conditions

Chapter Contents

Section 30.1

Allergic Bronchopulmonary Aspergillosis

Text in this section is excerpted from "Allergic Bronchopulmonary
Aspergillosis," National Center for Advancing Translational
Sciences (NCATS), May 21, 2015.

Overview

Allergic bronchopulmonary aspergillosis is an allergic lung reaction
to a type of fungus (Aspergillus fumigatus). Symptoms vary, but may
include wheezing, bronchial hyperreactivity, hemoptysis, productive
cough, low-grade fever, malaise, and weight loss. It is more common
in people who have asthma or cystic fibrosis. The recommended treatment for allergic bronchopulmonary aspergillosis is itraconazole, a
prescription antifungal medication. Oral corticosteroids, like prednisone, may also be helpful. The clinical course of allergic bronchopulmonary aspergillosis is variable. Many people with this condition can
be stabilized for long periods when treated. However, only about 50%
of patients achieve long-lasting remission and many require recurrent
courses of treatment.

Symptoms

The Human Phenotype Ontology provides the following list of
signs and symptoms for Allergic bronchopulmonary aspergillosis. If
the information is available, the table below includes how often the
symptom is seen in people with this condition.

Table 30.1. Signs and Symptoms

Signs and Symptoms	Approximate number of patients (when available)
Abnormality of eosinophils	90.00%
Asthma	90.00%
Abnormality of temperature regulation	50.00%
Abnormality of the bronchi	50.00%

Table 30.1. Continued

Signs and Symptoms	Approximate number of patients (when available)
Weight loss	50.00%
Abnormality of the fingernails	7.50%
Emphysema	7.50%
Hemoptysis	7.50%
Pulmonary hypertension	7.50%
Respiratory insufficiency	7.50%
Abnormality of the immune system	—
Autosomal dominant inheritance	—

Section 30.2

Anaphylaxis

Text in this section is excerpted from "Anaphylaxis," National Institute of Allergy and Infectious Diseases (NIAID), April 23, 2015.

Causes

The most common causes of anaphylaxis are reactions to foods (especially peanuts), medications, and stinging insects. Other potential triggers include exercise and exposure to latex. Sometimes, anaphylaxis occurs without an identifiable trigger. This is called idiopathic anaphylaxis.

Symptoms

Anaphylaxis includes a wide range of symptoms that can occur in many combinations and may be difficult to recognize. Some symptoms are not life-threatening, but the most severe ones restrict breathing and blood circulation.

Many of the body's organs can be affected:

- Skin—itching, hives, redness, swelling

- Nose—sneezing, stuffy nose, runny nose
- Mouth—itching, swelling of the lips or tongue
- Throat—itching, tightness, difficulty swallowing, swelling of the back of the throat
- Chest—shortness of breath, cough, wheeze, chest pain, tightness
- Heart—weak pulse, passing out, shock
- Gastrointestinal (GI) tract—vomiting, diarrhea, cramps
- Nervous system—dizziness or fainting

How soon after exposure will symptoms occur?

Symptoms can begin within minutes to hours after exposure to the allergen. Sometimes the symptoms go away, only to return anywhere from 8 to 72 hours later. When you begin to experience symptoms, seek immediate medical attention because anaphylaxis can be life-threatening.

How do you know if a person is having an anaphylactic reaction?

1. Anaphylaxis is likely if a person experiences two or more of the following symptoms within minutes to several hours after exposure to an allergen:

2. Hives, itchiness, or redness all over the body and swelling of the lips, tongue, or back of the throat

3. Trouble breathing

4. Severe GI symptoms such as abdominal cramps, diarrhea, or vomiting

5 Dizziness or fainting (signs of a drop in blood pressure)

6. If you are experiencing symptoms of anaphylaxis, seek immediate treatment and tell your healthcare professional if you have a history of allergic reactions.

Can anaphylaxis be predicted?

Anaphylaxis caused by an allergic reaction is highly unpredictable. The severity of a one attack does not predict the severity of subsequent attacks. Any anaphylactic reaction can become dangerous quickly and must be evaluated immediately by a healthcare professional.

Timing

An anaphylactic reaction can occur as any of the following:

- A single reaction that occurs immediately after exposure to the allergen and gets better with or without treatment within minutes to hours. Symptoms do not recur later in relation to that episode.

- A double reaction. The first reaction occurs within minutes or hours. The initial symptoms seem to go away but later reappear in a second reaction, which typically occurs 8 to 72 hours after the first reaction.

- A single, long-lasting reaction that continues for hours or days.

Treatment

If you or someone you know is having an anaphylactic episode, health experts advise using an auto-injector, if available, to inject epinephrine into the thigh muscle, and calling 9-1-1 if you are not in a hospital. (Epinephrine is a hormone that increases heart rate, constricts the blood vessels, and opens the airways.) If you are in a hospital, summon a resuscitation team.

If epinephrine is not given promptly, rapid decline and death could occur within 30 to 60 minutes. Epinephrine acts immediately but does not last long in the body, so it may be necessary to give repeat doses.

After epinephrine has been given, the patient can be placed in a reclining position with feet elevated to help restore normal blood flow.

A healthcare professional also may give the patient any of the following secondary treatments:

- Medicines to open the airways

- Antihistamines to relieve itching and hives

- Corticosteroids (a class of drugs used to treat inflammatory diseases) to prevent prolonged inflammation and long-lasting reactions

- Additional medicines to constrict blood vessels and increase heart rate

- Supplemental oxygen therapy

- Intravenous fluids

Conditions such as asthma, chronic lung disease, and cardiovascular disease may increase the risk of death from anaphylaxis. Medicines such as those that treat high blood pressure also may worsen symptom severity and limit response to treatment.

Antihistamines should be used only as a secondary treatment. Giving antihistamines instead of epinephrine may increase the risk of a life-threatening allergic reaction.

Management

Before leaving emergency medical care, your healthcare professional should provide the following:

- An epinephrine auto-injector or a prescription for two doses and training on how to use the auto-injector

- A follow-up appointment or an appointment with a clinical specialist such as an allergist or immunologist

- Information on where to get medical identification jewelry or an anaphylaxis wallet card that alerts others of the allergy

- Education about allergen avoidance, recognizing the symptoms of anaphylaxis, and giving epinephrine

- An anaphylaxis emergency action plan

If you or someone you know has a history of severe allergic reactions or anaphylaxis, your healthcare professional should remember to keep you S.A.F.E.

- Seek support: Your healthcare professional should tell you the following:

- Anaphylaxis is a life-threatening condition.

- The symptoms of the current episode may occur again (sometimes up to three days later).

- You are at risk for anaphylaxis in the future.

- At the first sign of symptoms, give yourself epinephrine and then immediately call an ambulance or have someone else take you to the nearest emergency facility.

- Allergen identification and avoidance: Before you leave the hospital, your healthcare professional should have done the following:

- Made efforts to identify the allergen by taking your medical history

- Explained the importance of getting additional testing to confirm what triggered the reaction, so you can successfully avoid it in the future

- Follow-up with specialty care: Your healthcare professional should encourage you to consult a specialist for an allergy evaluation.

- Epinephrine for emergencies: Your healthcare professional should give you the following:

  - An epinephrine auto-injector or a prescription and training on how to use an auto-injector

  - Advice to routinely check the expiration date of the auto-injector

NIAID-funded research focuses on anaphylaxis induced by food allergens. NIAID supports basic research in allergy and immunology to understand how, in certain people, foods elicit allergic reactions that can range from mild to severe. NIAID also conducts clinical trials of therapies that may alter the body's immune response so that it no longer triggers an allergic response to food.

The Laboratory of Allergic Diseases (LAD) supports basic, translational, and clinical research on anaphylaxis. Researchers in LAD seek to better understand the various immune system components that are involved in anaphylaxis; identify molecular events that cause and characterize anaphylactic reactions to understand their triggers; and discover diagnostic markers or reveal targets for new therapies to help prevent and treat life-threatening allergic reactions.

In December 2010, comprehensive guidelines for the diagnosis and management of food allergy were published. The guidelines provide healthcare professionals with recommendations on the best ways to identify food allergy and help people manage this condition, even its most severe forms. NIAID helped lead the guidelines effort, working with 34 professional organizations, patient advocacy groups, and federal agencies.

Section 30.3

Churg Strauss Syndrome

Text in this section is excerpted from "Churg Strauss
Syndrome," National Center for Advancing Translational
Sciences (NCATS), March 9, 2015.

Overview

Churg Strauss syndrome is a condition characterized by asthma,
high levels of eosinophils (a type of white blood cell that helps fight
infection), and inflammation of small to medium sized blood vessels
(vasculitis). The inflamed vessels can affect various organ systems
including the lungs, gastrointestinal tract, skin, heart and nervous
system. The exact cause of Churg Strauss syndrome is unknown, but
it is thought to be an autoimmune disorder. Treatment may involve
the use of glucocorticoids and/or other immunosuppressive therapies.

Symptoms

**What are the signs and symptoms of Churg Strauss
syndrome?**

The specific signs and symptoms of Churg Strauss syndrome (CSS)
vary from person to person depending on the organ systems involved.
The severity, duration and age of onset also vary. CSS is considered
to have three distinct phases–prodromal (allergic), eosinophilic and
vasculitic–which don't always occur sequentially. Some people do not
develop all three phases.

The prodromal (or allergic) phase is characterized by various allergic reactions. Affected people may develop asthma (including a cough,
wheezing, and shortness of breath); hay fever (allergic rhinitis); and/
or repeated episodes of sinusitis. This phase can last from months to
many years. Most people develop asthma-like symptoms before any
other symptoms.

The eosinophilic phase is characterized by accumulation of eosinophils (a specific type of white blood cell) in various tissues of the body
–especially the lungs, gastrointestinal tract and skin.

The vasculitic phase is characterized by widespread inflammation of various blood vessels (vasculitis). Chronic vasculitis can cause narrowing of blood vessels, which can block or slow blood flow to organs. Inflamed blood vessels can also become thin and fragile (potentially rupturing) or develop a bulge (aneurysm).

People with CSS often develop nonspecific symptoms including fatigue, fever, weight loss, night sweats, abdominal pain, and/or joint and muscle pain. Neurological symptoms (such as pain, tingling or numbness) are common and depend on the specific nerves involved. About half of affected people develop skin abnormalities due to accumulation of eosinophils in skin tissue. Symptoms of skin involvement may include purplish skin lesions, a rash with hives, and/or small bumps, especially on the elbows. Gastrointestinal involvement may cause various symptoms also. Heart problems may include inflammation of heart tissues and in severe cases, heart failure. The kidneys can also become involved, eventually causing glomerulonephritis.

The Human Phenotype Ontology (HPO) provides the following list of signs and symptoms for Churg Strauss syndrome. If the information is available, the table below includes how often the symptom is seen in people with this condition. You can use the MedlinePlus Medical Dictionary to look up the definitions for these medical terms.

The Human Phenotype Ontology (HPO) has collected information on how often a sign or symptom occurs in a condition. Much of this information comes from Orphanet, a European rare disease database. The frequency of a sign or symptom is usually listed as a rough estimate of the percentage of patients who have that feature.

The frequency may also be listed as a fraction. The first number of the fraction is how many people had the symptom, and the second number is the total number of people who were examined in one study. For example, a frequency of 25/25 means that in a study of 25 people all patients were found to have that symptom. Because these frequencies are based on a specific study, the fractions may be different if another group of patients are examined.

Sometimes, no information on frequency is available. In these cases, the sign or symptom may be rare or common.

Prognosis

What is the long-term outlook for people with Churg Strauss syndrome?

The long-term outlook (prognosis) for people with Churg Strauss syndrome (CSS) has improved significantly since the use of systemic glucocorticoids and the use of immunosuppressant therapies for people with more severe disease. Most reports now suggest a survival rate of 70 to 90 percent at five years. However, the prognosis may still depend on the severity of the illness in each person and the specific organ systems that are affected. Although CSS can be progressive and serious, many affected people do extremely well.

Organ damage may be minimized if treatment is started promptly and is carefully monitored by a specialist. Even people with very severe cases can achieve remission when treated promptly and followed closely. After being in remission, it is possible for CSS to recur. People with asthma or nasal allergies often have worsening of these symptoms, independent of vasculitis. Relapses involving vasculitis occur in about 30% to 50% of affected people. The chance to have a severe relapse can be minimized by prompt reporting of any new symptoms. The treatment approach for relapses is similar to the approach when first diagnosed, and it is possible to achieve remission again after a relapse.

Most deaths in affected people are due to complications from the vasculitic phase of CSS and are most commonly due to cardiac failure and/or heart attack; renal failure; cerebral hemorrhage; gastrointestinal bleeding; and acute, severe asthma (status asthmaticus).

Section 30.4

Eczema

Text in this section is excerpted from "Eczema," National Institute of Allergy and Infectious Diseases (NIAID), August 28, 2015.

What Is Atopic Dermatitis?

Atopic dermatitis, also known as eczema, is a non-contagious inflammatory skin condition that affects an estimated 30 percent of the U.S. population, mostly children and adolescents. It is a chronic disease characterized by dry, itchy skin that can weep clear fluid when scratched. People with eczema also may be particularly susceptible to bacterial, viral, and fungal skin infections.

Researchers estimate that 65 percent of people with atopic dermatitis develop symptoms during the first year of life, sometimes as early as age 2 to 6 months, and 85 percent develop symptoms before the age of 5. Many people outgrow the disease by early adulthood.

Eczema (Atopic Dermatitis) Causes

A combination of genetic and environmental factors appears to be involved in the development of eczema. The condition often is associated with other allergic diseases such as asthma, hay fever, and food allergy. Children whose parents have asthma and allergies are more likely to develop atopic dermatitis than children of parents without allergic diseases. Approximately 30 percent of children with atopic dermatitis have food allergies, and many develop asthma or respiratory allergies. People who live in cities or drier climates also appear more likely to develop the disease.

The condition tends to worsen when a person is exposed to certain triggers, such as

- Pollen, mold, dust mites, animals, and certain foods (for allergic individuals)
- Cold and dry air
- Colds or the flu
- Skin contact with irritating chemicals
- Skin contact with rough materials such as wool
- Emotional factors such as stress
- Fragrances or dyes added to skin lotions or soaps

Taking too many baths or showers and not moisturizing the skin properly afterward may also make eczema worse.

Section 30.5

Gastroesophageal Reflux Disease and Asthma

Gastroesophageal Reflux Disease

Gastroesophageal Reflux Disease (GERD), or acid reflux, occurs when stomach acid flows back up into the esophagus, producing an uncomfortable burning sensation known as heartburn. GERD and asthma are closely linked. People with asthma—and especially hard-to-treat asthma—are twice as likely to have GERD as those who do not have asthma. GERD appears to worsen asthma symptoms for many people, while controlling GERD often helps improve asthma symptoms. Meanwhile, some asthma medications—including theophylline and bronchodilators—seem to increase heartburn. GERD affects people of all ages—from infants to older adults.

The main mechanism involved in GERD is a muscular valve at the bottom of the esophagus called the lower esophageal sphincter. Ordinarily, this valve closes after intake of food and digestive juices contained within the stomach. In people with GERD, however, the muscle relaxes, allowing stomach acid to reflux back into the esophagus. When this occurs, it can create symptoms of heartburn, including a burning sensation in the upper abdomen, chest, or throat as well as a bad taste in the mouth.

Medical researchers have not determined the exact nature of the connection between GERD and asthma, but they have come up with a few theories about why the two diseases often coincide. One possibility is that the acid entering the esophagus triggers a nerve reflex, which causes the airways to narrow in order to prevent the stomach contents from entering the lungs. The narrowing of the airways, in turn, leads to wheezing and other asthma symptoms. Another possibility is that reflux irritates the airways, making the lungs more sensitive to allergens, air pollution, and other asthma triggers. Finally, researchers believe that asthma episodes can relax the esophageal sphincter, which can cause heartburn. Postprandial consumption of chocolates causes reduction in mean lower esophageal sphincter pressure leading to GERD.

Managing Asthma and GERD

Asthma is most likely to be related to GERD in people whose asthma symptoms begin in adulthood, fail to respond to standard asthma treatments, and tend to worsen after eating, exercising, or lying down. For people who have both asthma and GERD, it is important to manage both conditions. Some recommended methods include:

- Avoiding exposure to asthma triggers as much as possible.

- Assessing whether asthma medications may be increasing heartburn and other symptoms of GERD, and switching medications if necessary.

- Controlling GERD in order to improve asthma symptoms. The first step in treating GERD is to take an over-the-counter acid reducer such as ranitidine. If no improvement occurs over several weeks, prescription-strength medications—such as proton pump inhibitors—are also available to reduce stomach acid.

- Adjusting behavior in order to reduce heartburn symptoms. Some things to avoid include overeating, eating too fast, eating right before bedtime, and lying down immediately after eating.

- Making dietary changes to reduce heartburn symptoms. Some things to avoid include fatty foods, spicy foods, chocolate, caffeine, alcohol, carbonated beverages, and acidic foods like citrus fruits, tomatoes, and vinegar.

- Elevating the head end of the bed by several inches to allow gravity to help keep stomach acid from flowing upward. Using pillows is not advisable, however, because sleeping in a bent position may put pressure on the abdomen and aggravate heartburn.

- Maintaining a healthy weight and avoiding wearing tight belts and clothing in order to eliminate pressure on the abdomen.

- Quitting smoking, because it can cause the lower esophageal sphincter to relax.

References

1. American College of Asthma, Allergy, and Immunology. "GERD and Asthma Management." Ask the Allergist, 2014.

2. "GERD and Asthma." Cleveland Clinic Foundation, 2015.

3. "Heartburn and Asthma." WebMD Asthma Health Center, January 21, 2015.

Section 30.6

Obesity

Text in this section is excerpted from "Tips for Parents—Ideas to Help Children Maintain a Healthy Weight," Centers for Disease Control and Prevention (CDC), June 5, 2015; and text excerpted from "Adult Obesity Causes & Consequences," Centers for Disease Control and Prevention (CDC), June 16, 2015.

Why is childhood obesity considered a health problem?

Doctors and scientists are concerned about the rise of obesity in children and youth because obesity may lead to the following health problems:

- Heart disease, caused by:
  - high cholesterol and/or
  - high blood pressure
- Type 2 diabetes
- Asthma
- Sleep apnea
- Social discrimination

Childhood obesity is associated with various health-related consequences. Obese children and adolescents may experience immediate health consequences and may be at risk for weight-related health problems in adulthood.

Adult Obesity Causes and Consequences

Obesity is a complex health issue to address. Obesity results from a combination of causes and contributing factors, including individual factors such as behavior and genetics. Behaviors can include dietary patterns, physical activity, inactivity, medication use, and other exposures. Additional contributing factors in our society include the food and physical activity environment, education and skills, and food marketing and promotion.

Obesity is a serious concern because it is associated with poorer mental health outcomes, reduced quality of life, and the leading causes of death in the United States and worldwide, including diabetes, heart disease, stroke, and some types of cancer.

Behavior

Healthy behaviors include a healthy diet pattern and regular physical activity. Energy balance of the number of calories consumed from foods and beverages with the number of calories the body uses for activity plays a role in preventing excess weight gain.A healthy diet pattern follows the Dietary Guidelines for Americans which emphasizes eating whole grains, fruits, vegetables, lean protein, low-fat and fat-free dairy products and drinking water. The Physical Activity Guidelines for Americans recommends adults do at least 150 minutes of moderate intensity activity or 75 minutes of vigorous intensity activity, or a combination of both, along with 2 days of strength training per week.

Having a healthy diet pattern and regular physical activity is also important for long term health benefits and prevention of chronic diseases such as Type 2 diabetes and heart disease.

Community Environment

People and families may make decisions based on their environment or community. For example, a person may choose not to walk or bike to the store or to work because of a lack of sidewalks or safe bike trails. Community, home, child care, school, health care, and workplace settings can all influence people's daily behaviors. Therefore, it is important to create environments in these locations that make it easier to engage in physical activity and eat a healthy diet.

Learn about strategies for a Healthy Food Environment and strategies to improve the environment to make it easier to be physically active.

Strategies to create a healthy environment are listed on the Strategies to Prevent Obesity web page. More specifically, strategies to create a healthy school environment are listed on the CDC Adolescent and School Health website.

Genetics

Do Genes Have a Role in Obesity?

Genetic changes in human populations occur too slowly to be responsible for the obesity epidemic. Nevertheless, the variation in how people respond to the environment that promotes physical inactivity and intake of high-calorie foods suggests that genes do play a role in the development of obesity.

How Could Genes Influence Obesity?

Genes give the body instructions for responding to changes in its environment. Studies have identified variants in several genes that may contribute to obesity by increasing hunger and food intake. Rarely, a clear pattern of inherited obesity within a family is caused by a specific variant of a single gene (monogenic obesity). Most obesity, however, probably results from complex interactions among multiple genes and environmental factors that remain poorly understood (multifactorial obesity).

What about Family History?

Health care practitioners routinely collect family health history to help identify people at high risk of obesity-related diseases such as diabetes, cardiovascular diseases, and some forms of cancer. Family health history reflects the effects of shared genetics and environment among close relatives. Families can't change their genes but they can change the family environment to encourage healthy eating habits and physical activity. Those changes can improve the health of family members—and improve the family health history of the next generation.

Other Factors: Diseases and Drugs

Some illnesses may lead to obesity or weight gain. These may include Cushing's disease, and polycystic ovary syndrome. Drugs such as steroids and some antidepressants may also cause weight gain. The science continues to emerge on the role of other factors in energy balance and weight gain such as chemical exposures and the role of the microbiome.

A health care provider can help you learn more about your health habits and history in order to tell you whether behaviors, illnesses, medications, and/or psychological factors are contributing to weight gain or making weight loss hard.

Consequences of obesity

Health Consequences

People who are obese, compared to those with a normal or healthy weight, are at increased risk for many serious diseases and health conditions, including the following:

- All-causes of death (mortality)
- High blood pressure (Hypertension)
- High LDL cholesterol, low HDL cholesterol, or high levels of tri-glycerides (Dyslipidemia)
- Type 2 diabetes
- Coronary heart disease
- Stroke
- Gallbladder disease
- Osteoarthritis (a breakdown of cartilage and bone within a joint)
- Sleep apnea and breathing problems
- Some cancers (endometrial, breast, colon, kidney, gallbladder, and liver)
- Low quality of life
- Mental illness such as clinical depression, anxiety, and other mental disorders
- Body pain and difficulty with physical functioning

Economic and Societal Consequences

Obesity and its associated health problems have a significant economic impact on the U.S. health care system. Medical costs associated with overweight and obesity may involve direct and indirect costs. Direct medical costs may include preventive, diagnostic, and treatment services related to obesity. Indirect costs relate to morbidity and mortality costs including productivity. Productivity measures include 'absenteeism' (costs due to employees being absent from work for obesity-related health reasons) and 'presenteeism' (decreased productivity of employees while at work) as well as premature mortality and disability.

National Estimated Costs of Obesity

The medical care costs of obesity in the United States are high. In 2008 dollars, these costs were estimated to be $147 billion.

The annual nationwide productive costs of obesity obesity-related absenteeism range between $3.38 billion ($79 per obese individual) and $6.38 billion ($132 per obese individual).

In addition to these costs, data shows implications of obesity on recruitment by the armed forces. An assessment was performed of the percentage of the U.S. military-age population that exceeds the U.S. Army's current active duty enlistment standards for weight-for-height and percent body fat, using data from the National Health and Nutrition Examination Surveys. In 2007-2008, 5.7 million men and 16.5 million women who were eligible for military service exceeded the Army's enlistment standards for weight and body fat.

Section 30.7

Depression

Studies show that having severe asthma more than doubles a person's risk of developing depression. Depression is a serious mental health condition characterized by persistent feelings of sadness, hopelessness, and worthlessness that cause people to lose interest in normal activities. Depression affects approximately 21 percent of women and 13 percent of men in the United States at some point in their lives. Asthma is one of many chronic illnesses that appear to be linked with an increased risk of depression and other mood and anxiety disorders.

The Link between Asthma and Depression

Researchers are uncertain about the exact nature of the connection between asthma and depression, but they have come up with a few theories. One possibility is that the chronic inflammation that characterizes asthma causes neural changes in the brain. These neural changes may create symptoms of depression, including sadness, lethargy, changes in appetite, and a lack of interest in social interaction. As the symptoms of depression improve, asthma symptoms are often alleviated as well.

Another possible connection between asthma and depression is stress. People with uncontrolled asthma experience frequent episodes of wheezing, coughing, and difficulty breathing. These symptoms can be extremely stressful, both physically and emotionally. Stress can lead to depression, and it is also known to trigger asthma symptoms. In addition, poorly managed asthma can prevent people from being active and participating in sports and other recreational activities. The inability to join in fun activities can lead to social isolation, a lack of motivation, and depression, as well as a worsening of asthma symptoms.

Depression and asthma may also be linked because people who are depressed are less likely to treat their asthma effectively. People with depression often have trouble with concentration, memory, motivation, and problem solving. These problems make it more difficult for them to recognize the need for medical attention, keep doctor appointments, and take medication as directed. Finally, depression, irritability, and suicidal thoughts are potential side effects of some types of asthma medications, including anti-inflammatory inhalers and oral steroids.

Treating Asthma and Depression

Depression and asthma are both treatable. Following diagnosis by a health professional, it is important to develop a treatment plan that addresses the symptoms of both diseases since they are so often interconnected. In addition to medication and therapy, there are other steps people can take to improve their breathing and maintain their mental health:

- Control asthma so that symptoms do not restrict activities. Managing asthma effectively includes seeing an asthma doctor regularly, adjusting medications or doses if symptoms worsen, using asthma inhalers correctly, being aware of the possible side effects of asthma medications, and discussing any depressive symptoms with a doctor.

- Reduce the risk of depression and treat any symptoms as they arise. Proven methods of combating depression and improving mood include getting physical exercise, building a strong social network, applying coping strategies to replace negative thoughts with positive statements, and learning relaxation techniques. If depressive symptoms occur, it is important to take antidepressant medication as directed and try different medications as needed to find one that works.

Chapter 31

Lifestyle Modifications for Asthma Control

Many people with asthma find that making changes to their lifestyle can help them gain control over their asthma symptoms. Lifestyle modifications range from avoiding allergens and other asthma triggers in the home environment to adjusting nutrition and exercise programs for optimal health. Even minor lifestyle changes can sometimes offer major benefits in reducing the incidence and severity of asthma attacks. Although lifestyle modifications cannot eliminate the need for asthma medications, they can aid in the management of symptoms and thus make treatments work more effectively.

Modifications for a Healthy Environment

Understanding and avoiding asthma triggers in the home environment is a key to controlling symptoms. For half of people with asthma, a common allergen is responsible for triggering most asthma attacks. Although it may be impossible to completely eliminate allergens from the home environment, the following suggestions can help people with asthma limit their exposure to specific allergens:

"Lifestyle Modifications for Asthma Control," © 2016 Omnigraphics, Inc. Reviewed January 2016.

Pollen and Mold

For people whose asthma is triggered by pollen and outdoor mold, it is important to keep windows closed during peak allergy seasons. Since pollen and mold counts tend to be highest in the morning hours, it is best to remain indoors as much as possible at this time of day. In addition, consider consulting with a doctor to adjust asthma medications during allergy season. To prevent exposure to indoor mold, fix leaky plumbing, attend to poor home drainage issues that could cause flooding, and use a dehumidifier to rid the home of excess moisture. Use a cleanser with bleach to kill mold on hard surfaces.

Dust Mites

Dust mites thrive in carpets, bedding, and upholstery. For people whose asthma is triggered by an allergy to dust mites, it is especially important to avoid prolonged exposure at night. To kill mites in sheets and blankets, the bedding must be washed once a week in water hotter than 130 degrees Fahrenheit. Mattresses and pillows should be encased in dust-proof zippered covers. Stuffed toys should be kept out of the bedroom or washed weekly in hot water. If possible, avoid carpeting and cloth cushions, especially in the bedroom. Finally, use air conditioning or dehumidifiers to keep indoor humidity below 60 percent in order to create inhospitable conditions for dust mites.

Pet Dander

The best way to avoid exposure to pet dander is to keep pets out of the home. If this is not possible, pets should at least be prevented from entering the bedroom or climbing on fabric-covered furniture. Removing carpeting from the home can also help reduce exposure to pet dander.

Pests

Allergies to cockroaches, mice, and other pests can also trigger asthma. To avoid exposure to these pests, put food away promptly in airtight containers and keep garbage receptacles securely closed. Traps, poison baits, or boric acid are good options for pest control, since people with asthma should not inhale pesticide sprays.

Airborne Irritants

Smoke, dust, chemicals, and other forms of indoor air pollution can irritate the airways of people with asthma. It is best to avoid exposure to products with strong smells, such as paints, cleaning solvents, and per-fumes, as well as to fumes from wood-burning stoves, fireplaces, or kero-sene heaters. People with asthma should also not smoke, permit smoking in their homes or cars, or go places where other people are smoking. Since dust from a vacuum cleaner can be an asthma trigger, it is best to wear a dust mask while vacuuming or have someone else run the vacuum.

Modifications for a Healthy Lifestyle

For people with chronic diseases like asthma, it is especially valuable to maintain overall health through proper nutrition and exercise. Seeing a doctor regularly, following the recommended treatment plan, paying attention to warning signs, and using medication as directed are also important components of controlling asthma through lifestyle choices.

Recognize Asthma Symptoms and Treat Them Promptly

Some of the common warning signs of worsening asthma include increased wheezing, shortness of breath, chest tightness or pain, cough-ing, difficulty sleeping, and declining expiratory flow measurements. Recognizing these symptoms and beginning treatment immediately can prevent asthma attacks or at least reduce their severity. A number of asthma-management tools are available online—from groups like the American Lung Association and the Asthma and Allergy Foun-dation of America—to help people track their symptoms and improve their asthma control.

Exercise Safely with Asthma

Regular exercise offers many health benefits, including more effi-cient heart and lung function, greater muscle strength and endurance, and improvements in mood. Although it can be tricky to avoid asthma triggers outdoors, the benefits of exercise almost always outweigh the risks. In addition, there are many steps people can take to increase their ability to exercise safely with asthma.

The first step in preventing exercise-induced asthma is to ensure that asthma is well managed. Using a reliever medication about fif-teen minutes ahead of time and warming up at a low intensity for at least ten minutes before exercising can also help prevent attacks. During exercise, it is important to watch for asthma symptoms, use a reliever medication if they appear, and only return to the activity if the symptoms go away. After completing an exercise session, experts recommend taking time to cool down and remaining alert for asthma symptoms for thirty minutes.

Although asthma should not prevent people from participating in sports, it may be best to avoid exercising outdoors on days when asthma triggers such as air pollution, pollen, high humidity, or cold temperatures are present. If exercise-induced asthma occurs frequently, varying the type, intensity, or duration of activity may be helpful. It is also a good idea to introduce new activities gradually while watching for asthma symptoms.

Follow a Healthy Diet

Although the evidence is unclear about whether eating specific foods can help control asthma, it is well known that good nutrition offers many health benefits. For instance, a healthy, well-balanced diet boosts the immune system, which may enable people with asthma to fight off respiratory viruses and other illnesses that can worsen their symptoms.

Nutritionists generally recommend eating a wide variety of colorful fruits and vegetables, which contain vitamins and antioxidants. Vitamins C, D, and E are especially important in controlling inflammation and supporting immune system function. Experts also suggest consuming foods rich in omega-3 fatty acids—such as salmon, tuna, sardines, and flaxseeds—which help combat inflammation of the airways. Finally, the live bacteria found in yogurt and probiotic supplements have been shown to improve digestion and reduce the likelihood of an inflammatory response in the gut.

Maintain a Healthy Body Weight

Both diet and exercise play a role in maintaining a healthy body weight, which is another important factor in asthma control. Excess weight—especially around the midsection—puts pressure on the lungs and impedes breathing. As a result, studies show that people who are obese have more severe asthma symptoms and need more medication than those who maintain a healthy weight.

Losing weight can also help eliminate gastroesophageal reflux disease (GERD), a condition in which stomach acid flows back into the esophagus, causing an uncomfortable burning sensation in the chest known as heartburn. GERD and asthma are often linked, with an estimated 75 percent of asthma patients also experiencing heartburn symptoms. Eating smaller meals, not eating before bedtime, elevating the head of the bed, and avoiding alcohol, caffeine, chocolate, fatty foods, spicy foods, and acidic foods can help eliminate GERD as well as control related asthma symptoms.

Check for Food Sensitivities

Sensitivities to certain foods can sometimes trigger an inflammatory response in the gut. If the inflammation affects the airways, it can cause an asthma attack. Some of the most common food sensitivities include dairy products, eggs, soy, wheat, shellfish, and sulfites, which are chemicals used as preservatives in wine, condiments, dried fruits, canned vegetables, and other processed foods. If consuming one of these foods seems to be associated with a worsening of asthma symptoms, it may be helpful to eliminate it from the diet for a few weeks to see if symptoms improve.

Take Care of the Airways

People with asthma may also benefit from alternative medical practices intended to clear the sinuses and nasal passages and improve breathing control and lung capacity. Sinus drainage can trigger asthma symptoms, especially at night. To avoid this problem, it may be helpful to use a neti pot or saline spray to clear out congested nasal passages. When the nasal passages are clear, it reduces strain on the airways and eliminates drainage that may trigger asthma attacks.

Practicing steady, rhythmic, deep-breathing techniques has also been found to reduce symptoms of asthma in some studies. Online resources and smartphone apps are available to guide patients through the steps of various techniques, such as the Papworth method, the Buteyeko breathing technique, and pranayama yogic breathing.

References

1. "Asthma and Diet." WebMD Asthma Health Center, 2015.

2. "Asthma and Exercise." Better Health Channel, March 2015.

3. Badash, Michelle. "Lifestyle Changes to Manage Asthma." LifeScript, 2013.

4. Wlody, Ellen. "Lifestyle Changes Can Help Control Asthma." MedShadow Foundation, August 2, 2013.

Chapter 32

Managing Your Medicines

Chapter Contents

Section 32.1

Traveling with Asthma

Text in this section is excerpted from "Travelers with
Chronic Illnesses," Centers for Disease Control and
Prevention (CDC), May 3, 2013.

Travelers with Chronic Illnesses

Travel can be relaxing and rewarding, but people with chronic illnesses, such as heart disease, diabetes, asthma, or arthritis, may face unique challenges when they travel overseas. With a little planning and preparation, however, people with chronic illnesses can have safe and enjoyable trips. If you have a chronic illness and are planning an international trip, visit a travel medicine specialist at least 4–6 weeks before you leave to talk about what you should do to prepare. Some chronic illnesses and some medicines, such as steroids, can weaken the immune system. See Travelers with Weakened Immune Systems for more information.

Medicines and Supplies

You might take medicines or use medical supplies (such as asthma inhalers, glucose test strips, or insulin needles) regularly or just for emergencies. If that's the case, make sure you take enough of a supply to last your whole trip, plus a little extra in case of delays. If you are going to be gone a long time, talk to your doctor about how you can get enough medicine for your trip; sometimes insurance companies will only pay for a 30-day supply at a time.

Pack all your medicines and medical supplies in your carry-on luggage. You don't want to be stuck without them if your suitcase gets lost! Medicines should be in their original prescription bottles, and you should also include copies of your original prescriptions. Note that medicines should be taken according to the time since the last dose, not the local time of day, so ask your doctor about scheduling doses when you cross time zones.

Don't plan on being able to buy your medicines at your destination. They may not be available or may not meet US standards. In many developing countries, counterfeit drugs are a big problem.

If you see a travel medicine specialist separately from your regular doctor, the travel medicine specialist may prescribe trip-specific medicines, such as drugs to prevent malaria or altitude sickness or to treat travelers' diarrhea. If the travel medicine specialist prescribes any medicine, make sure he or she knows what medicines you routinely take, to prevent drug interactions.

Insurance

There are 3 types of insurance every traveler should consider buying. These may be especially important for travelers with chronic illnesses:

Trip cancellation insurance covers the cost of your trip if, for example, you have to reschedule or cancel because you are too sick to travel.

Travel health insurance covers the cost of health care received in other countries. Even if you have health insurance in the United States, it might not cover you overseas.

Medical evacuation insurance covers the cost of transportation to high-quality health care facilities, in the event of an emergency. This type of insurance is important if you will be traveling in rural or remote areas.

When selecting an insurance policy, always read the fine print, so you are sure that it covers what you need it to cover.

Other Preparation

Before you go, make sure you have a plan to get care overseas, in case you need it. It's also a good idea to carry a card with information about your condition, including any drug or food allergies, written in the local language. If appropriate, wear a medical alert bracelet or other medical jewelry with this information on it. And don't forget to pack a travel health kit that includes anything you need to manage your chronic illness, as well as other items necessary to ensure a safe and healthy trip!

Section 32.2

Medicines at Home

Text in this section is excerpted from "So You Have Asthma,"
National Heart, Lung, and Blood Institute (NHLBI), March 2013.

How to Remember to Take Your Medicines?

- Put a favorite picture of yourself or a loved one on the refrigerator with a note that says, "Remember to take your asthma medicine."

- Keep your medicine on the nightstand next to your side of the bed so you can see it when you wake up and when you go to bed.

- Take your asthma medicine right before you brush your teeth.

- Put "sticky" notes in visible places to remind yourself to take your asthma medicine—on the refrigerator, on the cabinet where you keep your favorite morning mug (you might even keep the medicine inside the mug), on the mirror, on the front door.

- If you use the phone company's voice mail service, record a reminder for yourself, and the service can automatically call you every day at the same time.

- Establish a buddy system with a friend who also is on daily medicine and arrange to call each other every day with a reminder to "take your medicine."

- Ask one or more of your children or grandchildren to call you every day with a quick reminder. It's a great way to stay in touch, and little ones love to help the grownups.

- If you take pills for asthma, place your medicine in a weekly pillbox, available at most pharmacies.

- If you have a personal computer, program a start-up reminder to take your asthma medicine or sign up with one of the free services that will send you a reminder email every day.

- Set your phone or watch alarm to remind you to take your asthma medicine.

- Remember to refill your prescription. Each time you pick up a refill, make a note on your calendar to order and pick up the next refill one week before the medicine is due to run out.

Chapter 33

Medical Identification Critical for People with Life-Threatening Allergies

In an emergency, making quick decisions with regard to medical treatment may mean the difference between life and death. It is critical for medical response personnel to be aware of any allergies or medical conditions that the patient they are treating might have. But if the patient is unconscious or unable to answer questions, they cannot provide this vital information. As a result, medical care may be delayed, or the treatment provided may be inappropriate for the patient's condition or even dangerous to their health. Wearable medical identification (ID) can play a life-saving role in such emergencies.

An individual with a serious medical condition or a life-threatening allergy can carry the information on a bracelet or necklace that is immediately identifiable. Wearable medical IDs can warn medical responders about the presence of such conditions as Alzheimer's disease, asthma, autism, diabetes, epilepsy, heart disease, high blood pressure, or organ transplant. They can also carry information about allergies to pharmaceutical drugs, foods, insects, or substances such as latex. They also typically display the individual's blood type, along with specific medical treatment requests such as DNR (do not resuscitate), DNI (do not intubate), or organ donation.

Most medical IDs also list any medications the individual takes regularly as well as the names and phone numbers of people to contact in case of emergency. It has become common practice for emergency medical technicians (EMTs) and other first responders to look for medical IDs before proceeding with treatment.

Obtaining a Medical ID

Wearable medical IDs are available from many sources online. They come in a wide variety of attractive styles and are fully customizable for individual needs. Some wearable IDs are designed to inform emergency medical responders of the presence of a more detailed medical alert card. These cards are typically carried in a wallet, purse, or backpack and provide further information about the patient's allergies or other health issues. Patients can consult with their primary-care physicians to obtain guidance in deciding what information to include on their ID.

In addition to people with life-threatening allergies and other health conditions, parents of small children and people who serve as sole caregivers for elderly or disabled individuals should also consider wearing a medical ID bracelet or necklace. If the parent or caregiver is involved in an accident or has another type of medical emergency, the medical ID can provide contact information for alternate care providers to ensure that dependent family members will receive needed assistance and remain safe. Experts also recommend wearable medical IDs for solo travelers, athletes who run or bike alone outdoors over long distances, and people who have undergone recent surgery. At a minimum, these IDs should include contact information in case of emergency.

Reference

White, Jenna. "Top Ten Reasons People Wear Medical ID Jewelry." Lauren's Hope, February 27, 2013.

Part Five

Pediatric Asthma

Chapter 34

Basic Facts about Asthma in Children

Who Is at Risk for Asthma?

Asthma affects people of all ages, but it most often starts during childhood. In the United States, more than 22 million people are known to have asthma. Nearly 6 million of these people are children.

Young children who often wheeze and have respiratory infections— as well as certain other risk factors—are at highest risk of developing asthma that continues beyond 6 years of age. The other risk factors include having allergies, eczema (an allergic skin condition), or parents who have asthma.

Among children, more boys have asthma than girls. But among adults, more women have the disease than men. It's not clear whether or how sex and sex hormones play a role in causing asthma.

Most, but not all, people who have asthma have allergies.

This chapter includes excerpts from "Explore Asthma," National Heart, Lung, and Blood Institute (NHLBI), August 4, 2014; text from "Children's Health," Agency for Healthcare Research and Quality (AHRQ), October 2014; text from "Managing Asthma in the School Environment," U.S. Environmental Protection Agency (EPA), November 6, 2015; text from "Asthma-related Missed School Days among Children aged 5–17 Years," Centers for Disease Control and Prevention (CDC), October 5, 2015; text from "Asthma Severity among Children with Current Asthma," Centers for Disease Control and Prevention (CDC), February 17, 2015; and text from "2013 National Health Interview Survey (NHIS) Data," Centers for Disease Control and Prevention (CDC), February 13, 2015.

Some people develop asthma because of contact with certain chemical irritants or industrial dusts in the workplace. This type of asthma is called occupational asthma.

Children and Asthma

Back-to-school time is tough for the one child in every 15 who faces the challenge of asthma. Myths, misconceptions, and stereotypes about children with asthma hurt them as much or more than the disease itself.

The problem is growing in schools; the asthma rate is rising more rapidly in preschool-aged children than in any other group. Asthma is the second most common cause of chronic illness in children, after chronic sinusitis.

Asthma and Absenteeism

Asthma is the leading cause of school absenteeism due to a chronic condition, accounting for nearly **13 million** missed school days per year.

Asthma has reached epidemic proportions in the United States, affecting millions of people of all ages and races. An average of one out of every 10 school-age children now has asthma, and the percentage of children with asthma is rising more rapidly in preschool-age children than in any other age group.

Asthma is a leading cause of school absenteeism due to a chronic condition, accounting for nearly 13 million missed school days per year. Asthma also accounts for many nights of interrupted sleep, limits activity and disrupts family and caregiver routines.

Asthma symptoms that are not severe enough to require a visit to an emergency room or to a physician can still be serious enough to prevent a child with asthma from living a fully active life.

Asthma is a long-term, inflammatory disease that causes the airways of the lungs to tighten and constrict, leading to wheezing, breathlessness, chest tightness and coughing. The inflammation also causes the airways of the lungs to become especially sensitive to a variety of asthma triggers. The particular trigger or triggers and the severity of symptoms can differ for each person with asthma.

Because Americans spend up to 90 percent of their time indoors, exposure to indoor allergens and irritants may play a significant role in triggering asthma episodes. Some of the most common asthma triggers found in schools, as well as techniques to mitigate them.

Control Asthma Triggers

Each day, one in five Americans occupies a school building. The majority of these occupants are children. Environmental asthma triggers commonly found in school buildings include:

- respiratory viruses
- cockroaches and other pests
- mold resulting from excess moisture in the building
- dander from animals in the classroom
- dander brought in on clothing from animals at home

Secondhand smoke and dust mites are other known environmental asthma triggers found in schools. Children with asthma may be affected by other pollutants from sources found inside schools, such as:

- unvented stoves or heaters
- common products including:
  - chemicals
  - cleaning agents
  - perfumes
  - pesticides
  - sprays

In addition, outdoor environmental asthma triggers, like ozone and particle pollution, or bus exhaust, can affect children with asthma while at school.

Students with uncontrolled asthma often miss more school and have poorer academic performance than healthy students. With the help of strong school asthma management programs, students with asthma can have equally good school attendance. When asthma is well controlled, students are ready to learn.

Effectively managing a child's asthma is best accomplished through a comprehensive plan that addresses both the medical management of the disease and the avoidance of environmental triggers. Because children spend most of their time in schools, day care facilities or at home, it is important to reduce their exposure to environmental asthma triggers as much as possible in each of these environments. This publication focuses on steps that schools can take to help children breathe easier.

373

Asthma Statistics

Lifetime Asthma in children

Table 34.1. Lifetime Asthma Population Estimates—in thousands by Age, United States: National Health Interview Survey, 2013

Characteristic	Age (years)			
	Children Age <18	0–4	5–14	15–19
Total:	9304	1168	5924	3322
Male	5409	757	3369	1964
Female	3894	410	2554	1359
White Non-Hispanic:	4389	442	2838	1706
Male	2478	315	1557	1009
Female	1911	128	1281	697
Black Non-Hispanic:	1833	323	1157	564
Male	1089	198	649	384
Female	744	125	508	180
Other Non-Hispanic:	961	123	584	341
Male	591	83	356	171
Female	370	40	228	170
Hispanic:	2121	280	1345	712
Male	1252	162	808	400
Female	870	118	537	312
Puerto Rican:a	397	80	221	126*
Male	216	32	134	51
Female	181	48	88	Not available
Mexican/ Mexican-American:	1170	124	778	413
Male	683	94	442	231
Female	486	Not available	336	182
Region:				
Northeast	1586	223	944	575

Table 34.1. Continued

Characteristic	Children Age <18	Age (years)		
		0–4	5–14	15–19
Midwest	1879	186	1108	936
South	3820	541	2583	1072
West	2019	218	1288	740
Ratio of Family Income to				
Poverty Threshold:				
0–0.99	2642	493	1742	824
1.00–2.49	2932	317	1841	1110
2.50–4.49	2010	232	1346	611
4.50 and above	1720	125	995	777

Table 34.2. Lifetime Asthma Prevalence Percents by Age, United States: National Health Interview Survey, 2013

Characteristic	Children Age <18	Age (years)		
		0–4	5–14	15–19
Total:	12.7	5.9	14.3	16.2
Male	14.4	7.5	16	18.2
Female	10.8	4.2	12.6	13.9
White Non-Hispanic:	11.3	4.4	13	14.8
Male	12.5	6.1	14	17.3
Female	10	2.6	11.9	12.3
Black Non-Hispanic:	18.2	11.9	19.9	20.9
Male	21.7	14.7	22.4	25.9
Female	14.8	9.1	17.4	14.9
Other Non-Hispanic:	14.2	6.5	15.6	18.8
Male	16.3	7.9	18.6	17.3
Female	11.7	4.7*	12.5	20.5

Table 34.2. Continued

Characteristic	Children Age <18	Age (years)		
		0–4	5–14	15–19
Hispanic:	11.9	5.4	13.6	15.7
Male	13.8	6.2	16	16.3
Female	10	4.7	11.1	15
Puerto Rican:	29.9	21.2	31.3	34.3
Male	35.2	18.8	41.2	29.3
Female	25.3	23.1	23	38.8
Mexican/Mexican-American:	9.5	3.5	11.3	13.5
Male	11.2	5.4	12.8	14.2
Female	7.9	Not available	9.7	12.7
Region:				
Northeast	13.7	6.9	15.4	16.3
Midwest	11.3	4.3	11.7	18.2
South	13.7	7	16.3	15.6
West	11.6	4.7	13.1	14.7
Ratio of Family Income to				
Poverty Threshold:b				
0–0.99	15.9	9.4	18.7	18.3
1.00–2.49	12.7	5.4	14	16.1
2.50–4.49	11.1	4.9	13	12.8
4.50 and above	11.1	3.1	11.7	17.7

Asthma-Related Missed School Days among Children aged 5–17 Years

The percent of children with asthma who reported one or more missed school days in 2013 was significantly lower than in 2003.

Poorly controlled asthma may impair a child's ability to attend school, affect his or her academic performance, and cause parents to miss work to care for an ill child.

The number of reported missed school days among children with asthma was 12.4 million in 2003, 10.4 million in 2008, and 13.8 million in 2013.

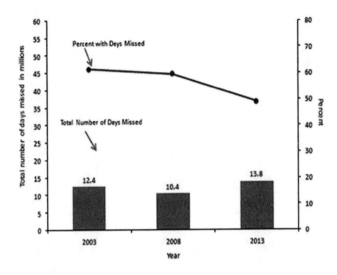

Figure 33.1. *Number and Percent of Asthma-related Missed School Days among Children aged 5–17 Years: United States, 2003, 2008, and 2013*

The percent of children with asthma who reported one or more asthma-related missed school days in 2013 (49.0%) was significantly lower than the percent in 2003 (61.4%). However, this percentage was similar to the percentage for 2008 (59.6%). The reported missed school days in each year did not differ by age, sex, race or ethnicity, and poverty level.

Table 34.3. Percent of Asthma-related Missed School Days

Percent of Asthma-Related Missed School Days among Children aged 5–17 years: United States, NHIS 2003, 2008, and 2013			
	2003	2008	2013
U.S. Total :	61.4	59.6	49
Male	64.2	59.4	51.3
Female	57.2	59.8	46
Age (years)			
11-May	61.9	65.9	52
17-Dec	60.8	51.1	45.5

Table 34.3. Continued

Percent of Asthma-Related Missed School Days among Children aged 5–17 years: United States, NHIS 2003, 2008, and 2013			
	2003	2008	2013
Race/Ethnicity			
NH White	57.1	54.3	43.8
NH Black	66.8	70	52.7
Hispanic	71.2	77.8	56.5
NH Other	61.3	40.9	50.3
Poverty Level			
0.0–0.99	61.6	57.6	54.8
1.00–2.49	64.2	58	47.7
2.50–4.49	64.7	65.7	45.1
4.50 and above	52.2	58.3	46.4

Asthma Severity among Children with Current Asthma

Asthma severity determines type and duration of treatment

Asthma severity is the inherent intensity of the disease process. Disease progression and symptoms vary among individuals and within an individual's experience over time. The population-based asthma severity prevalence estimate depends on whether the individual is treated or not and how well the individual responds to the treatment. Intermittent severity includes people who are well-controlled without long-term control medication.

Persistent severity includes people who are on long-term control medications and people with uncontrolled asthma (not well-controlled or very poorly controlled) who are not on long-term control medication. Nearly 60% of children with current asthma have persistent asthma; 40% have intermittent asthma. Intermittent and persistent asthma prevalence among children varied by state during the years 2006-2010, but did not follow a specific geographic pattern. Intermittent asthma prevalence ranged from 25.6% in Mississippi to 55.0% in Oregon (See table 33.2). Persistent asthma prevalence ranged from 45.0% in Oregon to 74.4% in Mississippi.

Table 34.4. Asthma Severity among Children with Current Asthma

Asthma Severity among Children with Current Asthma		
STATE	**Intermittent Severity**	**Persistent Severity**
U.S. Total	39.7	60.3
AZ	33	67
CA	32.5	67.5
CT	40.5	59.5
DC	46.9	53.1
GA	36.4	63.6
HI	52.6	57.4
IL	46.4	53.6
IN	34.9	65.1
IA	43.5	57.5
KS	33.7	66.3
LA	36.4	63.6
ME	39.8	60.2
MD	38.6	61.4
MA	40.2	59.8
MI	39.7	60.3
MS	25.6	74.4
MO	37	63
MT	43.4	56.6
NE	34.9	65.1
NH	50.6	49.4
NJ	42.5	57.5
NM	43.6	56.4
NY	42.6	57.4
ND	34.8	65.2
OH	39.8	60.2
OK	39.3	60.7
OR	55	45
PA	47.2	52.8
RI	37	63
TX	39.5	60.5
UT	42.2	57.8

Table 34.4. Continued

Asthma Severity among Children with Current Asthma		
STATE	**Intermittent Severity**	**Persistent Severity**
VT	42.5	57.5
VA	38.8	61.2
WA	53.3	46.7
WV	32.7	67.3
WI	43.7	56.3

Chapter 35

Diagnosing Asthma in Children

Most children who have asthma develop their first symptoms before 5 years of age. However, asthma in young children (aged 0 to 5 years) can be hard to diagnose.

Sometimes it's hard to tell whether a child has asthma or another childhood condition. This is because the symptoms of asthma also occur with other conditions.

Also, many young children who wheeze when they get colds or respiratory infections don't go on to have asthma after they're 6 years old.

A child may wheeze because he or she has small airways that become even narrower during colds or respiratory infections. The airways grow as the child grows older, so wheezing no longer occurs when the child gets colds. A young child who has frequent wheezing with colds or respiratory infections is more likely to have asthma if:

- One or both parents have asthma

- The child has signs of allergies, including the allergic skin condition eczema

This chapter includes excerpts from "How Is Asthma Diagnosed?" National Heart, Lung, and Blood Institute (NHLBI), August 4, 2014; and text from "What Are Lung Function Tests?" National Heart, Lung, and Blood Institute (NHLBI), September 17, 2012.

- The child has allergic reactions to pollens or other airborne allergens

- The child wheezes even when he or she doesn't have a cold or other infection

The most certain way to diagnose asthma is with a lung function test, a medical history, and a physical exam. However, it's hard to do lung function tests in children younger than 5 years. Thus, doctors must rely on children's medical histories, signs and symptoms, and physical exams to make a diagnosis.

Doctors also may use a 4–6 week trial of asthma medicines to see how well a child responds.

Testing in Infants and Young Children

Spirometry and other measures of lung function usually can be done for children older than 6 years, if they can follow directions well. Spirometry might be tried in children as young as 5 years. However, technicians who have special training with young children may need to do the testing.

Instead of spirometry, a growing number of medical centers measure respiratory system resistance. This is another way to test lung function in young children. The child wears nose clips and has his or her cheeks supported with an adult's hands.

The child breathes in and out quietly on a mouthpiece, while the technician measures changes in pressure at the mouth. During these lung function tests, parents can help comfort their children and encourage them to cooperate.

Very young children (younger than 2 years) may need an infant lung function test. This requires special equipment and medical staff. This type of test is available only at a few medical centers.

The doctor gives the child medicine to help him or her sleep through the test. A technician places a mask over the child's nose and mouth and a vest around the child's chest.

The mask and vest are attached to a lung function machine. The machine gently pushes air into the child's lungs through the mask. As the child exhales, the vest slightly squeezes his or her chest. This helps push more air out of the lungs. The exhaled air is then measured.

In children younger than 5 years, doctors likely will use signs and symptoms, medical history, and a physical exam to diagnose lung problems.

Doctors can use pulse oximetry and arterial blood gas tests for children of all ages.

Chapter 36

Treating Asthma in Children

Chapter Contents

Section 36.1

General Treatment Options for Children with Asthma

Text in this section is excerpted from "How Is Asthma Treated and Controlled?" National Heart, Lung, and Blood Institute (NHLBI), August 4, 2014.

It's hard to diagnose asthma in children younger than 5 years. Thus, it's hard to know whether young children who wheeze or have other asthma symptoms will benefit from long-term control medicines. (Quick-relief medicines tend to relieve wheezing in young children whether they have asthma or not.) Doctors will treat infants and young children who have asthma symptoms with long-term control medicines if, after assessing a child, they feel that the symptoms are persistent and likely to continue after 6 years of age.

Inhaled corticosteroids are the preferred treatment for young children. Montelukast and cromolyn are other options. Treatment might be given for a trial period of 1 month to 6 weeks. Treatment usually is stopped if benefits aren't seen during that time and the doctor and parents are confident the medicine was used properly.

Inhaled corticosteroids can possibly slow the growth of children of all ages. Slowed growth usually is apparent in the first several months of treatment, is generally small, and doesn't get worse over time. Poorly controlled asthma also may reduce a child's growth rate.

Many experts think the benefits of inhaled corticosteroids for children who need them to control their asthma far outweigh the risk of slowed growth.

Section 36.2

Do Inhaled Corticosteroids Stunt Children's Growth?

Text in this section is excerpted from "Inhaled Corticosteroids for Childhood Asthma May Affect Adult Height," National Heart, Lung, and Blood Institute (NHLBI), September 3, 2012.

Inhaled corticosteroids for childhood asthma may affect adult height.

Adults who had been treated previously with the inhaled corticosteroid budesonide as part of a children's clinical study were, on average, about half an inch shorter than their study counterparts who were not treated with inhaled corticosteroids, according to research funded by the National Institutes of Health (NIH). The half-inch difference had been observed when the study participants were children, showing that, while the effect on height does not go away, it also does not get worse, the researchers say.

These findings come from a continued follow-up of 1,041 participants in the Childhood Asthma Management Program (CAMP) clinical trial, sponsored by the NIH's National Heart, Lung, and Blood Institute (NHLBI). This is the first large prospective randomized study to follow children until they reached their final adult height since the association between inhaled corticosteroid use and decreased growth rate in children was first reported in the early 1990s.

"The study provides an answer to a longstanding question about what happens long-term to children who experience effects on their growth rate when they begin inhaled corticosteroids therapy for asthma," said Gary Gibbons, M.D., director of the NHLBI. "It clarifies that they do not eventually catch up as they age or fall further behind their peers."

Gibbons added that while the persistence of this effect on height is a noteworthy finding, it must be considered in the larger context that many studies have proven the superior benefits of inhaled corticosteroids on improving asthma control and preventing exacerbations in children.

The researchers also found that the height effect was dependent on medication dosage, as higher daily doses of the inhaled corticosteroid per weight of the child were associated with lower adult height.

"This suggests that finding the minimum dose required to control each child's asthma could help mitigate any potential effects on height," noted lead study researcher William Kelly, Pharm.D., professor emeritus of pediatrics and pharmacy at the University of New Mexico Health Sciences Center, Albuquerque.

"This study demonstrates the value of follow-up studies to clinical trials," said James Kiley, Ph.D., director of the NHLBI's Division of Lung Diseases. "By understanding the long-term benefits and potential side effects of inhaled corticosteroids, we can help parents and physicians make informed choices for treatment."

CAMP involved 1,041 children who were between 5 and 12 years old when they were enrolled in the study between 1993 and 1995. It compared the effects of daily therapies with the inhaled corticosteroid budesonide (400 micrograms per day), the non-steroidal inhaled therapy nedocromil, and a placebo on asthma control, lung development, and growth rate.

With four to six years of treatment, the nedocromil group had similar results as placebo, while children taking budesonide showed many improvements, such as fewer symptoms, fewer acute asthma attacks, fewer hospitalizations, and reduced airway hyperresponsiveness. The children in the budesonide group did experience a mild reduction in their growth rate during the first year of treatment that resulted in the group, on average, being about half an inch shorter than the children in the placebo and nedocromil groups. This effect persisted but did not increase over the duration of the clinical trial.

For this follow-up study, the researchers re-recruited the original CAMP participants and tracked their height, weight, and lung function every year for 12 more years, to an average participant age of 25. During that time, the participants were observed, but they were no longer treated for their asthma by study personnel; instead, they received asthma treatment from their personal physicians.

The researchers obtained adult height values for 943 of the original 1,041 CAMP participants, and observed a 0.47 inch difference in average height for those originally in the budesonide group, similar to the difference seen in the initial study. The deficit in growth rate was seen primarily in prepubertal children (girls 5–10 years of age and boys 5–11 years of age). These follow-up results confirmed that the effect on height during the initial treatment did not progress and was not cumulative, but it did persist to adulthood.

Section 36.3

Dealing with Asthma Flare-Ups in Children

Text in this section is excerpted from "Children and Asthma:
The Goal Is Control" U.S. Food and Drug Administration
(FDA), January 23, 2015.

Children and Asthma: The Goal Is Control

The news about children and asthma is both good and bad. Better treatments have banished the stereotype of the asthmatic child as frail and inactive, heavily relying on an inhaler to breathe. Children with asthma are now living active, independent lives.

The Food and Drug Administration (FDA) is working to make sure that the drugs and devices used to treat asthma—a chronic lung disease that inflames and narrows the airways—are safe and effective.

The bad news is that the number of reported cases of asthma in children has been rising. In 2010, there were 7 million children with asthma, 9.4% of Americans under 18, according to the Centers for Disease Control and Prevention, up from 6.5 million, or 8.9%, in 2005.

One reason may be that doctors are diagnosing more kids; illnesses once known as bronchitis or a croupy cough are now being recognized as asthma. Its symptoms may include coughing, wheezing (a whistling sound when you breathe), chest tightness and shortness of breath, according to the National Heart, Lung, and Blood Institute (NHLBI).

Uncontrolled asthma can lead to chronic lung disease and a poor quality of life, and may slow growth. Benjamin Ortiz, M.D., a medical officer in FDA's Office of Pediatric Therapeutics, recommends that parents work with a pediatrician, and an allergist or pulmonologist (lung specialist) if needed, to develop and follow an asthma action plan that details the treatment options when certain symptoms occur.

"Early intervention results in better health into adulthood," he says.

Knowing the Triggers

"We know what makes asthma worse or better, but don't know the primary cause," Ortiz says. The things that make asthma worse are known as "triggers."

They include:

- Season and climate changes
- High levels of air pollutants
- Tobacco smoke
- Mold
- Mites, roaches
- Plant pollen
- Pet dander
- Strong scents, like perfumes

In addition, certain factors may increase a child's risk of developing asthma:

- Family history of asthma
- Multiple episodes of wheezing before age 2
- Living in crowded housing
- A family member who smokes
- Obesity
- Early development of allergies or eczema

Treatment: Not One-Size-Fits-All

What makes asthma better? While asthma is never "cured," a variety of FDA-approved medications can help manage symptoms.

- For quick relief of severe symptoms, doctors will prescribe "rescue" medications, such as albuterol, which open up the bronchial tubes in the lungs. "The goal is not to use it, but have it available—at home, school, camp—just in case," says Anthony Durmowicz, M.D., a medical officer in the FDA's Center for Drug Evaluation and Research.

- To stabilize chronic and persistent symptoms, doctors will prescribe "controller" medications. The most common, safe and effective controller medications are the inhaled corticosteroids (ICS). With regular treatment, they improve lung function and prevent symptoms and flare-ups, reducing the need for rescue medications, according to NHLBI.

- Children whose asthma is triggered by airborne allergens (allergy-causing substances), or who cannot or will not use ICSs, might take a type of drug called a leukotriene modifier. These come in tablet and chewable forms, though for many people they tend to be less effective than ICSs, especially for more severe asthma, Ortiz says.

- For more severe cases that are not controlled with ICSs or leukotriene modifiers alone, adding long-acting beta agonists (LABAs) such as salmeterol or formoterol might be recommended. FDA cautions against using LABAs alone without an ICS, and recommends that if one must be used, it should be for the shortest time possible.

Most asthma medications are inhaled. Babies and toddlers use a nebulizer, a machine that delivers liquid medication as a fine mist through a tube attached to a face mask. Older children can use a metered dose inhaler or dry-powder inhaler.

To ensure that the proper dose of medication gets into a child's lungs, doctors might also prescribe a device called a spacer, or holding chamber which attaches to the inhaler. "There are practical advantages to using (spacers) in younger kids—the timing and coordination needed to use an inhaler is hard for them," Durmowicz says. Once the child can use the inhaler comfortably, it's no longer as critical, he adds. Clinical trials have shown that "the relative dose delivered to the lungs with and without the spacer is the same."

Health care providers also might recommend the use of a peak-flow meter to check how well a child's asthma is controlled by treatment over time. Peak flow meters measure the amount of air the child expels from the lungs.

The type and combination of medications and devices a doctor prescribes depends on severity, frequency of symptom flare-ups, the child's age, activity schedule and sometimes cost.

Adolescence Is Challenging

In adolescence, Durmowicz says, childhood symptoms might disappear, but they are likely to return or be different. When they disappear, teens might think they no longer need to pack medicines when they travel, or keep them at school.

Other pitfalls include less parental supervision, and reluctance to be seen by their peers taking medicine. Doctors can help with a medication schedule that allows for privacy. Also, dry powder inhalers may be small enough to tuck in a pocket or purse and use discreetly.

Ortiz says that following prescribed treatment when symptoms are present—at any age—is crucial, telling parents, "Your child will lead a normal life if their asthma is well controlled."

Section 36.4

Managing Your Child's Indoor Environment

Text in this chapter is excerpted from "If You Have a Child With Asthma, You're Not Alone," U.S. Environmental Protection Agency (EPA), August 2013.

How To Manage Your Child's Indoor Environment?

Americans spend about 90% of their time indoors. So, managing your child's indoor environment is an important step in reducing exposure to the things that can trigger asthma attacks. Asthma triggers vary from person to person. You and your doctor should determine a plan to reduce the triggers that most affect your child. Listed below are several common indoor environmental triggers and some actions you can take to reduce your child's exposure.

Secondhand Smoke

Asthma can be triggered by the smoke from the burning end of a cigarette, pipe, or cigar, or the smoke breathed out by a smoker.

What You Can Do: Choose not to smoke in your home or car, and do not allow others to do so either.

Pets

Your pet's skin flakes, urine, and saliva can be asthma triggers.

What You Can Do: Consider keeping pets outdoors or even finding a new home for your pets, if necessary. Keep pets out of the bedroom and other sleeping areas at all times, and keep the door closed. Keep pets away from fabric-covered furniture, carpets and stuffed toys.

Dust Mites

Dust mites are too small to be seen, but are found in every home. They live in mattresses, pillows, carpets, fabric-covered furniture, bedcovers, clothes, and stuffed toys.

What You Can Do: Wash sheets and blankets once a week in hot water. Choose washable stuffed toys, wash them often in hot water, and dry thoroughly. Keep stuffed toys off beds. Cover mattresses and pillows in dust-proof (allergen-impermeable) zippered covers.

Pets

Droppings or body parts of pests such as cockroaches or rodents can be asthma triggers.

What You Can Do: Do not leave food or garbage out. Store food in airtight containers. Clean all food crumbs or spilled liquids right away. Try using poison baits, boric acid (for cockroaches), or traps first before using pesticide sprays. If sprays are used, limit the spray to the infested area. Carefully follow instructions on the label. Make sure there is plenty of fresh air when you spray, and keep the person with asthma out of the room.

Molds

Molds grow on damp materials. The key to mold control is moisture control. If mold is a problem in your home, clean up the mold and get rid of excess water or moisture. Lowering the moisture also helps reduce other triggers, such as dust mites and cockroaches.

What You Can Do: Wash mold off hard surfaces and dry completely. Absorbent materials with mold, such as ceiling tiles and carpet, may need to be replaced. Fix leaky plumbing or other sources of water. Use exhaust fans or open windows in kitchens and bathrooms when showering, cooking, or using the dishwasher. Vent clothes dryers to the outside. Maintain low indoor humidity, ideally between 30-50%.

Keys To Preventing Your Child's Attack

- Work with a doctor to develop a written Asthma Management Plan that's right for you and your child.

- Learn what triggers your child's asthma and eliminate or reduce your child's exposure to those allergens and irritants.

- Make sure your child takes medications as prescribed and tell your doctor if there are any problems.

- Keep a daily symptom diary and use a peak flow meter every day to monitor your child's progress.

What Is An Asthma Management Plan?

Written details by your physician should include:

- A list of your child's asthma triggers

- Instructions for using asthma medication(s)

- Instructions for using a daily symptom diary and peak flow meter

- Details about how to stop an asthma attack or episode in progress

- Instructions for when to call the doctor

Chapter 37

Dealing with Asthma at School

Chapter Contents

Section 37.1

School and Asthma: The Basics

Text in this section is excerpted from "Asthma and Schools," Centers for Disease Control and Prevention (CDC), June 17, 2015.

Asthma and Schools

Asthma is a leading chronic illness among children and adolescents in the United States. It is also one of the leading causes of school absenteeism. On average, in a classroom of 30 children, about 3 are likely to have asthma. Low-income populations, minorities, and children living in inner cities experience more emergency department visits, hospitalizations, and deaths due to asthma than the general population.

When children and adolescents are exposed to things in the environment—such as dust mites, and tobacco smoke—an asthma attack can occur. These are called asthma triggers.

Asthma-friendly schools are those that make the effort to create safe and supportive learning environments for students with asthma. They have policies and procedures that allow students to successfully manage their asthma. Research and case studies that looked at ways to best manage asthma in schools found that successful school-based asthma programs

- Establish strong links with asthma care clinicians to ensure appropriate and ongoing medical care

- Target students who are the most affected by asthma at school to identify and intervene with those in greatest need

- Get administrative buy-in and build a team of enthusiastic people, including a full-time school nurse, to support the program

- Use a coordinated, multi-component and collaborative approach that includes school nursing services, asthma education for students and professional development for school staff

- Support evaluation of school-based programs and use adequate and appropriate outcome measures

Section 37.2

Why Schools Should Be Concerned about Asthma

Text in this section is excerpted from "Managing Asthma:
A Guide for Schools," National Heart, Lung, and Blood Institute
(NHLBI), February 24, 2015.

Asthma is common among students

Approximately 7 million children younger than 18 years of age in the United States have asthma. In a classroom of 30 students, about 3 currently have asthma. This rate may be higher in densely populated communities or among certain population groups. For instance, among African American children, 1 in 6 has asthma, an increase of nearly 50 percent from 2001 to 2009. Among Puerto Rican children, 1 in 5 has asthma, more than double the rate among Hispanic children overall. Additionally, there may be students who have asthma but have not been diagnosed.

Asthma is a leading cause of school absenteeism

Studies have shown that many students who have asthma miss school because of their disease. Asthma can lead to absenteeism for a variety of reasons, such as symptoms, doctor visits, hospitalizations, the need to avoid environmental triggers at school, and sleep deprivation due to nighttime asthma attacks. Nearly half of students who have asthma miss at least one day of school each year because of their disease. In 2008, on average, students missed 4 days of school because of asthma.

Uncontrolled asthma can lead to decreased academic performance

When compared with students who do not have a chronic condition, students who have asthma have decreased academic performance, according to standardized test scores and parental reports. More severe asthma is associated with poorer performance. Lower readiness scores were found among kindergarteners who have asthma; and entering school with asthma was found to be linked with lower reading scores after the first year. Effective management of asthma can eliminate potential challenges and obstacles to effective learning and academic success.

Asthma can be controlled—and schools can help

Through the use of well-coordinated asthma management programs, schools can play an effective role in helping students keep their asthma under control. Learn what your school can do to provide quality care for students who have asthma; be prepared to handle asthma emergencies; create an environment with fewer asthma triggers; and promote education and partnerships that support good asthma control.

Section 37.3

Asthma Management at School

This section includes excerpts from "Managing Asthma: A Guide for Schools," Centers for Disease Control and Prevention (CDC), February 24, 2015; and text from "Managing Asthma—A Guide for Schools," National Heart, Lung, and Blood Institute (NHLBI), December 2014.

Effective asthma management at school can help students with asthma stay healthy, learn better, and participate fully during their school day. Although asthma cannot be cured, it can be controlled with proper medical diagnosis and management, and the student's adherence to an individualized treatment regimen.

Good asthma care and control includes assessing asthma severity, assessing and monitoring asthma control, using inhaled corticosteroids (a long-term daily control medication) to reduce inflammation in children with more persistent symptoms, using an asthma action plan (a written plan from the student's health care provider to help manage asthma and prevent asthma attacks), controlling asthma triggers, and having routine follow-up visits with a health care provider. With good asthma management, almost all students who have asthma should:

1. Be free from troublesome symptoms day and night:

   - No coughing or wheezing

   - No difficulty breathing or chest tightness

   - No nighttime awakening due to asthma

2. Have the best possible lung function

3. Be able to participate fully in any activities of their choice

4. Not miss school or work because of asthma symptoms

5. Need fewer or no urgent care visits or hospitalizations for asthma

6. Use medications to control asthma with as few side effects as possible

7. Be satisfied with their asthma care

Keeping asthma under control is important so students can function at their maximum potential. School staff can work together with students, parents and guardians, and health care providers to provide a healthy and safe educational environment for students who have asthma—and, indeed, for all students.

What Effective Asthma Management at School Can Do

Effective asthma management at school can help students with asthma stay healthy, learn better, and participate fully during their school day. Although asthma cannot be cured, it can be controlled with proper medical diagnosis and management, and the student's adherence to an individualized treatment regimen.

Good asthma care and control includes assessing asthma severity, assessing and monitoring asthma control, using inhaled corticosteroids (a long-term daily control medication) to reduce inflammation in children with more persistent symptoms, using an asthma action plan (a written plan from the student's health care provider to help manage asthma and prevent asthma attacks), controlling asthma triggers, and having routine follow-up visits with a health care provider.

With good asthma management, almost all students who have asthma should:

- Be free from troublesome symptoms day and night:
- No coughing or wheezing
- No difficulty breathing or chest tightness
- No night time awakening due to asthma
- have the best possible lung function
- Be able to participate fully in any activities of their choice
- Not miss school or work because of asthma symptoms
- Need fewer or no urgent care visits or hospitalizations for asthma
- use medications to control asthma with as few side effects as possible
- Be satisfied with their asthma care

Keeping asthma under control is important so students can function at their maximum potential. School staff can work together with students, parents and guardians, and health care providers to provide a healthy and safe educational environment for students who have asthma—and, indeed, for all students.

Effective School Asthma Management Programs Can Produce the Following Positive Results:

- A healthier and supportive learning environment for students who have asthma.
- Reduced absences—students have fewer asthma attacks,and symptoms are treated earlier.
- Reduced disruption in the classroom—students have fewer symptoms and are more alert when their asthma is under control.
- Appropriate emergency care—school staff members know how to recognize and respond immediately to asthma emergencies.
- Improved access and adherence to appropriate asthma medications—students and parents feel comfortable asking the school for help if needed in obtaining or using prescribed medications.

- Full student participation in physical activities—physical education teachers,instructors,and coaches know how to prevent exercise-induced asthma or how to respond if symptoms appear. They also know how to help children who are having asthma symptoms and keep them involved in school activities.

Section 37.4

Developing an Asthma Management Program in Your School

Text in this section is excerpted from "Managing Asthma: A Guide for Schools," Centers for Disease Control and Prevention (CDC), February 24, 2015.

An asthma management program can help your school become more responsive to the needs of students who have asthma. Such a program establishes specific policies, procedures, and activities that promote the health, development, and achievement of students who have asthma. It also outlines staff roles and provides staff training on how to help students who have asthma, especially how to recognize and respond appropriately to an asthma attack.

Each school is unique, and some schools may not be able to implement all of these activities at once. It's important to start where you are and make strides toward better asthma management. Schools are encouraged to review the entire list of activities and decide which ones are most practical to implement and best fit the school's own needs and circumstances. Any activities that are not possible now can be viewed as future goals for improving asthma management.

An asthma management program may encompass the following key action items:

- Establish a team to develop, implement, and monitor the asthma management program

- Identify and track students who have asthma

- Provide care, support services, and resources for students who have asthma

- Ensure quick and easy access to prescribed medications, including supporting students who carry and self-administer their asthma medication

- Maintain a school-wide plan for asthma emergencies

- Provide a healthy school environment and reduce asthma triggers

- Enable full participation by students who have asthma

- Educate students, staff, and parents and guardians about asthma

- Promote partnerships among school staff, students, parents and guardians, health care providers, and the community

Each of these action items—and the specific activities related to them, detailed in this section—can contribute to the goal of improved asthma management at school. If your school is just beginning to develop an asthma management program, compare the information in this section with your planned program policies, procedures, and activities, before starting to implement your program. If your school is already engaged in asthma management efforts, reviewing the activities that follow can help you identify where gaps may exist and where you can strengthen your efforts.

It's important that your asthma management program consider federal, state, district, and local laws and requirements. All staff should be aware of and understand the school's responsibilities under these laws. Federal laws that apply to the needs and rights of students who have asthma include the Americans with Disabilities Act, Family Educational Rights and Privacy Act of 1974 (FERPA), Health Insurance Portability and Accountability Act (HIPAA), Individuals with Disabilities Education Act, and Section 504 of the Rehabilitation Act of 1973. Additional information about these laws is available from the Office for Civil Rights at the U.S. Department of Education (see Where to Learn More About Asthma Management). State, district, and local laws and requirements also address issues such as medication use at school, at off-site school-sponsored events, and during school-sponsored transportation.

The rest of this guide discusses in more detail the action items involved in managing asthma in the school. The guide also provides tools and resources that can help schools carry out the specific activities discussed.

Schools and districts are encouraged to monitor students who have asthma and to focus their asthma programs initially on students who have poorly controlled or uncontrolled asthma, as demonstrated by frequent school absences, visits to the school health office, worsening asthma symptoms, use of quick-relief medication more than twice a week for symptom relief, emergency department visits, hospitalizations, or other markers.

Section 37.5

Recognizing Warning Signs of an Asthma Attack

Text in this section is excerpted from "Managing Asthma:
A Guide for Schools," National Heart, Lung, and Blood Institute
(NHLBI), February 24, 2015.

Early Warning Signs and Symptoms of an Asthma Attack

Early warning signs and symptoms usually happen before more serious asthma symptoms occur. These signs can be different for each student who has asthma. Each student's early warning signs should be documented in his or her asthma action plan. Teachers, assistants, aides, and other educators should be aware of each student's early warning signs and watch for those signs.

Encourage students to speak up if they experience any of their early warning signs and symptoms. When you see those signs or a student reports them, act fast to stop symptoms and improve the chances of avoiding an asthma attack. Even mild asthma symptoms can get worse quickly and lead to a serious asthma attack.

These are lists some common early warning signs:

- Mild cough

- Itchy, scratchy, or sore throat

- Mild difficulty breathing

- Itchy, watery, or glassy eyes

- Mild wheezing

- Itchy or runny nose

- Chest starts to hurt or feel tight

- Waking up at night

- Cannot do all usual activities

- Need more quick-relief medication than usual

- Low peak flow readings

It's best to be prepared before asthma symptoms get worse or an asthma attack happens. Review students' asthma action plans so you know what to watch for and what to do in case of symptoms or an asthma attack. Keep asthma action plans where you can easily access them. In case of an asthma attack, follow the student's asthma action plan and call the school nurse or other school health staff to help the student right away.

Section 37.6

How Asthma-Friendly Is Your School?

Text in this section is excerpted from "Managing Asthma:
A Guide for Schools" Centers for Disease Control and
Prevention (CDC), February 24, 2015.

Students who have asthma need proper support at school to keep their asthma under control and be fully active. Use this checklist to find out how well your school serves students who have asthma:

- Are the school buildings and grounds free of tobacco smoke at all times?

- Are all school buses, vans, and trucks free of tobacco smoke?

- Are all school events, like field trips and team games (both "at-home" and "away") free from tobacco smoke?

- Does your school have a policy or rule that allows students to carry and use their own asthma medicines?

- If some students do not carry their asthma medicines, do they have quick and easy access to their medicines?

- Does your school have a written emergency plan for teachers and staff to follow to take care of a student who has an asthma attack?

- In an emergency, such as a fire, weather event, or lockdown, or if a student forgets his or her medicine, does your school have standing orders and quick-relief medicines for students to use?

- Do all students who have asthma have updated asthma action plans on file at the school? (An asthma action plan is a written plan from the student's doctor to help manage asthma and prevent asthma attacks.)

- Is there a school nurse or other school health staff in your school building during the school day?

- Does a nurse or other school health staff identify, assess, and monitor students who have asthma at your school?

- Does a nurse or other school health staff help students with their medicines, and help them to participate fully in exercise and other physical activity, including physical education, sports, recess, and field trips?

- If a school nurse or other school health staff is not full-time in your school, is a nurse readily and routinely available to write and review plans and give the school guidance on these issues?

- Does an asthma education expert teach all school staff about asthma, asthma action plans, and asthma medicines?

- Is asthma information incorporated into health, science, first aid, and other classes as appropriate?

- Can students who have asthma participate fully and safely in a range of exercise and other physical activity, including physical education, sports, recess, and field trips?

- Are students' quick-relief medicines nearby, before, during, and after they exercise?

- Can students who have asthma choose a physical activity that is different from others in the class when it is medically necessary?

- Can students who have asthma choose another activity without fear of being ridiculed or receiving reduced grades?

- Does the school have good indoor air quality?

- Does the school help to reduce or prevent students' contact with allergens or irritants--indoors and outdoors—that can make their asthma worse?

- Are any of the following present?

- Cockroach droppings

- Excessive dust and/or carpets, pillows, cloth-covered or uphol-stered furniture, or stuffed toys that harbor dust mites (tiny bugs too small to see)

- Mold or persistent moisture

- Pets with fur or hair

- Strong odors or sprays, such as paint, perfume, bug spray, and cleaning products

- Does your school have a no-idling policy for vehicles on school grounds, such as school buses and carpools?

- Does your school monitor daily local Air Quality Index (AQI) information to help reduce students' exposure to unhealthy air quality?

- Does your school partner with parents and health care providers to address students' asthma needs?

- Does your school work with an asthma specialist in the community?

If the answer to any question is "no," then it may be harder for students to have good control of their asthma. Uncontrolled asthma can hinder a student's attendance, participation, and progress in school.

School staff, health care providers, and families should work together to make schools more asthma-friendly to promote student health and education.

Section 37.7

Addressing Asthma within a Coordinated School Health Program

Text in this section is excerpted from "Guidelines & Strategies," Centers for Disease Control and Prevention (CDC), July 17, 2015.

Strategies for Addressing Asthma

A healthy student is a student ready to learn. Asthma-friendly schools are those that make the effort to create safe and supportive learning environments for students with asthma. They have policies and procedures that allow students to successfully manage their asthma. Chances for success are better when the whole school community takes part–school administrators, teachers, and staff, as well as students and parents.

CDC has identified six strategies for schools and districts to consider when addressing asthma within a coordinated school health program. These strategies can be effective whether your program is for the entire school district or just one school.

1. Establish **management and support systems** for asthma-friendly schools.

2. Provide appropriate **school health and mental health services** for students with asthma.

3. Provide **asthma education** and awareness programs for students and school staff.

4. Provide a safe and **healthy school environment** to reduce asthma triggers.

5. Provide safe, enjoyable **physical education and activity** opportunities for students with asthma.

6. Coordinate **school, family, and community efforts** to better manage asthma symptoms and reduce school absences among students with asthma.

The Six Strategies

1. Establish management and support systems for asthma-friendly schools.

- Identify your school's or district's existing asthma needs, resources for meeting those needs, and potential barriers.

- Designate a person to coordinate asthma activities at the district and school levels. If your school or district has a health coordinator, determine if asthma coordination can be integrated into his or her activities.

- Share these strategies with the district health council and school health team if they exist. If you do not have a council or team, help create them. Ensure that school-based asthma management is addressed as a high priority.

- Develop and implement written policies and procedures regarding asthma education and management. Promote asthma programs that are culturally and linguistically appropriate.

- Use or adapt existing school health records to identify all students with diagnosed asthma.

- Use health room and attendance records to track students with asthma. Focus particularly on students with poorly managed asthma as demonstrated by frequent school absences, school health office visits, emergency room visits, or hospitalizations. Avoid mass screening[*] and mass case detection[†] as methods for routine identification. These methods have not been shown to meet the World Health Organization's or American Academy of Pediatrics's criteria for population or school screening programs.

- Use 504 Plans or Individualized Education Plans (IEPs), as appropriate, especially for health services and physical activity modifications.

- Obtain administrative support and seek support from others in the school and community for addressing asthma within a coordinated school health program.

- Develop systems to promote ongoing communication among students, parents, teachers, school nurses, and health care providers to ensure that students' asthma is well-managed at school.

- Seek available federal, state, and private funding for school asthma programs.

- Evaluate asthma program strategies and policies annually. Use this information to improve programs.

  * *Screening for asthma (spirometry) can identify students who, in a test situation, exhibit signs and symptoms of asthma. These students may or may not truly have asthma.*

  † *Case detection (symptom questionnaires) can identify students with asthma symptoms who may or may not have the disease. Only testing and evaluation by a health professional can confirm which students truly have asthma.*

2. Provide appropriate school health and mental health services for students with asthma.

- Obtain a written asthma action plan for all students with asthma. The plan should be developed by a primary care provider and be provided by parents. It should include individualized emergency protocol, medications, peak flow monitoring, environmental triggers, and emergency contact information. Share the plan with appropriate faculty and staff in accordance with the Family Educational Rights and Privacy Act (FERPA) guidelines or with parental permission.

- Ensure that at all times students have immediate access to medications, as prescribed by a physician and approved by parents. Specific options, such as allowing students to self-carry and self-administer medications, should be determined on a case-by-case basis with input from the physician, parent, and school.

- Use standard emergency protocols for students in respiratory distress if they do not have their own asthma action plan.

- Ensure that case management is provided for students with frequent school absences, school health office visits, emergency department visits, or hospitalizations due to asthma.

- Provide a full-time registered nurse all day, every day for each school.

- Ensure access to a consulting physician for each school.

- Refer students without a primary care provider to child health insurance programs and providers.

- Provide and coordinate school-based counseling, psychological, and social services for students with asthma, as appropriate. Coordinate with community services.

‡ *Case management by a trained professional includes assessing needs and planning a continuum of care for students and families.*

3. Provide asthma education and awareness programs for students and school staff.

- Ensure that students with asthma receive education on asthma basics, asthma management, and emergency response. Encourage parents to participate in these programs.

- Provide school staff with education on asthma basics, asthma management, and emergency response as part of their professional development activities. Include classroom teachers, physical education teachers, coaches, secretaries, administrative assistants, principals, facility and maintenance staff, food service staff, and bus drivers

- Integrate asthma awareness and lung health education lessons into health education curricula.

- Provide and/or support smoking prevention and cessation programs for students and staff.

4. Provide a safe and healthy school environment to reduce asthma triggers.

- Prohibit tobacco use at all times, on all school property (including all buildings, facilities, and school grounds), in any form of school transportation, and at school-sponsored events on and off school property (for example, field trips).

- Prevent indoor air quality problems by reducing or eliminating allergens and irritants, including tobacco smoke; dust and debris from construction and remodeling; dust mites, molds, warmblooded animals, cockroaches, and other pests.

5. Provide safe, enjoyable physical education and activity opportunities for students with asthma.

- Encourage full participation in physical activities when students are well.

- Provide modified activities as indicated by a student's asthma action plan, 504 Plan, and/or IEP, as appropriate.

- Ensure that students have access to preventive medications before activity and immediate access to emergency medications during activity.

6. Coordinate school, family, and community efforts to better manage asthma symptoms and reduce school absences among students with asthma.

- Obtain written parental permission for school health staff and primary care providers to share student health information.

- Educate, support, and involve family members in efforts to reduce students' asthma symptoms and school absences.

- Work with local community programs. Coordinate school and community services, including community health care providers, community asthma programs and coalitions, community counselors, social workers, case managers, and before- and after-school programs. Encourage interested school staff to participate in community asthma coalitions.

Chapter 38

Physical Activity in Children with Asthma: Tips for Parents and Caregivers

Don't Let Asthma Keep You Out of the Game

Recently, more than ever, asthma is not a barrier to physical activity. In fact, if you keep your asthma under control, you can do it all! Need proof? Well, did you know that:

- At the 1984 summer Olympics, 67 of the 597 American athletes had asthma. Among them, they won 41 medals.

- Twenty percent of the athletes at the 1996 summer Olympics had asthma brought on by physical activity

- Almost 30% of the American swimmers on the 2000 summer Olympic team had asthma and used inhalers.

Asthma didn't hold them back, and it shouldn't hold you back, either!

Text in this section is excerpted from "Meeting The Challenge," Centers for Disease Control and Prevention (CDC), January 22, 2013.

Physical Activity → Asthma?

Things like cold or dry air, dust, pollen, pollution, cigarette smoke, or stress can "trigger" asthma. This can make your body pump out chemicals that close off your airways, making it hard for air to get into to your lungs, and causing an asthma attack.

Physical activity can trigger asthma attacks too. Experts don't know for sure why physical activity sometimes brings one on, but they suspect that fast breathing through the mouth (like what happens when you get winded) can irritate the airways. In addition, when air pollution levels are high, physical activity in the afternoon is harder on the lungs than morning activity — pollution levels rise later in the day.

Get Fit

So, should you get a doctor's note and skip gym class? Sorry, no. Doctors want their asthma patients to get active, especially in asthma-friendly activities like these: swimming, bicycling, golf, inline skating, and weightlifting.

Why are these good choices if you want to be physically active?

- They let you control how hard and fast you breathe
- They let you breathe through your nose at all times
- They don't dry out your airways
- They mix short, intense activities with long endurance workouts
- You can do them in a controlled environment (for example, a gym with air that's not too cold or dry)
- Usually you do them with other people, who can help you if an attack comes on

Getting regular physical activity can improve your breathing, and lead to fewer asthma attacks. Just remember to follow these tips. (In fact, this is good advice for everyone, not just those with asthma.)

- **Ease into it.**

Start your workout with a warm-up, and don't overdo it by running five miles on your first day if you get winded walking around the block! Finish up with a cool-down.

- **Take a buddy.**

It's more fun and a friend can help if you get into trouble.

- **Respect your body.**

Stay away from the things that trigger your asthma. Help out your airways by breathing through your nose instead of your mouth. Take it easy on days when your asthma symptoms are really bugging you. And stick to the medicine routine that your doctor has set up.

- **Take breaks.**

Treat yourself to rest and drink plenty of water.

- **Mix it up.**

For example, try going inline skating one day and taking a long walk the next.

Chapter 39

Parenting a Teen with Asthma

What's Happening at School?

Knowing the answers to the following questions can help you support your child's school to address asthma.. If you don't know the answers to these questions, check out the school handbook or school website, attend a school wellness meeting Parent-Teacher Association (PTA) meeting, or simply ask your child's teacher.

1. Is there a full-time registered nurse in the school building at all times, or a school-based health center to help children with chronic medical conditions or emergencies?

2. How does the school identify and share information about students with asthma?

3. Does the school require that each student with asthma have a current Asthma Action Plan on file?

4. Does the school allow students to carry their own medication, such as an inhaler, at school?

Text in this chapter is excerpted from "Children and Adolescents with Asthma," Centers for Disease Control and Prevention (CDC), November 1, 2015.

5. What are the school protocols if a student is having asthma symptoms at school, on the school bus, on a field trip, or in cases of emergency or lockdown?

6. Are other school staff, such as teachers, bus drivers, and food services staff, trained to recognize and respond to a student that may be having asthma symptoms

7. What is the policy for student participation in physical activity (e.g., recess or classroom activity breaks) or physical education at school if he or she has asthma?

8. Is there a bullying prevention policy in the school or district that discourages bullying or encourages awareness or anti-stigma of students with medical conditions?

9. Does the school or district have an indoor air quality management program to improve the school environment and reduce exposure to asthma triggers?

Ideas for Parents

You can be involved in your child's school by attending meetings, workshops, or training events offered by the school; communicating with school staff and other parents; volunteering for school events or in your child's classroom; reinforcing healthy messages and practices your child learns at school; helping make decisions about health in the school; and being part of community activities supported by the school. Here are some specific ideas for how you can support your child's school in addressing asthma

- Advocate for a full-time registered nurse in school

- Have an ongoing conversation with your child to discuss their asthma triggers, their feelings about having asthma, and if they feel safe and supported at school.

- Work with your child's health care provider to provide an Asthma Action Plan for the school and for the timely completion of required school forms. Encourage communication between school health services and your child's health care provider.

- Make sure that the school has your child's emergency asthma medication so that asthma symptoms can be managed at school.

- Keep your emergency contact information up to date with the teacher and school nurse.

Part Six

Asthma in Other Special Populations

Chapter 40

Asthma and Pregnancy

Discussing Current Medications

Some pregnant women must take medications to treat health conditions. For example, if a woman has asthma, epilepsy (seizures), high blood pressure, or depression, she might need to continue to take medication to stay healthy during pregnancy. If these conditions are not treated, a pregnant woman or her unborn baby could be harmed. It is important for a woman to discuss with her doctor which medications are needed during pregnancy. She also should talk to her doctor about which medications are likely to be the safest to take during pregnancy. It is important to balance the possible risks and benefits of any medication being considered. Suddenly stopping the use of a medication may be riskier than continuing to use the medication while under a doctor's care.

It also is important to know that dietary and herbal products, such as vitamins or herbs added to foods and drink, could be harmful to an unborn baby. These products can have other side effects when used during pregnancy. It's best for a woman to talk with her healthcare provider about everything she's taking or thinking about taking.

This chapter includes excerpts from "Medicine and Pregnancy," Centers for Disease Control and Prevention (CDC), December 3, 2014; text from "Maternal Asthma Medication Use and the Risk of Selected Birth Defects," Centers for Disease Control and Prevention (CDC), October 22, 2014; text from "Management of Asthma," Federal Bureau of Prisons (BOP), May 2013; and text from "Medications and Pregnancy," Centers for Disease Control and Prevention (CDC), December 3, 2014.

Accidental Exposure

Sometimes women take medication before they realize that they are pregnant. When this happens, they may worry about the effects of the medication on their unborn baby. The first thing a woman who is pregnant or who is planning on becoming pregnant should do is talk with her healthcare provider. Some medications are harmful when taken during pregnancy, but others are unlikely to cause harm.

Maternal Asthma Medication Use and the Risk of Selected Birth Defects

Recently, researchers used data from the National Birth Defects Prevention Study (NBDPS) to examine maternal asthma medication use during pregnancy and the risk of certain birth defects. The findings from this article are summarized in the following text.

Asthma—a disease that affects the lungs

Asthma is a common disease during pregnancy, affecting about 4%–12% of pregnant women. About 3% of pregnant women use asthma medications, including bronchodilators or anti-inflammatory drugs. Currently, guidelines recommend that women with asthma continue to use medication to control their condition during pregnancy. However, the safety data on using asthma medications during pregnancy are limited.

Main findings from studying pregnant women under medications

- Data from the study showed that using asthma medication during pregnancy

- Did not increase the risk for most of the birth defects studied.

- Might increase the risk for some birth defects, such as esophageal atresia (birth defect of the esophagus or food tube), anorectal atresia (birth defect of the anus), and omphalocele (birth defect of the abdominal wall).

- The most commonly reported asthma medications used during pregnancy were

- Albuterol (2%–3% of women)

- Fluticasone (About 1% of women)

- It was difficult to determine if asthma or other health problems related to having asthma increased the risk for these birth defects, or if the increased risk was from the medication use during pregnancy.

Medication during pregnancy: CDC activities

About 1 in every 33 babies is born with a birth defect. Birth defects are one of the leading causes of infant deaths, accounting for more than 20% of all infant deaths. Centers for Disease Control and Prevention (CDC) is committed to working with its partners and the public to build a comprehensive approach to understanding and communicating the risks of birth defects that potentially are associated with the use of medications during pregnancy.

- Research: CDC funds a large study of birth defects called the National Birth Defects Prevention Study. This study is working to identify risk factors for birth defects and to answer questions about some medications taken during pregnancy.

- Technical expertise: CDC works with staff from the U.S. Food and Drug Administration (FDA) and other professionals to help conduct studies on the effects of medication use during pregnancy and ways to prevent harmful effects.

Medicine and Pregnancy

Not all medicines are safe to take when you are pregnant. Even aspirin or ibuprofen could cause problems if you take it during the last 3 months of your pregnancy. Here are some tips to help you learn more about how prescription and over-the-counter medicines might affect you and your baby.

Ask Questions.

Always talk to your healthcare provider before you take any medicines, herbs, or vitamins. Don't stop taking your medicines until your healthcare provider says that it is OK.

Use these questions:

- **What should I do if I want to get pregnant?** Before you get pregnant, work with your doctor to make a plan to help you safely use your medicines.

- **How might this medicine affect my baby?** Ask about the benefits and risks for you and your baby.

- **What medicines should I avoid?** Some drugs can harm your baby during different stages of your pregnancy. At these times, your doctor may have you take something else.

- **Will I need to take more or less of my medicine?** Your heart and kidneys work harder when you are pregnant. This makes medicines pass through your body faster than usual.

- **What kind of vitamins should I take?** Ask about special vitamins for pregnant women. Do not take regular vitamins. They may have too much or too little of the vitamins that you need. Also ask about how much folic acid you should take before you become pregnant through the first part of your pregnancy. Folic acid helps to prevent birth defects of the baby's brain or spine.

- **Can I keep taking this medicine when I start breastfeeding?** Some drugs can get into your breast milk and affect your baby.

Read the Label.

Check the drug labels and other information you get with your medicine to learn about the possible risks for women who are pregnant or breastfeeding. The labels tell you what is known about how the drugs might affect pregnant women. Your healthcare provider can help you decide if you should take the drug.

The prescription drug labels are changing. The new labels will replace the old A, B, C, D, and X categories with more helpful information about a medicine's risks. The labels will also have more information on whether the medicine gets into breast milk and how it can possibly affect the baby.

Be Smart Online.

Double check the information you get online with your doctor, nurse, or pharmacist. Some websites say that drugs are safe, but they cannot know if it safe for you. Every woman's body is different.

- Do not trust that a product is safe just because it says "natural."

- Ask before you use a product that you heard about in a chat room or group.

Know the risks.

Report Problems.

Tell FDA about any serious problems you have after taking a medicine.

- Call 1-800-FDA-1088 to get a reporting form sent to you by mail.

- Report problems online (www.accessdata.fda.gov/scripts/med-watch/index.cfm?action=reporting.home).

Treatment in Pregnancy

- Providers should monitor pregnant patients' asthma status during prenatal visits.

- Albuterol is the preferred SABA because it has an excellent safety profile; furthermore, the most data related to safety during human pregnancy are available for this medication.

- ICSs are the preferred treatment for long-term control medication in pregnant patients. Budesonide is the preferred ICS, as it has been studied more in pregnant patients than other ICSs.

- For the treatment of comorbid conditions, intranasal corticosteroids are recommended for treating allergic rhinitis because they have a low risk of systemic effect.

Chapter 41

Asthma in Seniors: An Overview

Asthma affects people of every race, sex, and age. Currently in the United States, more than 23 million people have asthma. Approximately 13.6 million adults have been diagnosed with chronic obstructive pulmonary disease (COPD), and an approximately equal number have not yet been diagnosed. The burden of respiratory diseases affects individuals and their families, schools, workplaces, neighborhoods, cities, and states. Because of the cost to the health care system, the burden of respiratory diseases also falls on society; it is paid for with higher health insurance rates, lost productivity, and tax dollars. Annual health care expenditures for asthma alone are estimated at $20.7 billion.

What is Asthma?

Asthma is a chronic inflammatory disorder of the airways characterized by episodes of reversible breathing problems due to airway narrowing and obstruction. These episodes can range in severity from mild to life threatening. Symptoms of asthma include wheezing, coughing, chest tightness, and shortness of breath. Daily preventive treatment

This chapter includes excerpts from "COPD," National Institutes Of Health (NIH) Senior Health, March 2013; and text from "Respiratory Diseases," Office of Disease Prevention and Health Promotion (ODPHP), October 1, 2014; and text from "Quitting Smoking for Older Adults," National Institutes of Health (NIH) Senior Health, April 26, 2014; and text from "Talking With Your Doctor: A Guide for Older People," National Institute of Aging (NIA), January 22, 2015.

can prevent symptoms and attacks and enable individuals who have asthma to lead active lives.

What is COPD?

Chronic obstructive pulmonary disease, or COPD, is a progressive lung disease in which the airways of the lungs become damaged, making it harder to breathe. With COPD, airways become blocked, making it harder to get air in and out.

What causes COPD?

Cigarette smoking is the most common cause of COPD. Most people with COPD are smokers or have been smokers in the past. Breathing in other fumes and dusts over long periods of time can also lead to COPD.

Pipe, cigar, and other types of tobacco smoking can cause COPD, especially if the smoke is inhaled. Exposure to secondhand smoke can play a role in causing COPD. Most people with COPD are at least 40 years old or around middle age when symptoms start.

How is COPD diagnosed?

To confirm a COPD diagnosis, a doctor will use a breathing test called spirometry. The test is easy and painless. It shows how well the lungs are working.

The spirometer measures how much air the lungs can hold and how fast air is blown out of the lungs. Other tests, such as bronchodilator reversibility testing, a chest X-ray, and arterial blood gas test, may be ordered.

What are the treatments for COPD?

Treatment for COPD can be different for each person and is based on whether symptoms are mild, moderate or severe. Treatments include medication, pulmonary or lung rehabilitation, oxygen treatment, and surgery. There are also treatments to manage complications or a sudden onset of symptoms.

Asthma and COPD

Asthma and chronic obstructive pulmonary disease (COPD) are significant public health burdens. Specific methods of detection, intervention, and treatment exist that may reduce this burden and promote health.

Asthma is a chronic inflammatory disorder of the airways characterized by episodes of reversible breathing problems due to airway narrowing and obstruction. These episodes can range in severity from mild to life threatening. Symptoms of asthma include wheezing, coughing, chest tightness, and shortness of breath. Daily preventive treatment can prevent symptoms and attacks and enable individuals who have asthma to lead active lives.

COPD is a preventable and treatable disease characterized by airflow limitation that is not fully reversible. The airflow limitation is usually progressive and associated with an abnormal inflammatory response of the lung to noxious particles or gases (typically from exposure to cigarette smoke). Treatment can lessen symptoms and improve quality of life for those with COPD.

How Smoking Affects Older People's Health

The damage from smoking affects most parts of your body, from your skin to your brain, to all of your organs, to your immune system function. In fact, there are very few parts of your body that are spared the negative effects of tobacco.

Among people 50 and older, smokers are more likely to report health problems such as coughing, trouble breathing, and getting tired more easily than nonsmokers. Smoking could be making an existing medical condition worse, or it could be causing conditions that you might not have if you didn't smoke.

Smoking Is Linked to Many Diseases

Smoking is linked to many diseases besides cancer, including

- heart disease
- high blood pressure
- stroke
- emphysema, chronic bronchitis, chronic obstructive pulmonary disease (COPD), or asthma
- diabetes complications
- bone disease
- bone density loss
- cataracts (cloudiness in the eyes)

- pain or tightness in the chest

- stomach ulcers

Dangers of Secondhand Smoke

Smoking can also affect the health of nonsmokers. Smoke that comes from the burning of a tobacco product or smoke that is exhaled by smokers is called secondhand smoke.

The same cancer-causing chemicals that tobacco smokers breathe in are also inhaled in lower amounts by people exposed to secondhand tobacco smoke. Nonsmokers who are breathing in secondhand smoke have a higher risk of lung cancer and coronary heart disease.

Talking with Your Doctor: A Guide for Older People

Why Does It Matter?

How well you and your doctor talk to each other is one of the most important parts of getting good health care. But, talking to your doctor isn't always easy. It takes time and effort on your part as well as your doctor's.

In the past, the doctor typically took the lead and the patient followed. Today, a good patient-doctor relationship is more of a partnership. You and your doctor can work as a team, along with nurses, physician assistants, pharmacists, and other healthcare providers, to solve your medical problems and keep you healthy.

This means asking questions if the doctor's explanations or instructions are unclear, bringing up problems even if the doctor doesn't ask, and letting the doctor know if you have concerns about a particular treatment or change in your daily life. Taking an active role in your health care puts the responsibility for good communication on both you and your doctor.

All of this is true at any age. But, when you're older, it becomes even more important to talk often and comfortably with your doctor. That's partly because you may have more health conditions and treatments to discuss. It's also because your health has a big impact on other parts of your life, and that needs to be talked about too.

Choosing a Doctor You Can Talk To

- Decide what you are looking for in a doctor.

- Identify several possible doctors.
- Consult reference sources, including those online.
- Talk to office staff to learn more about the doctors you are considering.
- Make a choice.

Getting Ready for an Appointment

- Be prepared: make a list of concerns.
- Take information with you.
- Consider bringing a family member or friend.
- Make sure you can see and hear as well as possible.
- Plan to update the doctor on what has happened since your last visit.

Giving Information

- Share any symptoms.
- Give information about your medications.
- Tell the doctor about your habits.
- Voice other concerns.

Getting Information

- Learn about medical tests.
- Discuss your diagnosis and what you can expect.
- Find out about your medications.
- Understand how to take your prescriptions.

Making Decisions with Your Doctor

- Ask about different treatments.
- Ask about prevention.
- Talk about exercise.

Talking to Doctors in Special Situations

- Ask questions if you are unclear.

- Try to write down as much information as possible.

- Tell your primary care doctor if you see a specialist, need surgery, or have gone to the emergency room.

Practical Matters

- Don't hesitate to bring up concerns, even if they don't seem directly related to a medical condition.

- You and your doctor can make better decisions together if the doctor knows about your non-medical concerns.

- If the doctor can't help solve your non-medical problems, he or she may be able to refer you to other resources that can help.

Discussing Sensitive Subjects

- Don't hesitate to discuss sensitive subjects with your doctor.

- Use brochures or booklets as props to introduce topics you may feel awkward discussing.

- If you feel the doctor doesn't take your concerns seriously, it might be time to think about changing doctors.

Involving Your Family and Friends

- A family member or friend can be helpful during a doctor's visit.

- Remember you are still in control of the appointment.

Chapter 42

Asthma and Minority Populations

Chapter Contents

Section 42.1

Asthma and African Americans

This section includes excerpts from "Asthma and African Americans," Office of Minority Health (OMH), April 22, 2015; and text from "Minority Women's Health," Office on Women's Health (OWH), July 16, 2012.

In 2012, almost 2.8 million non-Hispanic Blacks reported that they currently have asthma.

- African Americans were 20 percent more likely to have asthma than non-Hispanic whites, in 2012.

- In 2013, African Americans were three times more likely to die from asthma related causes than the white population.

- From 2003-2005, African American children had a death rate 7 times that of non-Hispanic white children.

- Black children are 3 times more likely to be admitted to the hospital for asthma, as compared to non-Hispanic white children.

- While all of the causes of asthma remain unclear, children exposed to secondhand tobacco smoke exposure are at increased risk for acute lower respiratory tract infections, such as asthma. Children living below or near the poverty level are more likely to have high levels of blood cotinine, breakdown product of nicotine, than children living in higher income families.

Anybody can get asthma, but it is seen more often in African-Americans. More than 3 million African-Americans have asthma. African-Americans go to the hospital emergency room more than whites because of asthma. They also are almost three times more likely to die from asthma-related causes than whites. Asthma most often starts in childhood, and it is a top health problem for African-American children. Asthma is a leading reason why kids miss school.

Table 42.1. Current asthma prevalence percentage, adults ages 18 and over

	Non-Hispanic Black	Non-Hispanic White	Non-Hispanic Black/ Non-Hispanic White Ratio
Men	7.2	5.4	1.3
Women	9.9	9.2	1.1
Both Sexes	8.6	7.3	1.2

Source: CDC 2014. National Health Interview Survey Data 2013.

Table 42.2. Percentage of asthma among persons 18 years of age and over, ever being told they had asthma

	Non-Hispanic Black	Non-Hispanic White	Non-Hispanic Black/ Non-Hispanic White Ratio
Men	12.6	11.3	1.1
Women	16.4	15.4	1.1
Both Sexes	14.7	13.4	1.1

Source: CDC 2014. Summary Health Statistics for U.S. Adults: 2012.

Table 42.3. Percentage of current asthma prevalence

	Non-Hispanic Black	Non-Hispanic White	Non-Hispanic Black/ Non-Hispanic White Ratio
Men	8	6.1	1.3
Women	12.2	10.2	1.2
Both Sexes	10.3	8.2	1.3

Source: CDC 2014. Summary Health Statistics for U.S. Adults: 2012.

Table 42.4. Deaths per 100,000, with asthma as the underlying cause, National Vital Statistics System

Non-Hispanic Black	Non-Hispanic White	Non-Hispanic Black/ Non-Hispanic White Ratio
2.6	0.8	3.3

Source: CDC 2014. Deaths: Final Data for 2013.

Table 42.5. Age-adjusted percentages for children under 18 years of age, ever being told they had asthma

Non-Hispanic Black	Non-Hispanic White	Non-Hispanic Black/Non-Hispanic White Ratio
21.8	12.9	1.8

Source: CDC, 2013. Summary Health Statistics for U.S. Children: National Health Interview Survey, 2012.

Table 42.6. Age-adjusted percentages for children under 18 years of age, who currently have asthma

Non-Hispanic Black	Non-Hispanic White	Non-Hispanic Black/Non-Hispanic White Ratio
16.1	7.9	2

Source: CDC, 2013. Summary Health Statistics for U.S. Children: National Health Interview Survey, 2012.

Table 42.7. Current asthma prevalence percentage, children ages 18 and under

	Non-Hispanic Black	Non-Hispanic White	Non-Hispanic Black/Non-Hispanic White Ratio
Boys	15.7	8.1	1.9
Girls	11.1	6.9	1.6
Both Sexes	13.4	7.5	1.8

Source: CDC 2014. National Health Interview Survey Data 2013.

Table 42.8. Hospital admissions rate for asthma, children ages 2-17, United States

Non-Hispanic Black	Non-Hispanic White	Non-Hispanic Black/Non-Hispanic White Ratio
363.9	83.8	4.3

Source: National Healthcare Quality and Disparities Reports.

Section 42.2

Asthma and Asian Americans

Text in this section is excerpted from "Asthma and Asian Americans," Office of Minority Health (OMH), April 22, 2015.

- In 2012, 591,000 Asian Americans reported that they currently have asthma.

- Asian Americans generally have lower rates of asthma than the white population, however their death rate is higher.

- Data on asthma conditions for Asian Americans is limited.

- While all of the causes of asthma remain unclear, children exposed to secondhand tobacco smoke exposure are at increased risk for acute lower respiratory tract infections, such as asthma. Children living below or near the poverty level are more likely to have high levels of blood cotinine, a breakdown product of nicotine, than children living in higher income families.

Table 42.9. Percentage of asthma among persons 18 years of age and over, currently have asthma

Asian	Non-Hispanic White	Asian/Non-Hispanic White Ratio
4.9	8.2	0.6

Source: CDC 2014. Summary Health Statistics for U.S. Adults: 2012.

Table 42.10. Percentage of asthma among persons 18 years of age and over, ever being told they had asthma

Asian	Non-Hispanic White	Asian/Non-Hispanic White Ratio
7.6	13.4	0.6

Source: CDC 2014. Summary Health Statistics for U.S. Adults: 2012.

Table 42.11. Hospital admissions rate for asthma, adults age 18 and over, United States

Asian	Non-Hispanic White	Asian/Non-Hispanic White Ratio
65.4	90.5	0.7

Source: National Healthcare Quality and Disparities Reports.

Table 42.12. Deaths per 100,000, with asthma as the underlying cause, National Vital Statistics System

Asian	Non-Hispanic White	Asian/ Non-Hispanic White Ratio
1.1	0.8	1.4

Source: CDC 2014. Deaths: Final Data for 2013.

Table 42.13. Age-adjusted percentages for children under 18 years of age, ever being told they had asthma

Asian	Non-Hispanic White	Asian/ Non-Hispanic White Ratio
9	12.4	0.7

Source: CDC, 2013. Summary Health Statistics for U.S. Children: National Health Interview Survey, 2012.

Table 42.14. Age-adjusted percentages for children under 18 years of age, who currently have asthma

Asian	Non-Hispanic White	Asian/ Non-Hispanic White Ratio
4.9	7.9	0.6

Source: CDC, 2013. Summary Health Statistics for U.S. Children: National Health Interview Survey, 2012.

Section 42.3

Asthma and Hispanic Americans

Text in this section is excerpted from "Asthma and Hispanic Americans," Office of Minority Health (OMH), April 22, 2015.

- In 2012, 2,145,000 Hispanics reported that they currently have asthma.

- Puerto Rican Americans have almost twice the asthma rate as compared to the overall Hispanic population.

- Hispanics are 60 percent more likely to visit the hospital for asthma, as compared to non-Hispanic whites.

- Puerto Rican children are almost three times more likely to have asthma, as compared to non-Hispanic whites.

- Hispanic children are 40 percent more likely to die from asthma, as compared to non-Hispanic whites.

- While all of the causes of asthma remain unclear, children exposed to secondhand tobacco smoke exposure are at increased risk for acute lower respiratory tract infections, such as asthma. Children living below or near the poverty level are more likely to have high levels of blood cotinine, a breakdown product of nicotine, than children living in higher income families.

Table 42.15. Current asthma prevalence percentage, adults ages 18 and over

	Population	Non-Hispanic White	Population / Non-Hispanic White Ratio
All Hispanic	5.2	7.3	0.7
Puerto Rican	12.2	7.3	1.7
Mexican	4.1	7.3	0.6

Source: CDC 2014. National Health Interview Survey Data 2013.

Table 42.16. Percentage of asthma among persons 18 years of age and over, ever being told they had asthma

	Hispanic	Non-Hispanic White	Hispanic/ Non-Hispanic White Ratio
Men	8.6	11.3	0.8
Women	11.8	15.4	0.8
Both Sexes	10.4	13.4	0.8

Source: CDC 2014. Summary Health Statistics for U.S. Adults: 2012.

Table 42.17. Percentage of current asthma prevalence

	Hispanic	Non-Hispanic White	Hispanic/ Non-Hispanic White Ratio
Men	4.2	6.1	0.7
Women	8.5	10.2	0.8
Both Sexes	6.5	8.2	0.8

Source: CDC 2014. Summary Health Statistics for U.S. Adults: 2012.

Table 42.18. Deaths per 100,000, with asthma as the underlying cause, National Vital Statistics System

Hispanic	Non-Hispanic White	Hispanic/Non-Hispanic White Ratio
0.9	0.8	1.1

Source: CDC 2014. Deaths: Final Data for 2013.

Table 42.19. Age-adjusted percentages for children under 18 years of age, ever being told they had asthma

	Population	Non-Hispanic White	Population/Non-Hispanic White Ratio
Hispanic	13.5	12.4	1.1
Mexican	11.8	12.4	1

Source: CDC, 2013. Summary Health Statistics for U.S. Children: National Health Interview Survey, 2012.

Table 42.20. Age-adjusted percentages for children under 18 years of age, who currently have asthma

	Population	Non-Hispanic White	Population/Non-Hispanic White Ratio
Hispanic	8.9	7.9	1.1
Mexican	7.7	7.9	1

Source: CDC, 2013. Summary Health Statistics for U.S. Children: National Health Interview Survey, 2012.

Table 42.21. Current asthma prevalence percentage, children ages 18 and under

	Hispanic	Non-Hispanic White	Hispanic/ Non-Hispanic White Ratio
Boys	8.2	8.1	1
Girls	6.5	6.9	0.9
Both Sexes	7.4	7.5	1

Source: CDC 2014. National Health Interview Survey Data 2013.

Table 42.22. Current asthma prevalence percentage, children ages 18 and under

	Population	Non-Hispanic White	Population / Non-Hispanic White Ratio
Hispanic	7.4	7.5	1
Puerto Rican	20.7	7.5	2.8
Mexican	5.6	7.5	0.7

Source: CDC 2014. National Health Interview Survey Data 2013.

Section 42.4

Asthma and American Indians and Alaska Natives

Text in this section is excerpted from "Asthma and
American Indians/Alaska Natives," Office of Minority
Health (OMH), April 22, 2015.

Asthma and American Indians and Alaska Natives

- In 2012, 147,000 American Indian/Native American adults
  reported that they currently have asthma.

- American Indian/Alaska Native children are 80% more likely to
  have asthma as non-Hispanic white children.

- Data on asthma conditions for American Indian/Alaska Natives
  is limited.

- While all of the causes of asthma remain unclear, children
  exposed to secondhand tobacco smoke exposure are at increased
  risk for acute lower respiratory tract infections, such as asthma.
  Children living below or near the poverty level are more likely to
  have high levels of blood cotinine, a breakdown product of nicotine, than children living in higher income families.

Table 42.23. Percentage of asthma among persons 18 years of age
and over, ever being told they had asthma

American Indian/Alaska Native	Non-Hispanic White	American Indian/Alaska Native Non-Hispanic White Ratio
12.6	13.4	0.9

Source: CDC 2014. Summary Health Statistics for U.S. Adults: 2012.

Table 42.24. Percentage of current asthma prevalence

American Indian/Alaska Native	Non-Hispanic White	American Indian/Alaska Native Non-Hispanic White Ratio
7.1	8.2	0.9

Source: CDC 2014. Summary Health Statistics for U.S. Adults: 2012.

Table 42.25. Deaths per 100,000, with asthma as the underlying cause, National Vital Statistics System

American Indian/Alaska Native	Non-Hispanic White	American Indian/Alaska Native Non-Hispanic White Ratio
1.1	0.8	1.4

Source: CDC 2014. Deaths: Final Data for 2013.

Table 42.26. Age-adjusted percentages for children under 18 years of age, ever being told they had asthma

American Indian/Alaska Native	Non-Hispanic White	American Indian/Alaska Native Non-Hispanic White Ratio
21.6	12.4	1.7

Source: CDC, 2013. Summary Health Statistics for U.S. Children: National Health Interview Survey, 2012.

Table 42.27. Age-adjusted percentages for children under 18 years of age, who currently have asthma

American Indian/Alaska Native	Non-Hispanic White	American Indian/Alaska Native Non-Hispanic White Ratio
14.5	7.9	1

Source: CDC, 2013. Summary Health Statistics for U.S. Children: National Health Interview Survey, 2012.

Section 42.5

Asthma and Native Hawaiians / Pacific Islanders

This section includes excerpts from "Asthma and Native Hawaiians/Pacific Islanders," Office of Minority Health (OMH), April 22, 2015; and text from "Minority Women's Health," Office on Women's Health (OWH), July 16, 2012.

- Native Hawaiians / Pacific Islanders are twice as likely to have asthma as non-Hispanic whites.

- National data for this population is very limited.

- While all of the causes of asthma remain unclear, children exposed to secondhand tobacco smoke exposure are at increased risk for acute lower respiratory tract infections, such as asthma. Children living below or near the poverty level are more likely to have high levels of blood cotinine, a breakdown product of nicotine, than children living in higher income families.

The number of people with asthma keeps rising. When Native Hawaiians and other Pacific Islanders are counted as "Asian-Americans," their rate of asthma appears low. But surveys of Native Hawaiians and other Pacific Islanders suggest much higher rates. For example, in Hawaii, Native Hawaiians are twice as likely to have asthma as any other ethnic group in the state. Some research suggests that Native Hawaiians and other Pacific Islanders are also more likely to die from asthma.

Table 42.28. Percentage of asthma among persons 18 years of age and over, ever being told they had asthma

Native Hawaiian/Pacific Islander	Non-Hispanic White	Native Hawaiian/Pacific Islander/Non-Hispanic White Ratio
27.2	13.4	2

Source: CDC 2014. Summary Health Statistics for U.S. Adults: 2012.

Table 42.29. Percentage of current asthma prevalence

Native Hawaiian/Pacific Islander	Non-Hispanic White	Native Hawaiian/Pacific Islander/Non-Hispanic White Ratio
17	8.2	2.1

Source: CDC 2014. Summary Health Statistics for U.S. Adults: 2012.

Table 42.30. Age-adjusted percentages for children under 18 years of age, ever being told they had asthma

Native Hawaiian/Pacific Islander	Non-Hispanic White	Native Hawaiian/Pacific Islander/Non-Hispanic White Ratio
10.9	12.4	0.9

Source: CDC, 2013. Summary Health Statistics for U.S. Children: National Health Interview Survey, 2012.

Table 42.31. Age-adjusted percentages for children under 18 years of age, who currently have asthma

Native Hawaiian/Pacific Islander	Non-Hispanic White	Native Hawaiian/Pacific Islander/Non-Hispanic White Ratio
7.9	7.9	1

Source: CDC, 2013. Summary Health Statistics for U.S. Children: National Health Interview Survey, 2012.

Chapter 43

Asthma Disproportionately Affects Low-Income Populations

Introduction

Many children with asthma do not get the care they need, despite the existence of asthma care guidelines and evidence about effective treatments. For example, the appropriate use of controller medications is very important in the treatment of asthma. By helping to reduce the underlying inflammation of the airways in a person with asthma, controller medications diminish asthma symptoms and prevent attacks.

However, among children and adults with persistent asthma, approximately 29 percent are not receiving appropriate controller medications from providers, and some patients are not using the medications appropriately. Among Medicaid-enrolled children with persistent asthma, the underuse of controller medications is widespread, reaching as high as 73 percent. As a result, there are more acute episodes, greater use of emergency rooms and hospitals, and increased treatment costs.

Text in this chapter is excerpted from "Chronic Care for Low-Income Children with Asthma," Agency for Healthcare Research and Quality (AHRQ), October 2014; and text from "Most Recent Asthma Data," Centers for Disease Control and Prevention (CDC), April 23, 2015.

Research has shown that reorganizing the way chronic care is delivered can increase the appropriate use of controller medications among children with asthma and have other positive results. Preliminary evidence also suggests that disparities in asthma care can be decreased through the use of strategies sensitive to the needs of racial and ethnic minorities.

The research provides promising strategies that could help policymakers and purchasers of health care and health insurance improve care for children with asthma. Other related topics discussed are:

- Patterns of use/underuse of controller medications.

- Effects of proper use of controller medications.

- Practices and policies used by managed care organizations (MCOs) and clinics and their effects on quality of care.

It is addressed to:

- Administrators of State Medicaid programs.

- Executives of Medicaid managed care organizations.

- Managers of provider organizations.

- Health plan executives.

- Employers who purchase health care for their employees.

Background

Almost half of hospitalizations for asthma among children are billed to Medicaid. States are increasingly contracting with Medicaid managed care programs in various forms and giving them the responsibility for providing care to many Medicaid-enrolled children. Managed care, with its emphasis on the organization and coordination of care, has increased expectations about the quality of care that can be provided for those with asthma and other chronic conditions. At the same time, another feature of managed care, fixed prepaid budgets, has raised questions about the ability of these organizations to deliver on their promise.

Data on Asthma Care Show Gaps in Quality

Asthma care guidelines and evidence about effective treatments are available. The National Asthma Education and Prevention Program (NAEPP) Expert Panel issued its revised Guidelines for Diagnosis and Management of Asthma (EPR-2) in 1997 and an Update in 2002. However, many children with asthma do not get the care they need.

In addition, even when providers deliver appropriate care, children may not be using controller medications correctly because their parents do not understand the purpose of the medication. According to the 2004 survey on the quality of care in commercial managed care plans from the National Committee for Quality Assurance, about 29 percent of children and adults (ages 5–56) with persistent asthma are not receiving inhaled corticosteroids to control their condition.

The problem of underuse was even more serious among children with persistent asthma enrolled in Medicaid managed care, according to researchers from the Asthma Care Quality Assessment (ACQA) Study. In 1999, these children experienced a very high rate (73 percent) of underuse of controller therapy, with 49 percent of parents reporting no controller use and 24 percent reporting less than daily use.

A related issue is the significant racial/ethnic disparities in asthma status and home management practices. For example, African-American and Hispanic children with similar insurance and sociodemographic characteristics have more severe asthma than white children based on number of symptom days, school days missed, and health status scores. Also, compared to white children, in 1999 African-American and Hispanic children were 31 percent and 42 percent less likely, respectively, to be using controller medications (including inhaled corticosteroids). Finally, African-American children are about three times as likely to be admitted to a hospital for asthma as white children.

Table 43.1. Federal Poverty Threshold

Characteristic	Number with Current Asthma (in thousands)	Percent with Current Asthma
Below 100% of poverty level	5,321	10.90%
100% to less than 250% of poverty level	6,260	7.00%
250% to less than 450% of poverty level	5,208	6.20%
450% of poverty level or higher	5,859	6.60%

Part Seven

Additional Help and Information

Chapter 44

Glossary of Terms Related to Asthma

action plan: A list of specific instructions drawn up by a healthcare professional for a person with asthma to follow at home. An asthma action plan includes a normal schedule for asthma medicines, as well as what to do if peak flow readings or asthma symptoms become worse than usual. Asthma action plans are usually split into zones green zone, yellow zone, and red zone.

acute: Brief, not ongoing. Usually also implies relatively high intensity. For example, acute asthma symptoms may be ones that last a short time but are worse than a person's usual (*see* chronic) symptoms.

airways: Hollow tubes to and within the lungs through which air passes during breathing. Airways include the trachea, bronchi, and bronchioles.

allergen: Something that causes an allergic reaction.

allergy: A type of excessive immune system reaction to a substance in a person's environment. (Can also be called "hypersensitivity reaction.") Allergies can be triggered by eating, touching, or breathing in an allergen. Allergies are often associated with asthma, especially in children.

alveoli: The millions of tiny compartments within the lungs at the ends of the airways. (To imagine the shape, picture bunches of hollow

This glossary contains terms excerpted from documents produced by several sources deemed reliable.

grapes at the ends of hollow stems.) Also called "air sacs." Alveoli are where gas exchange takes place—that is, where the blood picks up oxygen (from the air a person has breathed in) and releases carbon dioxide (to be breathed out).

anti-inflammatory: medication that reduces inflammation (swelling in the airway and mucus production).

antibiotic: medication used to treat infection caused by bacteria. Antibiotics do not protect against viruses and do not prevent the common cold.

anticholinergics: (also called cholinergic blockers or "maintenance" bronchodilators). This type of medicine relaxes the muscle bands that tighten around the airways. This action opens the airways, letting more air out of the lungs to improve breathing. Anticholinergics also help clear mucus from the lungs.

antihistamine: medication that stops the action of histamine, which causes symptoms of allergy such as itching and swelling.

atopy: The genetically determined tendency to be allergic to things.

atropine: A poisonous white crystalline alkaloid, $C_{17}H_{23}NO_3$, from belladonna and related plants, used to relieve spasms of smooth muscles. It is an anticholinergic agent.

bacteria: Infectious organisms that might cause sinusitis, bronchitis, or pneumonia.

beta-agonist: Also called $beta_2$ agonist or beta-adrenergic agonist. The most common type of bronchodilator medication. Albuterol is a beta-agonist. The name beta-agonist comes from the way the medicine works, which is to enhance the stimulation of a certain kind of autonomic nerve (the $beta_2$ type), which is responsible for relaxing the airway smooth muscle (thereby opening the airways).

breathing rate: The number of breaths per minute.

bronchi: The airways that lead from the trachea to each lung, and then subdivide into smaller and smaller branches. They connect to the bronchioles. The walls of the bronchi are made of smooth lining tissue (called endothelium) over fibrous connective tissue, cartilage, and smooth muscle. They also have many glands to produce mucus.

bronchial tubes: Airways in the lung that branch from the trachea.

bronchiole: The tiny, branching airways that lead from the bronchi to the alveoli. Most bronchioles also produce mucus.

bronchiolitis: Inflammation of the bronchioles that may be acute or chronic. If the etiology is known, it should be stated. If permanent occlusion of the lumens is present, the term bronchiolitis obliterans may be used.

bronchitis: A non-neoplastic disorder of structure or function of the bronchi resulting from infectious or noninfectious irritation. The term bronchitis should be modified by appropriate words or phrases to indicate its etiology, its chronicity, the presence of associated airways dysfunction, or type of anatomic change. The term chronic bronchitis, when unqualified, refers to a condition associated with prolonged exposure to nonspecific bronchial irritants and accompanied by mucous hypersecretion and certain structural alterations in the bronchi. Anatomic changes may include hypertrophy of the mucous-secreting apparatus and epithelial metaplasia, as well as more classic evidences of inflammation. In epidemiologic studies, the presence of cough or sputum production on most days for at least three months of the year has sometimes been accepted as a criterion for the diagnosis.

bronchoalveolar lavage: A clinical technique which removes cell samples from the lower lungs to allow assessment of inflammation and other respiratory conditions.

bronchoconstriction: The reduction in the diameter of the bronchi, usually due to squeezing of the smooth muscle in the walls. This reduces the space for air to go through and can make breathing difficult.

bronchodilator: A medicine that relaxes the smooth muscles of the airways. This allows the airway to open up (to dilate) since the muscles are not squeezing it shut. Bronchodilator medicines do not help inflammation, however.

bronchospasm: The tightening of the muscle bands that surround the airways, causing the airways to narrow.

challenge test: A test done to determine whether or not a person's bronchi are hyperresponsive. The subject breathes in air containing carefully controlled amounts of a substance known to cause bronchoconstriction. (Common substances used include methacholine, histamine, and vaporized salt water.) The bronchi of people with asthma respond to much smaller amounts of the substance than the bronchi of people who do not have asthma. This test is often used to confirm a diagnosis of asthma if there is uncertainty.

chronic: Lasting a long time. Asthma is a chronic illness because it is ongoing and does not just go away in a few days or weeks.

chronic obstructive pulmonary disease (COPD): This term refers to chronic lung disorders that result in blocked air flow in the lungs. The two main COPD disorders are emphysema and chronic bronchitis, the most common causes of respiratory failure. Emphysema occurs when the walls between the lung's air sacs become weakened and collapse. Damage from COPD is usually permanent and irreversible.

contributing factors: Risk factors that either augment the likelihood of asthma developing upon exposure to them, or may even increase susceptibility to asthma. These factors including smoking, viral infections, small size at birth, and environmental pollutants.

corticosteroids: A type of medicine used to reduce inflammation. Corticosteroid drugs mimic a substance produced naturally by the body. In asthma, corticosteroids are often taken through an inhaler for long-term control. They may also be taken orally or given intravenously for a short time if asthma symptoms get out of control.

dry powder inhaler (DPI): This variety of device provides a new way of taking inhaled medicine. The propellants used in regular metered dose inhalers can be bad for the environment. For this reason, drug companies are in the process of switching over to DPIs, which do not use a propellant at all. The medicine is in the form of a very fine powder, which is easily inhaled without the use of an aerosol spray device. There are advantages for patients, too. DPIs can be easier to use because the patient doesn't have to coordinate the timing of activating the inhaler and breathing in, and the problems of bad taste and unpleasant "feel" are also greatly reduced.

dust mites: Very tiny creatures (microscopic, or just barely visible) that live in the dust in people's homes. They are present both in visible dust (under the bed or behind the couch, for example) and in soft places like pillows, mattresses, blankets, and stuffed animals. They thrive especially when the air is humid. Many people are allergic to dust mites, and trying to reduce the number of them in the home is part of many asthma control plans.

eosinophil: A type of white blood cell whose major useful role seems to be in protecting against parasitic infections. It is also associated, however, with the inflammation that is at the root of asthma. People with asthma tend to have more eosinophils in their blood and, in addition, have an unusual number of eosinophils "migrate" into their lungs. It is

454

still not entirely clear whether eosinophils cause some of the problems that asthmatics experience, or whether they are just associated with the process without doing damage themselves.

episode: In asthma, a period of markedly worsened symptoms. This may be brought on by exposure to a known trigger or by an upper respiratory infection (a cold), or it may not have a known explanation. An episode may come on suddenly or may develop gradually over days. Asthma episodes, at their worst, can be life threatening, and should always be taken seriously.

FEV1: The "forced expiratory volume in one second." In other words, this is the amount of air you are able to blow out in one second of blowing as hard as you can. This measurement, obtained through spirometry, gives your doctor an idea of the level of blockage you have in your airways due to inflammation, mucus, or bronchoconstriction.

forced expiratory volume: Denotes the volume of gas that is exhaled in a given time interval during the execution of a forced vital capacity. Conventionally, the times used are 0.5, 0.75, or 1 sec, symbolized FEV0.5, FEV0.75, FEV1. These values are often expressed as a percent of the forced vital capacity, e.g. (FEV1 /VC) x 100.

gas exchange: Movement of oxygen from the alveoli into the pulmonary capillary blood as carbon dioxide enters the alveoli from the blood. In broader terms, the exchange of gases between alveoli and lung capillaries.

gastroesophageal reflux disease: GERD is a chronic disorder in which some of the acid and enzymes that belong in the stomach are allowed to get up into the esophagus. This leads to the sensation of "heartburn" and sometimes also an unpleasant sour taste in the mouth. GERD and asthma can make a vicious circle—GERD is more common among people with asthma, and it also seems to make asthma worse in people who have it. Treatment of GERD can lead to an improvement in asthma symptoms.

histamine: A chemical made naturally in the body that is involved in inflammation, particularly inflammation related to an allergic reaction. Antihistamines, as the name suggests, are medicines that block the effect of histamine. (Histamine made in a laboratory is sometimes also used in challenge testing.)

holding chamber: A device much like a spacer, which is also intended to help medicine from an MDI get into the lungs. The difference between a spacer and a holding chamber is that a holding chamber has a special valve on it that allows a person more time to breathe in the medicine (the breath does not need to be coordinated with the puff). In the real world, holding chambers are often called "spacers" also, even though they are slightly different things.

house dust mite: Either of two widely distributed mites of the genus Dermatophagoides (D. farinae and D. pteronyssinus) that commonly occur in house dust and often induce allergic responses, especially in children.

hyperresponsiveness: The "twitchiness" of the airways of people with asthma, resulting in excessive reaction to substances, smells, and activity. Even little things that would have no effect on the airways of nonasthmatic people cause the smooth muscle of the asthmatic's airway to squeeze and squeeze.

immunoglobulin: A class of proteins produced in lymph tissue in vertebrates that function as antibodies in the immune response.

inflammation: A complex process in the body involving many types of cells (especially white blood cells) and chemicals (such as cytokines and leukotrienes). Inflammation may be protective or may be harmful. The typical signs of inflammation are redness, swelling, warmth, and pain. Loss of function (partial or complete) is often seen, and some kind of exudate is common. Inflammation of the airways is the main underlying problem in asthma.

inhaled corticosteroid: Anti-inflammatory medicine breathed directly into the lungs. The advantage to this is that the medicine goes directly to where the inflammation is, and has minimal effects on the rest of the body (and therefore fewer side effects than corticosteroids taken orally).

irritant: A substance that triggers asthma symptoms by irritating the airway when breathed in. Examples include cigarette smoke, fumes from a harsh cleaning fluid, or strong perfume. (Allergens are a different type of asthma trigger, which cause symptoms through an allergic reaction rather than by irritation.)

leukotriene: A type of chemical involved in inflammation. Leukotrienes seem to play a particularly important role in the inflammation associated with asthma. Recently some asthma medicines have been developed that work to reduce leukotrienes or their effects (these are called "leukotriene modifiers" or "leukotriene inhibitors").

lung volume: Actual volume of the lung, including the volume of the conducting airways.

metered dose inhaler: Often called "MDI." A device that allows delivery of medicine directly into the lungs. The medicine is in the form of a very, very fine powder, and a propellant is used to get the powder out in a cloud to be inhaled. Unfortunately, the propellant used in the standard MDI's is composed of CFC's (chlorofluorocarbons), which are involved in the destruction of the ozone layer. Different types of devices to deliver medicine to the lungs are now being designed, and some are already available to consumers (*see* DPI).

methacholine: A type of chemical used in challenge testing. Everybody's airways respond to it, but the airways of a person with asthma respond much more and at lower doses.

minute ventilation: Volume of air breathed in one minute. It is a product of tidal volume and breathing frequency.

mold: A fungus. Molds are plants that make spores instead of seeds; these spores float in the air and are a common trigger for allergies. Molds are found in damp areas, such as the basement or bathroom, as well as in the outdoor environment in grass, leaf piles, hay, and mulch.

mucociliary transport: The process by which mucus is transported, by ciliary action, from the lungs.

mucus: A substance secreted by various tissues in the body (the mucous membranes) made up of water, mucin (a glycoprotein), salts, and some cells. In the lungs, mucus serves to lubricate the insides of the airways and to trap inhaled foreign particles so that they can be coughed out. In asthma, however, an excess of mucus is produced and can actually block airways. Mucus also tends to be thicker and more viscous in asthmatics.

nasal spray: Medicine used to prevent and treat nasal allergy symptoms. It is available by prescription or over-the-counter in decongestant, corticosteroid, or salt-water solution form.

nebulizer: A machine for getting medicine into the lungs. A nebulizer makes a mixture of liquid medicine and water into a mist that a person then inhales (through a mask or a mouthpiece). Nebulizers are often used for babies and children too small to be able to coordinate using a metered dose inhaler. They are also sometimes used for people having severe asthma symptoms, as many people find it easier to take in the medicine this way when they are having a lot of trouble breathing.

nitrogen oxides (NOx): Compounds of nitrogen (N) and oxygen (O) in ambient air; i.e., nitric oxide (NO) and others with a higher oxidation state of N, of which NO_2 is the most important toxicologically.

nonsteroidal anti-inflammatory drug: Generally used to treat mild to moderate pain, especially pain that has a component of inflammation (such as arthritis pain). Some people (about 10 to 20 percent of all asthmatics) have their asthma symptoms triggered by these drugs (along with aspirin). Episodes triggered in this way can be quite severe and even life threatening. NSAID's include such medicines as ibuprofen (Motrin, Advil), naproxen (Naprosyn, Aleve, Anaprox), and a few related prescription medicines (such as Relafen, Daypro, Feldene, and Indocin).

oxidant: A chemical compound that has the ability to remove, accept, or share electrons from another chemical species, thereby oxidizing it.

particle pollution: Particle pollution (also known as "particulate matter") consists of a mixture of solids and liquid droplets. Some particles are emitted directly; others form when pollutants emitted by various sources react in the atmosphere.

parts per billion: A unit commonly used to express a concentration ratio (proportion) equal to 10-9. As an example, 60 ppb is equal to 0.06 ppm.

pathogen: Any virus, microorganism, or etiologic agent causing disease.

peak expiratory flow: The highest forced expiratory flow measured with a peak flow meter.

peak flow: The very fastest you can move air by blowing out as hard as you can. This measurement correlates pretty well with FEV-1 (a measurement obtained through spirometry in a doctor's office) but doesn't require expensive equipment and can be obtained easily at home with a peak flow meter.

peak flow meter: A device to measure how hard and fast a person can blow air out. This is an indication of how well the lungs and airways are doing. A peak flow meter is an important part of an asthma home-monitoring plan.

plethysmograph: A rigid chamber placed around a living structure for the purpose of measuring changes in the volume of the structure. In respiratory measurements, the entire body is ordinarily enclosed ("body plethysmograph") and the plethysmograph is used to measure changes in volume of gas in the system produced 1) by solution and volatilization (e.g., uptake of foreign gases into the blood), 2) by changes in pressure or temperature (e.g., gas compression in the lungs, expansion of gas upon passing into the warm, moist lungs), or 3) by breathing through a tube to the outside. Three types of plethysmograph are used

polymorphonuclear leukocyte: One of several types of white blood cells that is involved in the inflammatory response following ozone-induced cell damage.

pulmonary function tests: Often called "PFT's." A series of tests done (usually in a lab in a hospital) to determine whether a person has breathing problems, and precisely what those problems are. These are used to differentiate among different diseases and disorders. It is sometimes hard for a doctor to tell just by a regular exam whether a person has asthma or another condition, and pulmonary function tests can help clarify the diagnosis. PFT's do not hurt. They involve things like holding your breath, blowing into a tube as hard as you can, and exercising while wearing a special mask.

quick-relief medicine: A medicine that opens the airways right away to relieve symptoms of asthma. Quick relief medicines are usually used only when symptoms occur.

severity: How bad or serious a disease is. In asthma, severity is generally broken up into four categories—mild intermittent, mild persistent, moderate persistent, and severe persistent. (Some experts also include a category for "severe intermittent" for those unusual people who most of the time have no asthma symptoms at all but occasionally have very serious or life-threatening asthma episodes.) Just as we do not know what causes asthma, we do not understand why individuals differ so much one from another in asthma severity.

sinusitis: An inflammation of the sinuses (hollow spaces in the bone of the cheeks and forehead) due to infection. Common symptoms of sinusitis include pain in the face, colored (not white or clear) secretions from the nose, and headache. A lot of people who have asthma also have problems with recurrent sinusitis. There is some evidence that a flare-up of sinusitis can trigger a worsening of asthma symptoms, but this is still not certain.

smooth muscle: Sometimes called involuntary muscle. A type of muscle found many places in the body, including the walls of the airways. (It is called smooth muscle simply because of how it looks under a microscope, to distinguish it from striated muscle, which is what makes up the heart as well as voluntary (skeletal) muscle).

spacer: A device usually consisting of a plastic chamber that attaches to a metered dose inhaler on one end, with a mouthpiece on the other end. A spacer is intended to help medicine from a metered dose inhaler get into the lungs. Without a spacer, much of the medicine in an inhaler "puff" gets deposited on the tongue or in the back of the throat.

spirometry: The most commonly used pulmonary function test, done in a doctor's office or pulmonary function laboratory. The machine used measures how fast a person can blow out air, and how much air is blown. The results of this test include the FEV-1, the peak flow, and the FVC.

sputum: Expectorated matter; saliva mixed with discharges from the respiratory passages.

status asthmaticus: A severe episode of asthma that is not helped (or only partially helped) by inhaled bronchodilators, and that threatens a person's ability to breathe altogether. May require intensive bronchodilator therapy, systemic corticosteroids (oral or intravenous [IV]), or even intubation.

steroids: A general term for a wide variety of chemicals, natural and synthetic. In the context of asthma, "steroids" is usually a shorthand way of referring to corticosteroid medicines (taken to reduce asthma inflammation). Other steroids, including natural and synthetic sex hormones (such as the testosterone-like compounds sometimes used by athletes to build their muscles), are generally unrelated to asthma.

sulfur dioxide (SO_2): Colorless gas with pungent odor, released primarily from burning of fossil fuels, such as coal, containing sulfur.

systemic: Relating to or affecting the body as a whole (rather than one specific organ or part).

trachea: The largest breathing tube in the body, passing from the throat down to the chest (where it connects to the two bronchi leading to the lungs).

trigger: Anything that causes asthma symptoms to worsen in a given person. Different things are triggers for different people. Common triggers include exercise, cigarette smoke, pollen, dust, cold air, and aspirin/NSAIDs. Upper respiratory infections are perhaps the most common trigger for asthma symptoms.

valved holding chamber: A chamber with a one-way valve that is used with a metered dose inhaler to help the medicine get into the airways better and make it easier to use the inhaler. Sometimes these are referred to as "spacers."

ventilation: Physiological process by which gas is renewed in the lungs. The word ventilation sometimes designates ventilatory flow rate (or ventilatory minute volume) which is the product of the tidal volume by the ventilatory frequency. Conditions are usually indicated as modifiers; i.e., VE = Expired volume per minute (BTPS), and VI = Inspired volume per minute (BTPS). Ventilation is often referred to as "total ventilation" to distinguish it from "alveolar ventilation."

volatile organic compound: Any organic compound that participates in atmospheric photochemical reactions except those designated by EPA as having negligible photochemical reactivity.

wheeze: A breathing sound that may be squeaky, whistling, or musical. Wheezes are often (but not always) a symptom of asthma. (Some people have asthma but never wheeze, and some people wheeze for reasons other than asthma.) Wheezes are due to air passing through a narrowed opening and are therefore usually accompanied by difficulty breathing.

wood smoke: Smoke is made up of a complex mixture of gases and fine, microscopic particles produced when wood and other organic matter burn. The biggest health threat from wood smoke comes from fine particles (also called particulate matter).

zones: The way that asthma signs and symptoms are classified in an asthma action plan. Usually, the zones are the green zone (all is well, continue with regular medicines and activities); the yellow zone (trouble starting; follow doctor's instructions for yellow zone); and red zone (DANGER! Get to the emergency room as quickly as possible). These are determined by symptoms and peak flow readings.

Chapter 45

Directory of Asthma-Related Resources

Government Organizations

Centers for Disease Control and Prevention
1600 Clifton Rd.
Atlanta, GA 30333
Toll-Free: 800-CDC-INFO
(800-232-4636)
TTY: 888-232-6348
Website: www.cdc.gov
E-mail: cdcinfo@cdc.gov

Environmental Protection Agency
Ariel Rios Bldg., 1200
Pennsylvania Ave. N.W.
Washington, DC 20460
Phone: 202-272-0167
TTY: 202-272-0165
Website: www.epa.gov

Indoor Air Quality Information Clearinghouse
1301 Constitution Ave. N.W.
Washington, DC 20004
Phone: 703-356-4020
Fax: 703-356-5386
Toll-Free: 800-438-4318
Website: www.epa.gov
E-mail: iaqinfo@aol.com

National Center for Environmental Health
4770 Buford Hwy N.E.
Atlanta, GA 30341-3717
Toll-Free: 800-CDC-INFO
(800-232-4636)
TTY: 888-232-6348
Website: www.cdc.gov/nceh

Resources in this chapter were compiled from several sources deemed reliable, January 2016.

National Heart, Lung, and Blood Institute
P.O. Box 30105
Bethesda, MD 20824-0105
Phone: 301-592-8573
Fax: 240-629-3246
TTY: 240-629-3255
Website: www.nhlbi.nih.gov
E-mail: nhlbiinfo@nhlbi.nih.gov

National Institute of Allergy and Infectious Diseases
5601 Fishers Ln.
Bethesda, MD 20892-9806
Phone: 301-496-5717
Fax: 301-402-3573
Toll-Free: 866-284-4107
Website: www.niaid.nih.gov
E-mail: ocpostoffice@niaid.nih.gov

National Institute of Enviromental Health Sciences
P.O. Box 12233
Research Triangle Park, NC 27709-2233
Phone: 919-541-3345
Fax: 301-480-2978
Website: www.niehs.nih.gov

National Institute on Aging
P.O. Box 8057
Gaithersburg, MD 20898-8057
Toll-Free: 800-222-2225
TTY: 800-222-4225
Website: www.nia.nih.gov

Private Organizations

Allergy & Asthma Network Mothers of Asthmatics
8229 Boone Blvd.
Ste. 260
Vienna, VA 22182
Phone: 800-878-4403
Fax: 703-288-5271
Website: www. allergyasthmanetwork.org/main

Allergy/Asthma Information Association
17 Four Season Pl., Ste. 200
Toronto, Ontario M9B 6E6
Canada
Phone: 416-621-4571
Fax: 416-621-5034
Toll-Free: 800-611-7011
Website: www.aaia.ca
E-mail: admin@aaia.ca

American Academy of Allergy, Asthma & Immunology
555 E. Wells St.
Ste. 1100
Milwaukee, WI 53202-3823
Phone: 414-272-6071
Toll-Free: 800-822-2762
Website: www.aaaai.org

The American Academy of Pediatrics
141 N.W. Point Blvd.
Elk Grove Village, IL 60007-1098
Phone: 847-434-4000
Fax: 847-434-8000
Website: https://www. healthychildren.org

American Association for Respiratory Care
9425 N. MacArthur Blvd.
Ste. 100
Irving, TX 75063-4706
Phone: 972-243-2272
Fax: 972-484-2720
Website: www.aarc.org
E-mail: info@aarc.org

American College of Allergy, Asthma & Immunology
85 W. Algonquin Rd.
Ste. 550
Arlington Heights, IL 60005
Phone: 847-427-1200
Fax: 847-427-1294
Toll-Free: 800-842-7777
Website: www.acaai.org

American College of Chest Physicians
2595 Patriot Blvd.
Glenview, IL 60026
Phone: 224-521-9800
Fax: 224-521-9801
Toll-Free: 800-343-2227
Website: www.chestnet.org

American College of Preventive Medicine
455 Massachusetts Ave. N.W.
Ste. 200
Washington, DC 20001
Phone: 202-466-2044
Fax: 202-466-2662
Website: www.acpm.org
E-mail: info@acpm.org

American Lung Association
55 W. Wacker Dr.
Ste. 1150
Chicago, IL 60601
Phone: 202-785-3355
Fax: 202-452-1805
Toll-Free: 800-LUNGUSA or
800-548-8252
Website: www.lungusa.org
E-mail: info@lung.org

American Medical Association
330 N. Wabash Ave.
Ste. 39300
Chicago, IL 60611-5885
Toll-Free: 800-262-3211
Website: www.ama-assn.org

Association of Asthma Educators (AAE)
70 Buckwalter Rd., Ste. 900
Royersford, PA 19468
Phone: 888-988-7747
Website: www.asthmaeducators.org
E-mail: admin@asthmaeducators.org

Asthma and Allergy Foundation of America
8201 Corporate Dr., Ste. 1000
Landover, MD 20785
Toll-Free: 800-7-ASTHMA
(800-727-8462)
Website: www.aafa.org
E-mail: info@aafa.org

Asthma Center Education and Research Fund
205 N. Broad St.
Ste. 300
Philadelphia, PA 19107
Phone: 215-569-1111
Website: www.theasthmacenter.
org

Asthma Initiative of Michigan
Website: www.getasthmahelp.
org
E-mail: info@getasthmahelp.org

Asthma Society of Canada
124 Merton St.
Ste. 401
Toronto, Ontario M4S 2Z2
Canada
Phone: 416-787-4050
Fax: 416-787-5807
Toll-Free: 866-787-4050
Website: www.asthma.ca
E-mail: info@asthma.ca

Chicago Asthma Consortium (CAC)
P.O. Box 31757
Chicago, IL 60631
Phone: 888-268-8334
Fax: 773-628-7663
Website: chicagoasthma.org
E-mail: info@chicagoasthma.org

Children's Asthma Education Centre
FE125-685 William Ave.
Winnipeg, Manitoba R3E 0Z2
Canada
Phone: 204-787-2551
Fax: 204-787-5040
Website: www.asthma-
education.com
E-mail: caec@hsc.mb.ca

Cleveland Clinic
9500 Euclid Ave.
Cleveland, Ohio 44195
Toll-Free: 800-223-2273
TTY: 216-444-0261
Website: www.
myclevelandclinic.org

Food Allergy Research & Education, Inc.
7925 Jones Branch Dr., Ste. 1100
McLean, VA 22102
Phone: 703-691-3179
Fax: 703-691-2713
Toll-Free: 800-929-4040
Website: www.foodallergy.org

Merck Childhood Asthma Network (MCAN)
601 Pennsylvania Ave. N.W.
Ste. 1200
Washington, DC 20004
Website: www.mcanonline.org

National Environmental Education Foundation
4301 Connecticut Ave. N.W.
Ste. 160
Washington, DC 20008
Phone: 202-833-2933
Website: https://www.neefusa.org

National Jewish Health
1400 Jackson St.
Denver, CO 80206
Toll-Free: 877-CALL-NJH
(877-225-5654)
Website: www.nationaljewish.org

Ontario Lung Association
18 Wynford Dr.
Ste. 401
Toronto,Ontario M3C 0K8
Canada
Fax: 416-864-9911
Toll-Free: 888-344-LUNG
(888-344-5864)
Website: www.on.lung.ca
E-mail: info@on.lung.ca

Partners Asthma Center
15 Francis St.
Boston, MA 02115
Phone: 617-732-7419
Toll-Free: 800-9PARTNERS
(800-972-7863)
Website: www.asthma.partners.
org
E-mail: asthma@partners.org

*Respiratory Health
Association*
1440 W. Washington Blvd.
Chicago, IL 60607
Phone: 312-243-2000
Fax: 312-243-3954
Website: www.lungchicago.org
E-mail: info@lungchicago.org

*University of Chicago
Asthma and COPD Center*
5841 S. Maryland Ave.
Chicago, IL 60637
Phone: 773-702-0880
Website: asthma.bsd.uchicago.
edu
E-mail: asthma@medicine.bsd.
uchicago.edu

Index

Index